UNDOING THE DEMOS

Undoing the Demos:
Neoliberalism's Stealth Revolution

Wendy Brown

ZONE BOOKS

near futures

© 2015 Wendy Brown
ZONE BOOKS
633 Vanderbilt Street, Brooklyn, New York 11218

A version of Chapter Six was previously published
as "The End of Educated Democracy" in *Representations*,
Volume 116 (Fall 2011).

Printed in the United States of America.
Distributed by Princeton University Press,
Princeton, New Jersey, and Woodstock, United Kingdom.

Library of Congress Cataloging-in-Publication Data
Brown, Wendy, 1955–
    Undoing the demos: neoliberalism's stealth
revolution / by Wendy Brown. — First edition.
        pages   cm.
    Includes bibliographical references and index.
    ISBN 978-1-935408-54-3
    1. Neoliberalism. 2. Democracy. 3. Foucault, Michel,
1926–1984. I. Title.
    JC574.B766 2015
    320.51'3–dc23
                                        2014018378

CONTENTS

Undoing the Demos

In a century heavy with political ironies, there may have been none greater than this: at the end of the Cold War, as mainstream pundits hailed democracy's global triumph, a new form of governmental reason was being unleashed in the Euro-Atlantic world that would inaugurate democracy's conceptual unmooring and substantive disembowelment. Within thirty years, Western democracy would grow gaunt, ghostly, its future increasingly hedged and improbable.

More than merely saturating the meaning or content of democracy with market values, neoliberalism assaults the principles, practices, cultures, subjects, and institutions of democracy understood as rule by the people. And more than merely cutting away the flesh of liberal democracy, neoliberalism also cauterizes democracy's more radical expressions, those erupting episodically across Euro-Atlantic modernity and contending for its future with more robust versions of freedom, equality, and popular rule than democracy's liberal iteration is capable of featuring.

The claim that neoliberalism is profoundly destructive to the fiber and future of democracy in any form is premised on an understanding of neoliberalism as something other than a set of economic policies, an ideology, or a resetting of the relation between state and economy. Rather, as a normative order of reason developed over three decades into a widely and deeply disseminated governing rationality, neoliberalism transmogrifies every human domain and endeavor, along with humans themselves, according to a specific image of the economic. All conduct is economic conduct; all spheres of existence are framed and measured by economic terms and metrics, even when those spheres are not directly monetized. In neoliberal reason and in domains governed by it, we are only and everywhere *homo oeconomicus,* which itself has a historically specific form. Far from Adam Smith's creature propelled by the natural urge to "truck, barter, and exchange," today's *homo oeconomicus* is an intensely constructed and governed bit of human capital tasked with improving and leveraging its competitive positioning and with enhancing its (monetary and nonmonetary) portfolio value across all of its endeavors and venues. These are also the mandates, and hence the orientations, contouring the projects of neoliberalized states, large corporations, small businesses, nonprofits, schools, consultancies, museums, countries, scholars, performers, public agencies, students, websites, athletes, sports teams, graduate programs, health providers, banks, and global legal and financial institutions.

What happens when the precepts and principles of democracy are remade by this order of reason and governance? When the commitment to individual and collective self-rule and the institutions supporting it are overwhelmed and then displaced by the encomium to enhance capital value, competitive positioning, and credit ratings? What happens when the practices and principles of speech, deliberation, law, popular sovereignty, participation, education, public goods, and shared power entailed in rule by the people are submitted to economization? These are the questions animating this book.

To pose these questions is already to challenge commonplace notions that democracy is the permanent achievement of the West and therefore cannot be lost; that it consists only of rights, civil liberties, and elections; that it is secured by constitutions combined with unhindered markets; or that it is reducible to a political system maximizing individual freedom in a context of state-provisioned order and security. These questions also challenge the Western liberal democratic conceit that humans have a natural and persistent desire for democracy. They presume instead that democratic self-rule must be consciously valued, cultured, and tended by a people seeking to practice it and that it must vigilantly resist myriad economic, social, and political forces threatening to deform or encroach upon it. They presume the need to educate the many for democracy, a task that grows as the powers and problems to be addressed increase in complexity. Finally, these questions presume that the promise of shared rule by the people is worth the candle, both an end in itself and a potential, though uncertain, means to other possible goods, ranging from human thriving to planetary sustainability. Hardly the only salient political value, and far from insurance against dark trajectories, democracy may yet be more vital to a livable future than is generally acknowledged within Left programs centered on global governance, rule by experts, human rights, anarchism, or undemocratic versions of communism.

None of these contestable presumptions have divine, natural, or philosophical foundations, and none can be established through abstract reasoning or empirical evidence. They are convictions animated by attachment, scholarly contemplation of history and the present, and argument, nothing more.

———

Undoing the Demos has been richly enabled by colleagues, students, research assistants, loved ones, and strangers, only a few of whom I can acknowledge here. Antonio Vázquez-Arroyo years ago goaded me to specify neoliberalism more closely and more recently insisted that I write this book, rather than the one on Marx that remains unfinished. Many of the ideas in this book are Michel Feher's; others he disagrees with, but were much improved by his critiques and reading suggestions. Robert Meister and Michael MacDonald have been invaluable sources and interlocutors for me on the subject of neoliberalism. The Bruce Initiative's "Rethinking Capitalism" project, which Meister led, was also fecund for my thinking.

The ideas in the book were improved each time I had to expose them to daylight, and I am indebted to hosts and audiences in the many venues where this exposure took place. Julia Elyachar offered excellent commentary on the paper that was my initial foray into this project. Steve Schiffrin generously responded to a version of Chapter 5 with a sheaf of terrific criticisms and references. I am also grateful to students in two courses where I germinated some of the arguments, first at the 2011 Birkbeck Critical Theory Summer School, then in a magical 2012 Berkeley graduate seminar where we read Marx and Foucault together for fourteen luxurious weeks. Several draft chapters were also smartly engaged by members of a workshop organized by Mark Devenney at the University of Brighton.

The book benefitted immensely from a small platoon of research assistants and others who lent their labors. Early on, Jack Jackson tracked down sources and instructed me through his own remarkable work and thinking. In the later stages, Nina Hagel and William Callison went far beyond the usual library runs and endnote completion. Their detailed corrections, queries, and suggestions for reformulations were superb, and their patience, grace, and graciousness made them consistently wonderful to work with. Nina also prepared the index. Derin McCleod kindly loaned his Latin fluency to the task of inventing a feminine counterpart to *homo oeconomicus*. Sundar Sharma, a talented former Berkeley undergraduate, and Jason Koenig, a former graduate student with a passion for democracy shorn of its imbrication with capitalism, located sources for articles that were the precursors of Chapter 6. At Zone, I had the great luxury of working with Meighan Gale, who smoothed the path of production at every turn, Ramona Naddaff, who gave the final typescript her expert eye and generously consulted on many other aspects of the book, Julie Fry, whose designs are brilliant, and Bud Bynack, copyeditor extraordinaire. In addition to saving one from being a fool on the page, Bud channels his mastery of the art and science of editing into a companionable, often entertaining, and always enlightening tutorial for the author.

At home, Judith Butler embodies all the rich interiority, poetry, generosity, and commitment to worldly betterment that neoliberal reason turns aside. She is also a treasured interlocutor and critic. Isaac's fineness of spirit, extraordinary music, and exuberant openness to life counters my despair about the future. The extended "wolf pack" buoys us all; I am grateful to the dozen of us for the sustaining alternative kinship form we have made.

Finally, I had the good fortune to receive institutional support from the Class of 1936 First Chair at the University of California, Berkeley, and from the Society for the Humanities at Cornell University. I am especially indebted to Tim Murray for inviting me and to Brett de Bray for hosting me at Cornell's A. D. White House, where I spent a splendid Ithaca autumn completing a draft of the book.

NEOLIBERAL REASON
AND POLITICAL LIFE

CHAPTER ONE

Undoing Democracy:
Neoliberalism's Remaking of State and Subject

This book is a theoretical consideration of the ways that neoliberalism, a peculiar form of reason that configures all aspects of existence in economic terms, is quietly undoing basic elements of democracy. These elements include vocabularies, principles of justice, political cultures, habits of citizenship, practices of rule, and above all, democratic imaginaries. My argument is not merely that markets and money are corrupting or degrading democracy, that political institutions and outcomes are increasingly dominated by finance and corporate capital, or that democracy is being replaced by plutocracy—rule by and for the rich. Rather, neoliberal reason, ubiquitous today in statecraft and the workplace, in jurisprudence, education, culture, and a vast range of quotidian activity, is converting the distinctly *political* character, meaning, and operation of democracy's constituent elements into *economic* ones. Liberal democratic institutions, practices, and habits may not survive this conversion. Radical democratic dreams may not either. Thus, this book charts both a disturbing contemporary condition and the potential barrenness for future democratic projects contained in this troubled present. The institutions and principles aimed at securing democracy, the cultures required to nourish it, the energies needed to animate it, and the citizens practicing, caring for or desiring it—all of these are challenged by neoliberalism's "economization" of political life and of other heretofore noneconomic spheres and activities.

What is the connection between neoliberalism's hollowing out of contemporary liberal democracy and its imperiling of more radical democratic imaginaries? Liberal democratic practices and institutions almost always fall short of their promise and at times cruelly invert it, yet liberal democratic principles hold, and hold out, ideals of both freedom and equality universally shared and of political rule by and for the people. Most other formulations of democracy share these ideals, interpreting them differently and often seeking to realize them more substantively than liberalism's formalism, privatism, individualism, and relative complacency about capitalism makes possible. However if, as this book suggests, neoliberal reason is evacuating these ideals and desires from actually existing liberal democracies, from what platform would more ambitious democratic projects be launched? How would the desire for more or better democracy be kindled from the ash heap of its bourgeois form? Why would peoples want or seek democracy in the absence of even its vaporous liberal democratic instantiation? And what in dedemocratized subjects and subjectivities would yearn for this political regime, a yearning that is neither primordial nor cultured by this historical condition? These questions are reminders that the problem of what kinds of peoples and cultures would seek or build democracy, far from being one mainly pertinent to the non-West, is of driving importance in the contemporary West. Democracy can be undone, hollowed out from within, not only overthrown or stymied by antidemocrats And desire for democracy is neither given nor uncorruptible; indeed, even democratic theorists such as Rousseau and Mill acknowledge the difficulty of crafting democratic spirits from the material of European modernity.[1]

Any effort to theorize the relation of democracy and neoliberalism is challenged by the ambiguities and multiple significations of both words. "Democracy" is among the most contested and promiscuous terms in our modern political vocabulary. In the popular imaginary, "democracy" stands for everything from free elections to free markets, from protests against dictators to law and order, from the centrality of rights to the stability of states, from the voice of the assembled multitude to the protection of individuality and the wrong of dicta imposed by crowds. For some, democracy is the crown jewel of the West; for others, it is what the West has never really had, or it is mainly a gloss for Western imperial aims. Democracy comes in so many varieties—social, liberal, radical, republican, representative, authoritarian, direct, participatory, deliberative, plebiscite—that such claims often speak past one another. In political science, empirical scholars seek to stabilize the term with metrics and meanings that political theorists contest and problematize. Within political theory, scholars are sanguine or unhappy to different degrees about the contemporary monopoly on "democratic theory" by a single formulation (liberal) and method (analytic).

Even the Greek etymology of "democracy" generates ambiguity and dispute. *Demos/kratia* translates as "people rule" or "rule by the people." But who were the "people" of ancient Athens? The propertied? The poor? The uncounted? The many? This was a dispute in Athens itself, which is why for Plato, democracy is proximate to anarchy, while for Aristotle, it is rule by the poor. In contemporary Continental theory, Giorgio Agamben identifies a constant ambiguity—one that "is no accident"—about the demos as referring both to the entire political body and to the poor.[2] Jacques Rancière argues (through Plato's *Laws*) that the demos refers to neither, but instead to those unqualified to rule, to the "uncounted." Thus, for Rancière, democracy is always an eruption of "the part that has no part."[3] Etienne Balibar augments Rancière's claim to argue that democracy's signature equality and freedom are "imposed by the revolt of the excluded," but always then "reconstructed by citizens themselves in a process that has no end."[4]

Accepting the open and contestable signification of democracy is essential to this work because I want to release democracy from containment by any particular form while insisting on its value in connoting political self-rule by the people, whoever the people are. In this, democracy stands opposed not only to tyranny and dictatorship, fascism or totalitarianism, aristocracy, plutocracy or corporatocracy, but also to a contemporary phenomenon in which rule transmutes into governance and management in the order that neoliberal rationality is bringing about.

"Neoliberalism," too, is a loose and shifting signifier. It is a scholarly commonplace that neoliberalism has no fixed or settled coordinates, that there is temporal and geographical variety in its discursive formulations, policy entailments, and material practices.[5] This commonplace exceeds recognition of neoliberalism's multiple and diverse origins or the recognition that neoliberalism is a term mainly deployed by its critics, and hence its very existence is questionable.[6] Neoliberalism as economic policy, a modality of governance, and an order of reason is at once a global phenomenon, yet inconstant, differentiated, unsystematic, impure. It intersects in Sweden with the continued legitimacy of welfarism, in South Africa with a post-Apartheid expectation of a democratizing and redistributive state, in China with Confucianism, post-Maoism, and capitalism, in the United States with a strange brew of long-established antistatism and new managerialism. Neoliberal policies also come through different portals and agents. While neoliberalism was an "experiment" imposed on Chile by Augusto Pinochet and the Chilean economists known as "the Chicago Boys" after their 1973 overthrow of Salvador Allende, it was the International Monetary Fund that imposed "structural adjustments" on the Global South over the next two decades. Similarly, while Margaret Thatcher and Ronald Reagan sought bold free-market reforms when they first came to power, neoliberalism also unfolded more subtly in Euro-Atlantic nations through techniques of governance usurping a democratic with an economic vocabulary and social consciousness. Moreover, neoliberal rationality itself has altered over time, especially, but not only in the transition from a productive to an increasingly financialized economy.[7]

A paradox, then. Neoliberalism is a distinctive mode of reason, of the production of subjects, a "conduct of conduct," and a scheme of valuation.[8] It names a historically specific economic and political reaction against Keynesianism and democratic socialism, as well as a more generalized practice of "economizing" spheres and activities heretofore governed by other tables of value.[9] Yet in its differential instantiations across countries, regions, and sectors, in its various intersections with extant cultures and political traditions, and above all, in its convergences with and uptakes of other discourses and developments, neoliberalism takes diverse shapes and spawns diverse content and normative details, even different idioms. It is globally ubiquitous, yet disunified and nonidentical with itself in space and over time.

Notwithstanding these diverse instantiations, for reasons that will become clear, I will be more concerned to stipulate a meaning for "neoliberalism" than for "democracy" in this work. However, these aspects of neoliberalism—its unevenness, its lack of self-identity, its spatial and temporal variability, and above all, its availability to reconfiguration—are important to underscore in an argument focused on its iteration in the time we may call contemporary and the place we may call the Euro-Atlantic world. Alertness to neoliberalism's inconstancy and plasticity cautions against identifying its current iteration as its essential and global truth and against making the story I am telling a teleological one, a dark chapter in a steady march toward end times.

In the *Republic*, Plato famously offers a strict homology between the city and the soul. Each has the same constituent parts—reason (philosophers), spirit (warriors), and appetite (workers)—and each is properly or improperly ordered in the same way. If appetite or spirit, rather than reason, governs either the individual or political life, the cost is justice or virtue. Political theorists have challenged Plato's homology often enough, yet it has a way of recurring. This book will suggest that neoliberal reason has returned it with a vengeance: both persons and states are construed on the model of the contemporary firm, both persons and states are expected to comport themselves in ways that maximize their capital value in the present and enhance their future value, and both persons and states do so through practices of entrepreneurialism, self-investment, and/or attracting investors. Any regime pursuing another course faces fiscal crises, downgraded credit, currency or bond ratings, and lost legitimacy at the least, bankruptcy and dissolution at the extreme. Likewise, any individual who veers into other pursuits risks impoverishment and a loss of esteem and creditworthiness at the least, survival at the extreme.

Most striking about the new homology between city and soul is that its coordinates are economic, not political. As both individual and state become projects of management, rather than rule, as an economic framing and economic ends replace political ones, a range of concerns become subsumed to the project of capital enhancement, recede altogether, or are radically transformed as they are "economized." These include justice (and its subelements, such as liberty, equality, fairness), individual and popular sovereignty, and the rule of law. They also include the knowledge and the cultural orientation relevant to even the most modest practices of democratic citizenship.

Two examples, one concerning the soul and one concerning the state, will help to make this point.

Remaking the Soul. It is no news that European and North American universities have been radically transformed and revalued in recent decades. Rising tuition rates, declining state support, the rise of for-profit and online education, the remaking of universities through corporate "best practices," and a growing business culture of "competences" in place of "certificates" have cast the ivory tower of just thirty years ago as anachronistic, expensive, and indulgent. While Britain has semiprivatized most public institutions and tied remaining state funding to a set of academic productivity metrics that measure knowledge according to "impact," the icon of transformation in the United States is a bit different—proliferation of more informal ranking systems proximate to crowdsourcing. Older measures of college quality (themselves contestable insofar as they were heavily bound to the caliber and size of applicant pool, along with endowments) are being rapidly supplanted by a host of new "best bang for the buck" rankings.[10] Offered by venues ranging from *Kiplinger's Personal Finance* to the *Princeton Review* and *Forbes Magazine,* the algorithms may be complicated, but the cultural shift is plain: replacing measures of educational quality are metrics oriented entirely to return on investment (ROI) and centered on what kind of job placement and income enhancement student investors may expect from any given institution. The question is not immoral, but obviously shrinks the value of higher education to individual economic risk and gain, removing quaint concerns with developing the person and citizen or perhaps reducing such development to the capacity for economic advantage. More importantly, there is a government plan in the works to base allocations of $150 billion in federal financial aid on these new metrics, permitting schools that earn a high rating to offer more student aid than those at the bottom. If the plan materializes, which seems likely, institutions and students alike will not be vaguely interpellated or "incentivized" but forcefully remade by the metrics, as universities, like any other investment, are rated in terms of risk exposure and expected yield.[11] The rating system would have institutional ramifications vastly exceeding its expressed concerns with capping costs at universities, instead inciting rapid compression of general education requirements and time to degree, undermining whatever remains of both the liberal arts and recruitment of historically disadvantaged populations, and more broadly, remaking pedagogy, pathways, and standards for knowledge acquisition expected of college graduates. The new metrics, in short, both index and drive a higher-education revolution. Once about developing intelligent, thoughtful elites and reproducing culture, and more recently, enacting a principle of equal opportunity and cultivating a broadly educated citizenry, higher education now produces human capital, thereby turning classically humanist values on their head. As Chapter 6 argues at greater length, when higher education is revolutionized in this way, so are the soul, the citizen, and democracy.

Remaking the State. President Obama opened his second term in office with apparently renewed concern for those left out of the American dream by virtue of class, race, sexuality, gender, disability, or immigration status. His "We the People" inauguration speech in January 2013 sounded those concerns loudly; combined with his State of the Union address three weeks later, the president seemed to have rediscovered his Left base or perhaps even his own justice-minded spirit after a centrist, compromising, deal-making first term in office. Perhaps Occupy Wall Street could even claim a minor victory in shifting popular discourse on who and what America was for.

Certainly, it is true that the two speeches featured Obama's "evolution" on gay marriage and renewed determination to extricate the United States from its military quagmires in the Middle East. They expressed concern, too, with those left behind in the neoliberal race to riches while "corporate profits...rocketed to all-time highs."[12] In these ways, it seemed that the light of "hope and change" on which Obama had glided to power in 2008 had indeed been reignited. Close consideration of the State of the Union address, however, reveals a different placing of the accent marks. While Obama called for protecting Medicare; progressive tax reform; increasing government investment in science and technology research, clean energy, home ownership, and education; immigration reform; fighting sex discrimination and domestic violence; and raising the minimum wage, each of these issues was framed in terms of its contribution to economic growth or American competitiveness.[13]

"A growing economy that creates good, middle-class jobs—that must be the North Star that guides our efforts" the president intoned. "Every day," he added, "we must ask ourselves three questions as a nation."[14] What are these supervenient guides to law and policy formation, to collective and individual conduct? "How do we attract more jobs to our shores? How do we equip our people with the skills needed to do those jobs? And how do we make sure that hard work leads to a decent living?"[15]

Attracting investors and developing an adequately remunerated skilled workforce—these are the goals of the world's oldest democracy led by a justice-minded president in the twenty-first century. Success in these areas would in turn realize the ultimate goal of the nation and the government that stewards it, "broad-based growth" for the economy as a whole. More importantly, every progressive value—from decreasing domestic violence to slowing climate change—Obama represented as not merely reconcilable with economic growth, but as driving it. Clean energy would keep us competitive—"as long as countries like China keep going all-in on clean energy, so must we."[16] Fixing our aging infrastructure would "prove that there is no better place to do business than the United States of America."[17] More accessible mortgages enabling "responsible young families" to buy their first home will "help our economy grow."[18] Investing in education would reduce the drags on growth caused by teen pregnancy and violent crime, put "kids on a path to a good job," allow them to "work their way into the middle class," and provide the skills that would make the economy competitive. Schools should be rewarded for partnering with "colleges and employers" and for creating "classes that focus on science, technology, engineering and math—the skills today's employers are looking for."[19] Immigration reform will "harness the talents and ingenuity of striving, hopeful immigrants" and attract "the highly skilled entrepreneurs and engineers that will help create jobs and grow our economy."[20] Economic growth would also result "when our wives, mothers and daughters can live their lives free from discrimination...and...fear of domestic violence," when "we reward an honest day's work with honest wages" with minimum wage reform, when we rebuild decimated factory towns, and when we strengthen families through "removing financial deterrents to marriage for low-income couples and doing more to encourage fatherhood."[21]

Obama's January 2013 State of the Union speech thus recovered a liberal agenda by packaging it as economic stimulus, promising that it would generate competitiveness, prosperity, and continued recovery from the recessions induced by the 2008 finance-capital meltdown. Some might argue that this packaging was aimed at co-opting the opposition, not simply neutralizing, but reversing the charges against tax-and-spend Democrats by formulating social justice, government investment, and environmental protection as fuel for economic growth. That aim is patently evident. But exclusive focus on it elides the way that economic growth has become both the end and legitimation of government, ironically, at the very historical moment that honest economists acknowledge that capital accumulation and economic growth have gone separate ways, in part because the rent extractions facilitated by financialization are not growth inducing.[22] In a neoliberal era when the market ostensibly takes care of itself, Obama's speech reveals government as both responsible for fostering economic health and as subsuming all other undertakings (except national security) to economic health. Striking in its own right, this formulation means that democratic state commitments to equality, liberty, inclusion, and constitutionalism are now subordinate to the project of economic growth, competitive positioning, and capital enhancement. These political commitments can no longer stand on their own legs and, the speech implies, would be jettisoned if found to abate, rather than abet, economic goals.

What the Obama speech also makes clear is that the state's table of purposes and priorities has become indistinguishable from that of modern firms, especially as the latter increasingly adopts concerns with justice and sustainability. For firms and the state alike, competitive positioning and stock or credit rating are primary; other ends—from sustainable production practices to worker justice—are pursued insofar as they contribute to this end. As "caring" becomes a market niche, green and fair-trade practices, along with (minuscule) profit diversion to charity, have become the public face and market strategy of many firms today. Obama's State of the Union speech adjusts the semantic order of things only slightly, foregrounding justice issues even as they are tethered to competitive positioning. The conduct of government and the conduct of firms are now fundamentally identical; both are in the business of justice and sustainability, but never as ends in themselves. Rather, "social responsibility," which must itself be entrepreneurialized, is part of what attracts consumers and investors.[23] In this respect, Obama's speech at once depicts neoliberal statism and is a brilliant marketing ploy borrowed directly from business—increasing his own credit and enhancing his value by attracting (re)investment from an ecologically or justice-minded sector of the public.

These are but two examples of the contemporary neoliberal transformations of subjects, states, and their relation that animate this book: What happens to rule by and for the people when neoliberal reason configures both soul and city as contemporary firms, rather than as polities? What happens to the constituent elements of democracy—its culture, subjects, principles, and institutions—when neoliberal rationality saturates political life?

Having opened with stories, I hasten to add that this is mainly a work of political theory whose aim is to elucidate the large arc and key mechanisms through which neoliberalism's novel construction of persons and states are evacuating democratic principles, eroding democratic institutions and eviscerating the democratic imaginary of European modernity. It is, in the classic sense of the word, a critique—an effort to comprehend the constitutive elements and dynamics of our condition. It does not elaborate alternatives to the order it illuminates and only occasionally identifies possible strategies for resisting the developments it charts. However, the predicaments and powers it illuminates might contribute to the development of such alternatives and strategies, which are themselves vital to any future for democracy.

Neoliberalism is most commonly understood as enacting an ensemble of economic policies in accord with its root principle of affirming free markets. These include deregulation of industries and capital flows; radical reduction in welfare state provisions and protections for the vulnerable; privatized and outsourced public goods, ranging from education, parks, postal services, roads, and social welfare to prisons and militaries; replacement of progressive with regressive tax and tariff schemes; the end of wealth redistribution as an economic or social-political policy; the conversion of every human need or desire into a profitable enterprise, from college admissions preparation to human organ transplants, from baby adoptions to pollution rights, from avoiding lines to securing legroom on an airplane; and, most recently, the financialization of everything and the increasing dominance of finance capital over productive capital in the dynamics of the economy and everyday life.

Critics of these policies and practices usually concentrate on four deleterious effects. The first is *intensified inequality*, in which the very top strata acquires and retains ever more wealth, the very bottom is literally turned out on the streets or into the growing urban and suburban slums of the world, while the middle strata works more hours for less pay, fewer benefits, less security, and less promise of retirement or upward mobility than at any time in the past half century. While they rarely use the term "neoliberalism," this is the emphasis of the valuable critiques of Western state policy offered by economists Robert Reich, Paul Krugman, and Joseph Stiglitz and of development policy offered by Amartya Sen, James Ferguson, and Branko Milanović, among others.[24] Growing inequality is also among the effects that Thomas Piketty establishes as fundamental to the recent past and near future of post-Keynesian capitalism.

The second criticism of neoliberal state economic policy and deregulation pertains to the *crass or unethical commercialization* of things and activities considered inappropriate for marketization. The claim is that marketization contributes to human exploitation or degradation (for example, Third World baby surrogates for wealthy First World couples), because it limits or stratifies access to what ought to be broadly accessible and shared (education, wilderness, infrastructure), or because it enables something intrinsically horrific or severely denigrating to the planet (organ trafficking, pollution rights, clear-cutting, fracking). Again, while they do not use the term "neoliberalism," this is the thrust of the critiques forwarded in Debra Satz's *Why Some Things Should Not Be for Sale* and Michael Sandel's *What Money Can't Buy.*[25]

Thirdly, critics of neoliberalism understood as state economic policy are also distressed by the *ever-growing intimacy of corporate and finance capital with the state*, and corporate domination of political decisions and economic policy. Sheldon S. Wolin emphasizes this in *Democracy, Incorporated*, although Wolin, too, avoids the descriptor "neoliberalism."[26] These themes are also the signature of filmmaker Michael Moore, and are developed in a different way by Paul Pierson and Jacob Hacker in *Winner-Take-All Politics.*[27]

Finally, critics of neoliberal state policy are often concerned with the *economic havoc* wreaked on the economy by the ascendance and liberty of finance capital, especially the destabilizing effects of the inherent bubbles and other dramatic fluctuations of financial markets. Made vivid by the immediate shock as well as the long tail of the 2008–2009 finance-capital meltdown, these effects are also underscored by the routinely widening discrepancies between the fates of Wall Street and the so-called "real" economy. They are charted by a range of thinkers including Gérard Duménil and Dominique Lévy in *The Crisis of Neoliberalism*, Michael Hudson in *Finance Capitalism and Its Discontents*, Yves Smith in *E-CONned: How Unrestrained Self-Interest Undermined Democracy and Corrupted Capitalism*, Matt Taibbi in *Griftopia: A Story of Bankers, Politicians and the Most Audacious Power Grab in American History*, and Philip Mirowski in *Never Let a Serious Crisis Go to Waste: How Neoliberalism Survived the Financial Meltdown*.[28]

Intensified inequality, crass commodification and commerce, ever-growing corporate influence in government, economic havoc and instability—certainly all of these are consequences of neoliberal policy, and all are material for loathing or popular protest, as indeed, Occupy Wall Street, the Southern European protests against austerity policies, and, earlier, the "Antiglobalization" movement loathed and protested them. However, in this book, neoliberalism is formulated somewhat differently and focuses on different deleterious effects. In contrast with an understanding of neoliberalism as a set of state policies, a phase of capitalism, or an ideology that set loose the market to restore profitability for a capitalist class, I join Michel Foucault and others in conceiving neoliberalism as an order of normative reason that, when it becomes ascendant, takes shape as a governing rationality extending a specific formulation of economic values, practices, and metrics to every dimension of human life.[29]

This governing rationality involves what Koray Çalışkan and Michel Callon term the "economization" of heretofore noneconomic spheres and practices, a process of remaking the knowledge, form, content, and conduct appropriate to these spheres and practices.[30] Importantly, such economization may not always involve monetization. That is, we may (and neoliberalism interpellates us as subjects who do) think and act like contemporary market subjects where monetary wealth generation is not the immediate issue, for example, in approaching one's education, health, fitness, family life, or neighborhood.[31] To speak of the relentless and ubiquitous economization of all features of life by neoliberalism is thus not to claim that neoliberalism literally *marketizes* all spheres, even as such marketization is certainly one important effect of neoliberalism. Rather, the point is that neoliberal rationality disseminates the *model of the market* to all domains and activities—even where money is not at issue—and configures human beings exhaustively as market actors, always, only, and everywhere as *homo oeconomicus*.

Thus, one might approach one's dating life in the mode of an entrepreneur or investor, yet not be trying to generate, accumulate, or invest monetary wealth in this domain.[32] Many upscale online dating companies define their clientele and offerings in these terms, identifying the importance of maximizing return on investment of affect, not only time and money.[33] The Supreme Court might construe free speech as the right to advance or advertise one's worth without this worth being monetized; we will see an instance of this in *Citizens United*, discussed in Chapter 5. A student might undertake charitable service to enrich her college application profile; however, the service remains unwaged, and the desire for a particular college may exceed its promise of income enhancement. Similarly, a parent might choose a primary school for a child based on its placement rates in secondary schools who have high placement rates in elite colleges, yet not be calculating primarily either the monetary outlays for this child or the income that the grown child is expected to earn.

Widespread economization of heretofore noneconomic domains, activities, and subjects, but not necessarily marketization or monetization of them, then, is the distinctive signature of neoliberal rationality. However, "economization" is itself a broad term, with no constant content or force across different historical and spatial instantiations of "economy." To say that neoliberalism construes subjects as relentlessly economic actors does not tell us in what roles. Producers? Merchants? Entrepreneurs? Consumers? Investors? Similarly, the economization of society and politics could occur through the model of the household, a nation of laborers, a nation of clients or consumers, or a world of human capitals. These are among the possibilities carried by economization in recent histories of state socialism, welfare statism, social democracy, national socialism, and neoliberalism Indeed, Carl Schmitt argued that liberal democracy was already a form of economizing the state and the political, and for Hannah Arendt and Claude Lefort, the economization of society, politics, and man was a signature of Marxism in theory and practice.[34] So what is distinctive about neoliberal economization?

Part of the story pertains to economization's enlarged domain—it reaches to practices and crevices of desire heretofore unimaginable. But the shift is more than a matter of degree. Contemporary neoliberal rationality does not mobilize a timeless figure of economic man and simply enlarge its purview. That is, *homo oeconomicus* does not have a constant shape and bearing across the centuries. Two hundred years ago, the figure famously drawn by Adam Smith was that of a merchant or trader who relentlessly pursued his own interests through exchange. One hundred years ago, the principle of *homo oeconomicus* was reconceived by Jeremy Bentham as avoidance of pain and pursuit of pleasure, or endless cost-benefit calculations. Thirty years ago, at the dawn of the neoliberal era, *homo oeconomicus* was still oriented by interest and profit seeking, but now entrepreneurialized itself at every turn and was formulated as human capital. As Foucault puts it, the subject was now submitted to diffusion and multiplication of the enterprise form within the social body.[35] Today, *homo oeconomicus* maintains aspects of that entrepreneurialism, but has been significantly reshaped as financialized human capital: its project is to self-invest in ways that enhance its value or to attract investors through constant attention to its actual or figurative credit rating, and to do this across every sphere of its existence.[36]

The contemporary "economization" of subjects by neoliberal rationality is thus distinctive in at least three ways. First, in contrast with classical economic liberalism, we are everywhere *homo oeconomicus* and only *homo oeconomicus*. This is one of the novelties that neoliberalism introduces into political and social thought and is among its most subversive elements. Adam Smith, Nassau Senior, Jean-Baptiste Say, David Ricardo, and James Steuart devoted a great deal of attention to the relationship of economic and political life without ever reducing the latter to the former or imagining that economics could remake other fields of existence in and through its own terms and metrics.[37] Some even went so far as to designate the danger or impropriety of allowing the economy too great an influence in political, not to mention moral and ethical life.

Second, neoliberal *homo oeconomicus* takes its shape as human capital seeking to strengthen its competitive positioning and appreciate its value, rather than as a figure of exchange or interest. This, too, is novel and distinguishes the neoliberal subject from the subject drawn by classical or neoclassical economists, but also by Jeremy Bentham, Karl Marx, Karl Polanyi, or Albert O. Hirschman.

Third, and related, today, the specific model for human capital and its spheres of activity is increasingly that of financial or investment capital, and not only productive or entrepreneurial capital. Marketeering based on profitable exchange and entrepreneurializing one's assets and endeavors has not entirely vanished and remains part of what contemporary human capital is and does. Increasingly, however, as Michel Feher argues, *homo oeconomicus* as human capital is concerned with enhancing its portfolio value in all domains of its life, an activity undertaken through practices of self-investment and attracting investors.[38] Whether through social media "followers," "likes," and "retweets," through rankings and ratings for every activity and domain, or through more directly monetized practices, the pursuit of education, training, leisure, reproduction, consumption, and more are increasingly configured as strategic decisions and practices related to enhancing the self's future value.

Of course, many contemporary firms continue to be oriented by interest, profit, and market exchange; commodification has not disappeared from capitalist economies, nor has entrepreneurialism. The point, however, is that finance capital and financialization bring about a new model of economic conduct, one that is not only reserved to investment banks or corporations. Even entrepreneurial firms that continue to seek profits through cost reduction, development of new markets, or adaptation to changing environments also pursue careful strategies of risk management, capital enhancement, leveraging, speculation, and practices designed to attract investors and enhance credit ratings and portfolio value. Thus, the conduct and subjectivity of *homo oeconomicus* shaped in the era of finance capital differs significantly from Smithian truck, barter, and exchange, and from Benthamite pursuit of pleasure and avoidance of pain. As neoliberal rationality remakes the human being as human capital, an earlier rendering of *homo oeconomicus* as an interest maximizer gives way to a formulation of the subject as both a member of a firm and as itself a firm, and in both cases as appropriately conducted by the governance practices appropriate to firms. These practices, as Chapter 4 will explore in detail, substitute ever-evolving new management techniques for top-down rule in state, firm, and subject alike. Centralized authority, law, policing, rules, and quotas are replaced by networked, team-based, practice-oriented techniques emphasizing incentivization, guidelines, and benchmarks.

When the construction of human beings and human conduct as *homo oeconomicus* spreads to every sphere, including that of political life itself, it radically transforms not merely the organization, but the purpose and character of each sphere, as well as relations among them. In political life, the focus of this book, neoliberalization transposes democratic political principles of justice into an economic idiom, transforms the state itself into a manager of the nation on the model of a firm (Thailand's prime minister, Thaksin Shinawatra, declared himself "CEO of Thailand Inc." in the 1990s), and hollows out much of the substance of democratic citizenship and even popular sovereignty. Thus, one important effect of neoliberalization is the vanquishing of liberal democracy's already anemic *homo politicus*, a vanquishing with enormous consequences for democratic institutions, cultures, and imaginaries.

How do human beings come to be figured as *homo oeconomicus* and more specifically as "human capital" across all spheres of life? How does the distinctive form of reason that is neoliberalism become a governing rationality saturating the practices of ordinary institutions and discourses of everyday life? While neoliberal policy was often imposed through fiat and force in the 1970s and 1980s, neoliberalization in the Euro-Atlantic world today is more often enacted through specific techniques of governance, through best practices and legal tweaks, in short, through "soft power" drawing on consensus and buy-in, than through violence, dictatorial command, or even overt political platforms. Neoliberalism governs as sophisticated common sense, a reality principle remaking institutions and human beings everywhere it settles, nestles, and gains affirmation. Of course, there are dust-ups, including protests and political altercations with police, over the privatization of public goods, union busting, benefits reductions, public-service cuts, and more. But neoliberalization is generally more termitelike than lionlike... its mode of reason boring in capillary fashion into the trunks and branches of workplaces, schools, public agencies, social and political discourse, and above all, the subject. Even the termite metaphor is not quite apt: Foucault would remind us that any ascendant political rationality is not only destructive, but brings new subjects, conduct, relations, and worlds into being.

Within neoliberal rationality, human capital is both our "is" and our "ought"—what we are said to be, what we should be, and what the rationality makes us into through its norms and construction of environments. We have already seen that one way neoliberalism differs from classical economic liberalism is that all domains are markets, and we are everywhere presumed to be market actors. Another difference, underscored by Foucault, is that in neoliberal reason, competition replaces exchange as the market's root principle and basic good.[39] (As we will see in Chapter 2, Foucault also argues that neoliberal reason formulates competition as normative, rather than natural, and thus requires facilitation and legal support.) This subtle shift from exchange to competition as the essence of the market means that all market actors are rendered as little capitals (rather than as owners, workers, and consumers) competing with, rather than exchanging with each other. Human capital's constant and ubiquitous aim, whether studying, interning, working, planning retirement, or reinventing itself in a new life, is to entrepreneurialize its endeavors, appreciate its value, and increase its rating or ranking. In this, it mirrors the mandate for contemporary firms, countries, academic departments or journals, universities, media or websites: entrepreneurialize, enhance competitive positioning and value, maximize ratings or rankings.

This figure of the human as an ensemble of entrepreneurial and investment capital is evident on every college and job application, every package of study strategies, every internship, every new exercise and diet program. The best university scholars are characterized as entrepreneurial and investment savvy, not simply by obtaining grants or fellowships, but by generating new projects and publications from old research, calculating publication and presentation venues, and circulating themselves and their work according to what will enhance their value.[40] The practice of networking now so ubiquitous in all fields of endeavor is a practice Michel Feher calls "attracting investors."[41] These examples remind us again that as neoliberal rationality disseminates market values and metrics to new spheres, this does not always take a monetary form; rather, fields, persons, and practices are economized in ways that vastly exceed literal wealth generation. This point will be crucial to understanding the neoliberal remaking of democracy.

Rendering human beings as human capital has many ramifications. Here, I focus only on those relevant to my argument.

First, we are human capital not just for ourselves, but also for the firm, state, or postnational constellation of which we are members. Thus, even as we are tasked with being responsible for ourselves in a competitive world of other human capitals, insofar as we are human capital *for* firms or states concerned with their own competitive positioning, we have no guarantee of security, protection, or even survival. A subject construed and constructed as human capital both for itself and for a firm or state is at persistent risk of failure, redundancy and abandonment through no doing of its own, regardless of how savvy and responsible it is. Fiscal crises, downsizing, outsourcing, furloughs—all these and more can jeopardize us, even when we have been savvy and responsible investors and entrepreneurs. This jeopardy reaches down to minimum needs for food and shelter, insofar as social-security programs of all kinds have been dismantled by neoliberalism. Disintegrating the social into entrepreneurial and self-investing bits removes umbrellas of protection provided by belonging, whether to a pension plan or to a citizenry; only familialism, discussed in Chapter 3, remains an acceptable social harbor, even as public supports for family life, from affordable housing to education, have themselves been degraded by neoliberalism. Moreover, as a matter of political and moral meaning, human capitals do not have the standing of Kantian individuals, ends in themselves, intrinsically valuable. Nor do specifically political rights adhere to human capital; their status grows unclear and incoherent. As Chapter 5 will argue, rights themselves can be economized, sharply recast in meaning and application. As human capital, the subject is at once in charge of itself, responsible for itself, yet an instrumentalizable and potentially dispensable element of the whole. In this regard, the liberal democratic social contract is turning inside out.

Second, inequality, not equality, is the medium and relation of competing capitals. When we are figured as human capital in all that we do and in every venue, equality ceases to be our presumed natural relation with one another. Thus, equality ceases to be an a priori or fundament of neoliberalized democracy. In legislation, jurisprudence, and the popular imaginary, inequality becomes normal, even normative. A democracy composed of human capital features winners and losers, not equal treatment or equal protection. In this regard, too, the social contract is turning inside out.

Third, when everything is capital, labor disappears as a category, as does its collective form, class, taking with it the analytic basis for alienation, exploitation, and association among laborers. Dismantled at the same time is the very rationale for unions, consumer groups, and other forms of economic solidarity apart from cartels among capitals. This paves the way for challenging several centuries of labor law and other protections and benefits in the Euro-Atlantic world and, perhaps as important, makes illegible the foundations of such protections and benefits. One instance of this illegibility is the growing popular opposition to pensions, security of employment, paid holidays, and other hard-won achievements by public-sector workers in the United States. Another measure of it is the absent sympathy for the effects of life-threatening austerity measures imposed on Southern Europeans amid the 2011–2012 European Union crises. German Chancellor Merkel's infamous "lazy Greeks" speech during this crisis was important not only for fueling reactionary populist sentiments in Northern

Europe, but also for delivering as common sense the charge that Spanish, Portuguese, and Greek workers should not enjoy comfortable lives or retirements.[42]

Fourth, when there is only *homo oeconomicus*, and when the domain of the political itself is rendered in economic terms, the foundation vanishes for citizenship concerned with public things and the common good. Here, the problem is not just that public goods are defunded and common ends are devalued by neoliberal reason, although this is so, but that citizenship itself loses its *political* valence and venue. Valence: *homo oeconomicus* approaches everything as a market and knows only market conduct; it cannot think public purposes or common problems in a distinctly political way. Venue: Political life, and the state in particular (about which more in a moment), are remade by neoliberal rationality. The replacement of citizenship defined as concern with the public good by citizenship reduced to the citizen as *homo oeconomicus* also eliminates the very idea of a people, a demos asserting its collective political sovereignty.

As neoliberalism wages war on public goods and the very idea of a public, including citizenship beyond membership, it dramatically thins public life without killing politics. Struggles remain over power, hegemonic values, resources, and future trajectories. This persistence of politics amid the destruction of public life and especially educated public life, combined with the marketization of the political sphere, is part of what makes contemporary politics peculiarly unappealing and toxic—full of ranting and posturing, emptied of intellectual seriousness, pandering to an uneducated and manipulable electorate and a celebrity-and-scandal-hungry corporate media. Neoliberalism generates a condition of politics absent democratic institutions that would support a democratic public and all that such a public represents at its best: informed passion, respectful deliberation, aspirational sovereignty, sharp containment of powers that would overrule or undermine it.

Fifth, as the legitimacy and task of the state becomes bound exclusively to economic growth, global competitiveness, and maintenance of a strong credit rating, liberal democratic justice concerns recede. The economy becomes the organizing and regulative principle of the state and of postnational constellations such as the European Union. This is what Obama's January 2013 State of the Union speech made clear: justice, peace, or environmental sustainability may be pursued to the extent that they advance economic purposes. It was also underscored by the EU bailouts in Southern Europe: the welfare of millions was sacrificed to avert debt default and currency downgrades—such is the fate of citizenship converted to human capital. Similarly, not shuttered public services, but the effect on the stock market, on America's credit rating, and on the growth rate dominated pundits' worries about the fall 2013 government shutdown and the congressional fracas over lifting the debt ceiling.

The success of neoliberal rationality in remaking citizenship and the subject is indexed by the lack of a scandalized response to the state's new role in prioritizing, serving, and propping a supposedly free-market economy. The economization of everything and every sphere, including political life, desensitizes us to the bold contradiction between an allegedly free-market economy and a state now wholly in service to and controlled by it. As the state itself is privatized, enfolded, and animated by market rationality in all of its own functions, and as its legitimacy increasingly rests in facilitating, rescuing, or steering the economy, it is measured as any other firm would be. Indeed, one of the paradoxes of the neoliberal transformation of the state is that it is remade on the model of the firm while compelled to serve and facilitate an economy it is not supposed to touch, let alone to challenge.

The absence of a scandalized response to the state's role in propping up capital and demoting justice and citizen well-being is also the effect of neoliberalism's conversion of basic principles of democracy from a political to economic semantic order. More than merely demoted, state enactments of the principles of justice are transformed by neoliberal rationality when, in Foucault's words, "neoliberalism models the overall exercise of political power on the principles of the market…and the economic grid tests action and gauges validity."[43] When such economization configures the state as the manager of a firm and the subject as a unit of entrepreneurial and self-investing capital, the effect is not simply to narrow the functions of state and citizen or to enlarge the sphere of economically defined freedom at the expense of common investment in public life and public goods. Rather, it is to transpose the meaning and practice of democratic concerns with equality, freedom, and sovereignty from a political to an economic register. Here is how this goes.

As liberty is relocated from political to economic life, it becomes subject to the inherent inequality of the latter and is part of what secures that inequality. The guarantee of equality through the rule of law and participation in popular sovereignty is replaced with a market formulation of winners and losers. Liberty itself is narrowed to market conduct, divested of association with mastering the conditions of life, existential freedom, or securing the rule of the demos. Freedom conceived minimally as self-rule and more robustly as participation in rule by the demos gives way to comportment with a market instrumental rationality that radically constrains both choices and ambitions. With the vanquishing of *homo politicus*, the creature who rules itself and rules as part of the demos, no longer is there an open question of how to craft the self or what paths to travel in life. This is one of many reasons why institutions of higher education cannot now recruit students with the promise of discovering one's passion through a liberal arts education. Indeed, no capital, save a suicidal one, can freely choose its activities and life course or be indifferent to the innovations of its competitors or parameters of success in a world of scarcity and inequality. Thus, in the neoliberal *political* imaginary that has taken a responsibilized turn, we are no longer creatures of moral autonomy, freedom, or equality. We no longer choose our ends or the means to them. We are no longer even creatures of interest relentlessly seeking to satisfy ourselves.[44] In this respect, the construal of *homo oeconomicus* as human capital leaves behind not only *homo politicus*, but humanism itself.

As the province and meaning of liberty and equality are recalibrated from political to economic, political power comes to be figured as their enemy, an interference with both. This open hostility to the political in turn curtails the promise of the modern liberal democratic state to secure inclusion, equality, and freedom as dimensions of popular sovereignty. Again, as each term is relocated to the economy and recast in an economic idiom, inclusion inverts into competition, equality into inequality, freedom into deregulated marketplaces, and popular sovereignty is nowhere to be found. There, compressed to a formula, is the means by which neoliberal rationality hollows out both liberal democratic reason and a democratic imaginary that would exceed it.

Moreover, in their newly economized form, neoliberal states will shed as much as possible the cost of developing and reproducing human capital. Thus, they substitute individually debt-financed education for public higher education, personal savings and interminable employment for social security, individually purchased services for public services of all kinds, privately sponsored research for public research and knowledge, fees for use for public infrastructure. Each of these intensifies inequalities and further constrains the liberty of neoliberalized subjects required to procure individually what was once provisioned in common.

It is difficult to overstate the significance for democracy of these remakings of the purpose and orientations of both states and citizens. Of course, they entail the dramatic curtailment of public values, public goods, and popular participation in political life. They facilitate the increasing power of large corporations to fashion law and policy for their own ends, not simply crowding out, but overtly demoting the public interest. Obviously, too, governance according to market metrics displaces classic liberal democratic concerns with justice and balancing diverse interests. But neoliberalization extinguishes something else. As economic parameters become the only parameters for all conduct and concern, the limited form of human existence that Aristotle and later Hannah Arendt designated as "mere life" and that Marx called life "confined by necessity"—concern with survival and wealth acquisition—this limited form and imaginary becomes ubiquitous and total *across* classes.[45] Neoliberal rationality eliminates what these thinkers termed "the good life" (Aristotle) or "the true realm of freedom" (Marx), by which they did not mean luxury, leisure, or indulgence, but rather the cultivation and expression of distinctly human capacities for ethical and political freedom, creativity, unbounded reflection, or invention. Here is Marx:

> Just as the savage must wrestle with Nature to satisfy his wants, to maintain and reproduce life, so must civilized man.... Freedom in this field can only consist in...the associated producers, rationally regulating their interchange with Nature, bringing it under their common control, instead of being ruled by it as by the blind forces of Nature; and achieving this...under conditions most favorable to, and worthy of, their human nature. But it nonetheless still remains a realm of necessity. Beyond it begins that development of human energy which is an end in itself, the true realm of freedom, which however can blossom forth only with the realm of necessity as its basis.[46]

For Aristotle, Arendt, and Marx, the potential of the human species is realized not through, but beyond the struggle for existence and wealth accumulation. We need not even reach outside liberalism for this point: for John Stuart Mill, too, what makes humanity "a noble and beautiful object of contemplation" is individuality, originality, "fullness of life," and above all, cultivation of our "higher nature."[47] Neoliberalism retracts this "beyond" and eschews this "higher nature": the normative reign of *homo oeconomicus* in every sphere means that there are no motivations, drives, or aspirations apart from economic ones, that there is nothing to being human apart from "mere life." Neoliberalism is the rationality through which capitalism finally swallows humanity—not only with its machinery of compulsory commodification and profit-driven expansion, but by its form of valuation. As the spread of this form evacuates the content from liberal democracy and transforms the meaning of democracy *tout court*, it subdues democratic desires and imperils democratic dreams.

Of course, liberal democracy has never been untainted by capitalist powers and meanings. The story is well known: repeatedly marginalizing or co-opting various republican and radical democratic insurgencies and experiments, it emerged across modern Europe and North America as a very constrained and conscripted form of democracy. Contoured by nation-state sovereignty, capitalism, and bourgeois individualism, the content of this form has been everywhere (differently) rife with internal exclusions and subordinations—in addition to class, those pertaining to gender, sexuality, race, religion, ethnicity, and global origin. Liberal democracy has featured both imperial and colonial premises. It has secured private property and thus the propertyless, facilitated capital accumulation and thus mass exploitation, and presumed and entrenched privileges for a bourgeois white heterosexual male subject. All of this is common knowledge.

However, for several centuries, liberal democracy has also carried—or monopolized, depending on your view—the language and promise of inclusive and shared political equality, freedom, and popular sovereignty. What happens when this language disappears or is perverted to signify democracy's opposite? What happens to the aspiration for popular sovereignty when the demos is discursively disintegrated? How do subjects reduced to human capital reach for or even wish for popular power? What do radical aspirations for democracy, for humans crafting and controlling their fates together, draw upon as subjective desires, mobilizable as paradoxes or legitimating precepts? What if neoliberal rationality were to succeed in completely recasting both city and soul in its terms? What then?

Foucault's *Birth of Biopolitics* Lectures: Charting Neoliberal Political Rationality

How are we to specify and understand our novel world in the making today, the neoliberalization not only of markets, institutions, and everyday life, but of democracy and the democratic citizen? What precisely is happening to subjects, citizens, families, states, social norms, and institutions of all kinds that has both continuity and rupture with previous modalities of capitalism? How are we to comprehend this at its dawn, rather than at its dusk? Scholars have been struggling with these questions since the early 1970s IMF-and-US-imposed neoliberal experiments in the Global South, followed by the surprise ascendency of neoliberal policy, reason, and governance in the Global North almost two decades later. While neoliberalism in the South was and continues to be violently imposed through coups d'état and juntas, occupations, structural adjustments (now jumping north across the Strait of Gibraltar), and militarized disciplining of populations, its dissemination in the Euro-Atlantic world came about more subtly, through transformations of discourse, law, and the subject that comport more closely with Foucault's notion of governmentality. In the North, while policing and security are certainly both the subject and the object of neoliberal transformations, its main instruments of implementation have been soft, rather than hard power. As a consequence, neoliberalism has taken deeper root in subjects and in language, in ordinary practices and in consciousness. This, too, makes it more difficult to apprehend and articulate, offering perhaps one reason why neoliberalism has met with greater resistance in, say, Latin America over the past several decades than in the United States or Britain.

What, precisely, is neoliberalism as a worldview—what does it want, aspire to, dream? What are its transformations of state, economy, citizen, and value? What is its theory of the state and governance? What is its utopia? What relationship do its lived practices have to its founding theoreticians and contemporary exponents? What are its varieties, disunities, hybrids, local instantiations, phases, reckonings, regroupings? What are its rapid self-transformations and adaptations? What political deficits, potentials, and foreclosures emerge as labor rendered as a commodity transmogrifies into labor rendered as self-investing human capital?

Three decades out, rich accounts by geographers, economists, political theorists, anthropologists, sociologists, philosophers, and historians grappling with these questions have established that neoliberalism is neither singular nor constant in its discursive formulations and material practices. This recognition exceeds the idea that a clumsy or inapt name is draped over a busy multiplicity; rather, neoliberalism as economic policy, modality of governance, and order of reason is at once a global phenomenon, yet inconstant, morphing, differentiated, unsystematic, contradictory, and impure, what Stuart Hall calls a "field of oscillations" or Jamie Peck calls "unruly historical geographies of an evolving interconnected project."[1] Neoliberalism is a specific and normative mode of reason, of the production of the subject, "conduct of conduct," and scheme of valuation, yet in its differential instantiations and encounters with extant cultures and political traditions, it takes diverse shapes and spawns diverse content and normative details, even different idioms.

Thus the paradox of neoliberalism as a global phenomenon, ubiquitous and omnipresent, yet disunified and nonidentical with itself. This dappled, striated, and flickering complexion is also the face of an order replete with contradiction and disavowal, structuring markets it claims to liberate from structure, intensely governing subjects it claims to free from government, strengthening and retasking states it claims to abjure.[2] In the economic realm, neoliberalism aims simultaneously at deregulation and control. It carries purpose and has its own futurology (and futures markets), while eschewing planning. It seeks to privatize every public enterprise, yet valorizes public-private partnerships that imbue the market with ethical potential and social responsibility and the public realm with market metrics. With its ambition for unregulated and untaxed capital flows, it undermines national sovereignty while intensifying preoccupation with national GNP, GDP, and other growth indicators in national and postnational constellations.

There are also different temporal chapters of neoliberal reason, even in its short life to date. Differences that emerge from its diverse schools of origin—Ordo versus Chicago School intellectuals, F. A. Hayek versus Milton Friedman—or those representing different political modulations—Gary Becker or George Stigler, Nicolas Sarkozy or Angela Merkel, George Bush or Barack Obama. There are differences between the neoliberalism of the 1970s and the present, between neoliberalism as an experiment on and in the Third World and as the new enterprise society of Ronald Reagan and Margaret Thatcher, between the socialism of François Mitterrand, the Third Way of Gordon Brown and Bill Clinton, the ownership society of the second George Bush, and most recently…as austerity politics.

So neoliberalism is doubly impossible to grasp: on the one hand, as our present in the making, it shares with all such forces the difficulties of apprehending and theorizing it. On the other hand, it is not a stable or unified object, but rather ranges and changes temporally and geographically. This problem is not solved by Michel Foucault's account of neoliberalism, but it is bracketed by it in a certain way. Foucault argued for understanding neoliberalism as a normative order of reason that would become a governing rationality, a distinctive "art of government," a novel "reasoned way of governing best."[3] Neither a stage of capitalism nor formulated in response to crises of capitalism, neoliberalism for Foucault was an intellectually conceived and politically implemented "reprogramming of liberal governmentality" that first took hold in postwar Germany and was increasingly in evidence in other parts of Europe at the time of Foucault's lectures on the subject in the late 1970s. Understood as a distinctive form of reason that, when it becomes ascendant, will remake liberal governing and government, neoliberalism may comprise a variety of local instantiations and a range of different policies or techniques while hewing to discernible norms and principles that consistently distinguish it from classical economic and political liberalism, as well as from Keynesianism, social democracy, or state-owned and state-controlled economies. In other words, the norms and principles of neoliberal rationality do not dictate precise economic policy, but rather set out novel ways of conceiving and relating state, society, economy, and subject and also inaugurate a new "economization" of heretofore noneconomic spheres and endeavors. This conceptualization of neoliberalism is what makes Foucault's thinking a useful springboard for theorizing neoliberalism's dedemocratizing effects today.

FOUCAULT'S 1978–79 COLLÈGE DE FRANCE LECTURES, *THE BIRTH OF BIOPOLITICS*

Almost any reader of Foucault's 1978–79 lectures on neoliberal reason at the Collège de France will be struck by his extraordinary prescience about the contours and importance of a formation that was just then beginning to take shape, but that would come to dominate the future of Europe. At the time, critical intellectuals mainly characterized neoliberalism as something the Global North imposed on the

Global South—something that reconfigured as it intensified North-South inequalities, something that resecured the South as a source of cheap resources, labor, and production in the aftermath of colonialism, something that was perfectly compatible with coups, support of brutal dictatorships and other political interventions, and something that could also be carried out with the velvet glove of International Monetary Fund, World Bank, and World Trade Organization governance, and, eventually, NAFTA-like trade agreements.

While students of neoimperialism in the 1970s and early 1980s grasped the importance of neoliberal economic experiments in parts of Latin America, Africa, Asia, and the Caribbean, they rarely detected its presence back in the metropole. The "Washington Consensus" affirming free-market policies over Keynesian ones was still more than a decade off. Thatcher and Reagan had not yet come to power. European welfare states still appeared to be the beacon and the future of the civilized West, and the question for most of those leaning left in the mid-1970s was not how to defend them, but whether they could be pushed further toward—or beyond—social democracy.

This is the backdrop against which Foucault's lectures seem remarkable. Here we find Foucault tracking how liberalism had been transmogrifying into neoliberalism since the 1950s, how the theory was seeping into political practice and political reason, how its worms lived in the bowels of a hegemonic Keynesianism, indeed, how many European countries in the 1960s began to blend neoliberal principles into welfare statism. Here is Foucault showing how a new political and economic subject, a new form of political reason, and above all, a new form of governmental rationality and state legitimacy were articulated by a diverse set of postwar intellectuals and were beginning to appear in policy and political discourse as early as the 1950s. Here is Foucault formulating neoliberalism not as a 1980s political rebellion by new-Right populists, not as a vision heralded by a specific set of political leaders and economic craftsmen in the century's final decades, but rather as an "emergence" over the second and third quarters of the twentieth century, already "the program of most governments of capitalist countries"[4] at the time of his lectures. All these are clues that Foucault's neoliberalism differs significantly from conventional accounts.

Against the conventional story, Foucault's formulation of neoliberalism as a remaking of the liberal *art of government* is able to reveal the slow transformation of liberal into neoliberal formations, neoliberalism's continuities with *and* modifications of liberal political and economic theory; neoliberalism's nonunified character, even at its inception; the commonalities that nonetheless bind this modality of thought, governance, and reason into an identifiable and nameable one; and neoliberalism's cohabitation with certain other political rationalities, what he calls "a series of governmental rationalities [that] overlap, lean on each other, challenge each other, and struggle with each other: art of government according to truth...according to the rationality of the sovereign state...according to the rationality of economic agents...and according to the rationality of the governed themselves."[5]

These combined accomplishments suggest a remarkable confounding of Hegel's insistence that the owl of Minerva flies only at dusk, perhaps suggesting as well the advantages of genealogical over dialectical history for grasping the present. That said, just as Marx could not have anticipated some of the inventions, trajectories, and encounters of capital after attempting to theorize its foundations, Foucault could not anticipate neoliberalism's unfolding in the last part of the twentieth century in the Euro-Atlantic world—its unpredictable transformations and modifications, its imbrication with other discourses and developments. Hence, after contextualizing and reprising Foucault's account, I will identify some of the significant developments between Foucault's time and our own that generate distinctive contemporary features of neoliberal rationality, and I will identify as well several intrinsic limitations of his account.

Context

The 1978–79 Collège de France lectures are notoriously difficult to place in Foucault's thought. Testimony to his admirable willingness to go where his reading and thinking led him, rather than follow rigid research plans and hypotheses, they nonetheless stand out in several respects for their divergence from the rest of his work and its trajectory. While he opens with the idea that an appreciation of the rise of political economy will assist in understanding the transformation of the state and of *raison d'état* in modernity, this does not explain his specific turn to the intellectual history of twentieth-century neoliberalism, the only research Foucault ever undertook on contemporary theory. Moreover, the lectures, which travel under the title *The Birth of Biopolitics*, seem to have little to do with that subject, apart from his attention to the governance of civil society in the final lecture; that is, while the reprogramming of liberal governmentality he is tracking certainly has implications for biopolitics, it does not address its "birth."[6] Perhaps Foucault was wandering a bit that year, trying out various ways of opening historico-theoretical problems preoccupying him and also seeking to make sense of what he was reading in his daily newspapers.

The lectures on neoliberalism have another odd feature. Despite their prescience and rich insights, they largely comprise partial and speculative intellectual histories. As such, they do not abide by Foucault's own rules for grasping the complex emergence of governing rationalities and subject formations.[7] With one or two small exceptions, they do not study popular or political discourses contributing to, carrying, or disseminating neoliberal reason. They do not explore the polyvalence of discourses generating neoliberal rationality and, again with a minor exception or two, they do not explore how other discourses compromise, modify, or transform neoliberal reason. These absences are related and presumably issue in part from Foucault's quite partial foray into this field, in part from his express concern with a form of reason, rather than with "real governmental practice[s]…problems…tactics…and instruments," and partly from the fact that neoliberalism was not full-blown or hegemonic but merely whispering its emergence in Foucault's time. This last feature challenges genealogy's aim to offer a "history of the present," diverting it to discernment of a specter or adumbration in thought and thus contributing to something more like a history of the future. Thus, rather than tracking "substitutions, displacements, disguised conquests, and systematic reversals" played out as "a series of subjugations" on the body "as the inscribed surface of events"—exemplified in his genealogies of sexuality, punishment, and madness and formulated methodologically in "Nietzsche, Genealogy, History"—Foucault offers a quieter, less complete biographical, historical, geopolitical story of the emergence and dissemination of neoliberal reason.[8]

Not only is the archive and the approach to studying neoliberalism strikingly un-Foucauldian, relying, with few exceptions, on intellectual, even academic currents for its claims about government, the state, civil society, political economy, and more,[9] the lectures vacillate between marking neoliberalism's distinctiveness and establishing its continuity with liberalism. Thus, neoliberalism appears alternately (and inconsistently) as a break with, a swerve from, and a modification of liberalism. Indeed, the lecture series as a whole oscillates a bit awkwardly between liberalism and neoliberalism: lectures 1 through 4 discuss liberalism, lectures 5 through 10 address neoliberalism, and the final two lectures return to liberalism, even as they tender claims about the present.

All of this can be explained in part by the in-progress and relatively impromptu character of the research Foucault was presenting. (Some scholars have argued that several of the lectures appear to be almost extemporaneous.)[10] The lectures never became a book or even the substructure for one—Foucault would next turn to arts of the self and other researches for volumes 2 and 3 of *The History of Sexuality*. Thus, these lectures might be understood in the vein of some of Marx's early manuscripts—lines of inquiry and thought undertaken largely for self-edification and clarification that should not be taken as settled or polished formulations, let alone doctrine.

It is also unclear what Foucault's own normative stakes in and takes on neoliberalism were. How much is he engaged in an anti-Marxist rant in these lectures, invested in exposing the colossal failings (yet maddening persistence in the French intellectual scene) of Marxist categories, methods, lenses, and concrete historical enactments, an investment particularly manifest in lectures 4 and 8? How much is his interest in neoliberalism a reflection of his own attraction to it, conse-quent to what he describes at some points as its commitment to a cer-tain principle of freedom and "not being governed so much," even as he also describes the liberal/neoliberal subject as consummately gov-ernable and government itself as developing a complex new relation-ship with freedom—organizing and administering it, producing and consuming it?[11] How much is the research contoured by his contin-ued aim to map modern and contemporary governmentality or to get at something about contemporary biopolitics that he never quite man-aged to gather up from his exploration of neoliberal thought? Or do the lectures represent a kind of mashup of several of Foucault's ongoing concerns—the development of liberalism as a biopolitics operating through and on individual liberty, the instrumentalization of liberty by governmentality, the critique of Marxism and socialism, the continued problematization of the state and sovereignty—as well as an immediate interest in the emergence of neoliberal reason in 1970s Europe?[12]

I raise these questions not to pursue them, but because any close engagement with the lectures provokes them. And while I consider overstated the claim that Foucault's interest in neoliberalism was driven by his deep attraction to it,[13] I also reject the common perception that Foucault is offering a neo-Marxist critique of neoliberal rationality in these lectures, even if some of us draw on his work for such purposes.

Foucault was examining something that fascinated him in the present and whose twentieth-century intellectual origins—distinctive for their antipathy to certain kinds of governmental power—also intrigued him, yet he appeared relatively uninterested in what many would call the "politics" of neoliberalism—its gestation of new inequalities and concentrations of wealth, its deracinations and destitutions of populations, its dismantling of publics and social solidarities. Rather, he was interested in neoliberalism's transformations of the social, the state, and the subject and also in how neoliberalism brings liberalism more squarely into places, such as France, where liberal principles had heretofore nested somewhat uneasily with other governing rationalities, such as republicanism and socialism. He is interested in how this novel political rationality poses a new problem of "the relation between the subject of right and the economic subject."[14] Above all, he was fascinated by neoliberalism's "reprogramming" of liberalism, its radical reconfiguration of relations and purposes among state, economy, and subject.

These interests mean that Foucault's account of neoliberalism may not much impress critics on the Left. Here is how he formulates the central *political* problematic to which first liberal and then neoliberal arts of government respond: it is a question of

> how to govern in a space of sovereignty inhabited by economic subjects, since precisely...the juridical theory of the subject of right, of natural rights, and of the granting and delegation of rights does not fit together with...the very designation and characterization of *homo oeconomicus.* The governability...of these individuals, who inhabit the space of sovereignty as subjects of right and, at the same time, as economic men, can only be assured...by the emergence of a new object, a new domain or field.... These individuals...are only governable insofar as a new ensemble can be defined which will envelop them both as subjects of right and as economic actors...[I]t is this new ensemble that is characteristic of the liberal art of governing.[15]

The emergence of *homo oeconomicus*, the central character in Foucault's story of the emergence of liberalism, changes how sovereign power in government *must* work; it demands a new governing rationality, which is what Foucault believed Adam Smith, John Locke, and David Hume supplied for liberalism and Wilhelm Ropke, F. A Hayek, Milton Friedman, and others provided for neoliberalism.[16] Focus on this character is what permits Foucault to feature neoliberalism as a novel contemporary chapter in *liberal* governmentality, one that foregrounds the problem of governing *homo oeconomicus* (and the economy as a whole) "without touching it." I want to build this problem a little before turning to Foucault's broader characterization of neoliberalism.

Foucault begins his 1978–79 Collège de France lectures by considering different kinds of limits on state power. *Raison d'état* in early modern monarchical Europe, he argues, was an exercise in *external* self-limitation; competition among states made every state the limit of every other state's exercise of power.[17] On the other hand, internally, law or juridical practice functions as what Foucault calls a "multiplier" of state power, extending, rather than limiting the power of the king.[18] However, in the seventeenth century, with the rise of parliaments, the bourgeoisie, and their correlative challenges to monarchical and aristocratic authority, law and right came to be limits on, rather than extensions of intensifications of royal power; juridical reason began to move against *raison d'état*, to constitute its limits, rather than a source of its elaboration and force.[19] In the mid-eighteenth century, yet another principle of limitation arose, that of the market. Rights remained a constraint on sovereignty, but the principle of what Foucault terms "market veridiction" now animated an ontological, epistemological, and political reformulation of sovereignty, one that not only constrained, but produced a new form of the state and its legitimacy.[20] As the market became the new site of truth or veridiction, it simultaneously became that which must be left alone by the state and what came to construct, measure, and legitimate the state, substituting for law and edict in this regard.

Here we can spy one of Foucault's many implicit, but important quarrels with Marx in these lectures. Foucault is *not* saying that in the mid-eighteenth century, capital came to dominate government or that the state became an apparatus of capital. Rather, his point is that the market (tellingly, he never says "capitalism" here) become a new limit on the state even as it began to saturate and construe the state with its distinctive form of reason and that this limit and this form of reason are at the heart of what we call "liberalism." Without ever arguing that liberalism or neoliberalism actually usher in free markets, he argues that political economy becomes the new reason of state and establishes how not to govern too much: "the new art of government is 'the reason of the least state'" or "frugal government."[21] He adds, "the question of the frugality of government is indeed the question of liberalism."[22] In Foucault's telling, liberalism was born with a market governmentality, rather than the rights of man at its heart. However, in contrast with Marxism, this governmentality rested not on the liberal state's concern with property rights, disavowal of class, market ideology, or capture by the interests of capital, but other things altogether: on the one hand, the market was a new site of veridiction for governing and a new way of organizing, limiting, measuring, and legitimating government.[23] On the other hand, government acquired a new and complex relationship with freedom—it produced, organized, managed, and consumed individual freedom, all without touching the subject.[24] This is what makes liberal governmentality coterminous with the emergence of biopolitics.

Thus, while Foucault's account of liberalism includes a tributary from rights and their constitutionalization, that is, from social contract theory, it is fundamentally a political-economic construction refracting and organizing government through the truth and the limit of the market and establishing interest-driven *homo oeconomicus* as the subject it governs. Not Hobbes, Locke, and Rousseau, but Smith and

Bentham articulate liberalism's basic problematic and principles. Put another way, for Foucault, there is no significant divergence between economic and political liberalism when they are viewed from the perspective of the economic orientation, limitation, and legitimacy of government and from the perspective of the subject of interest. As I will argue in Chapter 3, there are some problematic ramifications of this relative neglect of liberalism's more political aspects and drives, ramifications pertaining especially to liberalism's imbrication with and inflection of a democratic imaginary, its own and more radical ones. But at this point, we are concerned only to establish the extent to which, for Foucault, neoliberalism emerged as a reprogramming of liberalism, one that responded to a series of crises in liberal governmentality gestated by Keynesianism, fascism, Nazism, state planning, and social democracy. For Foucault, neoliberalism was born not from crises of capitalist accumulation, as David Harvey and other Marxists would have it, but of liberal governmentality.[25]

Foucault's Neoliberalism

Foucault introduces the intellectual history of neoliberalism with an appreciation of its twin birthplaces separated by two decades, an ocean, and a world war. There was, first, the Ordoliberal or Freiburg School, comprising sociologists, economists, and philosophers, which emerged in Germany and Austria in the mid-1930s and gained serious traction at the close of World War II. On the other side of the Atlantic, the Chicago School of economics emerged in the 1950s. Foucault identifies F. A. Hayek as a critical intellectual link between the two schools and chief inspiration of "American anarcho-capitalism"; Hayek was raised on Ordoliberalism, but after spending time in the United States in the 1950s was eventually appointed at the University of Freiburg in 1962, "thus closing the circle."[26]

Foucault devotes much of lecture 5 to the major differences between the two schools. He notes that the Ordo School was reacting to Nazism and fascism, while the Chicago School was reacting to New Deal Keynesianism, and he elaborates their distinctive intellectual positions on the nature of the economy, state, and freedom. Among the most important of these is the Ordoliberals' deep appreciation of the state's role in facilitating competition and the Chicago School's development of the theory of human capital. The Ordoliberals, according to Foucault, also provide more latitude for state governance of the social, for protecting "warm moral and cultural values" antithetical to the "cold mechanism of competition."[27] (Ironically, this makes for greater conviviality between neoliberalism and neoconservatism in its European variant, yet it is in America that neoconservatism and neoliberalism became so thickly entwined in the 1980s.)[28] Foucault describes American neoliberalism as "more complete and exhaustive" in its promulgation of competition for every sphere, its unlimited extension of the market to every endeavor, activity and problem.[29]

There is much more separating the European and American schools of neoliberalism, but given the extent to which these separate intellectual influences have now intersected and even fused—for example, the Ordo emphasis on extending the formal rationality of the market and the Chicago emphasis on extending its concrete mechanisms have come together in a contemporary governing rationality that features both—I will not on dwell further on these differences. Instead, I will consider what distinguishes neoliberal from classical liberal reason in Foucault's understanding. Foucault himself proceeds this way toward the end of lecture 5:

> We should not be under any illusion that today's neoliberalism is, as is too often said, the resurgence or recurrence of old forms of liberal economics which were formulated in the eighteenth and nineteenth centuries and are now being reactivated by capitalism for a variety of reasons to do with its impotence and crises. . . . In actual fact, something much more important is at stake in modern neo-liberalism, whether this takes the German form . . . or the anarcho-liberal American form. What is at issue is whether

a market economy can in fact serve as the principle, form and model for a state which, because of its defects, is mistrusted by everyone on both the right and the left.... Can the market really have the power of formalization for both the state and society? This is the...crucial problem of present-day liberalism and to that extent it represents an absolutely important mutation [of] traditional liberal projects...it is not just a question of freeing the economy. It is a question of knowing how far the market economy's powers of political and social information extend. This is the stake.[30]

How far can the market become the figure and the mode of rationality for state and society, the political and the social? This question did not contour the ambition of liberalism either as an economic or a political doctrine; the former sought only to free the economic subject, the latter to free the political and civil subject. Neither raised the market itself to a principle of all life or of government.[31] The distinctiveness of neoliberalism, for Foucault, is that it "generalizes the economic form of the market" or "generalizes the 'enterprise' form within the social body," producing an "economization of the entire social field."[32] Thus, Foucault insists, neoliberalism is not just the "reactivation of old economic theories"; it is not "just a way of establishing strictly market relations in society"; nor is it "a cover for...generalized state power." In short, it is not "Adam Smith revived," the market society that is "decoded and denounced in Book I of *Capital*," or "Solzhenitsyn on a world scale."[33] He decries these analytic frameworks for grasping neoliberalism for several pages—each makes neoliberalism "always the same thing only worse" or "nothing at all."[34] Neoliberalism's distinctiveness, Foucault repeats, lies in "taking the formal principles of a market economy and referring and relating them to, projecting them on to a general art of government."[35] This move requires transforming, not merely extending, classical liberalism.

Above all, it means uncoupling the market economy from the political principle of laissez-faire, and here lies the radicalism of Foucault's scholarly intervention into the political debates that would unfold in the decade following his lectures.[36] Neoliberalism is not about the state leaving the economy alone. Rather, neoliberalism activates the state on behalf of the economy, *not* to undertake economic functions or to intervene in economic *effects*, but rather to facilitate economic competition and growth and to economize the social, or, as Foucault puts it, to "regulate society by the market."[37]

This point, which may seem small at first blush, unfolds new worlds. With neoliberalism, the political rationality of the state becomes economic in a triple sense: the economy is at once model, object, and project. That is, economic principles become the model for state conduct, the economy becomes the primary object of state concern and policy, and the marketization of domains and conduct is what the state seeks to disseminate everywhere. At the same time, the economy itself is denaturalized and loses its liberal status as autarkic. Instead, it is understood to require support and maintenance by the state. "Economy" is also detached from exclusive association with the production or circulation of goods and the accumulation of wealth. Instead, "economy" signifies specific principles, metrics, and modes of conduct, including for endeavors where monetary profit and wealth are not at issue. Again, neoliberal political rationality does not merely marketize in the sense of monetizing all social conduct and social relations, but, more radically, casts them in an exclusively economic frame, one that has both epistemological and ontological dimensions.

Neoliberalism achieves these broad effects through a specific set of departures, modifications, and inversions of the principles of classical and neoclassical economic liberalism. Here is a compressed account of Foucault's depiction of those departures, modifications, and inversions.

Competition as nonnatural. For neoliberalism, markets are good because they operate through competition, but competition itself is neither natural nor given. Foucault elaborates this curious and counterintuitive point:

> Competition is not the result of a natural interplay of appetites, instincts, behavior...the effects of competition are due only to the essence that characterizes and constitutes it...not to a pre-existing nature [but] to a formal privilege. Competition has an internal logic; it has its own structure. Its effects are only produced if this logic is respected. It is, as it were, a formal game between inequalities; it is not a natural game between individuals and behaviors.[38]

If, for neoliberals, economic competition is essential (an *eidos*, Foucault calls it at one point) and valuable, but not natural, then it must be continuously supported and corrected from outside, and this need defines one of the crucial functions of the neoliberal state.[39] Government intervenes to produce and reproduce competition, to facilitate or restore it. Again, nature is the province of classical liberalism, hence the importance of laissez-faire to its theorists. By contrast, convention, intervention, and even subvention are all key to neoliberalism.[40] The "juridical gives form to the economic," Foucault says of neoliberalism.[41] "Government must accompany the market from start to finish," he adds.[42] However, what distinguishes neoliberalism from liberalism here is that the state must "govern *for* the market, not *because* of the market."[43] Foucault calls this a complete reversal of classical liberalism, where government is hands-off and/or aims to offset market effects such as unemployment, poverty, resource depletion, or pollution.

The economization of the state and of social policy. The virtue of competition is that it generates economic growth, the promotion of which is "the only one and true fundamental *social* policy."[44] Foucault elaborates: In neoliberalism, "social policy must not be something that works against economic policy and compensates for it" or that "follows strong economic growth by becoming more generous." Instead, economic growth by itself should enable individuals to prosper and to protect themselves against risk, so economic growth *is* the state's social policy.[45] Competition is a means facilitating an end; the state primes this means so that the economy can generate the end.

Neoliberal states thus depart from liberal ones as they become radically economic in a triple sense: The state secures, advances, and props the economy; the state's purpose is to facilitate the economy, and the state's legitimacy is linked to the growth of the economy—as an overt actor on behalf of the economy, the state also becomes responsible for the economy. State action, state purpose, and state legitimacy: each is economized by neoliberalism. The Ordoliberals carried this even further: the market economy should also be the principle of the state's internal regulation and organization. Reversing the liberal formulation in which a free market is defined and supervised by the state, for them, the state should be defined and supervised by the market.[46] In short, the state itself should be economized.

Competition replaces exchange; inequality replaces equality. In neoliberalism, competition replaces the liberal economic emphasis on exchange as the fundamental principle and dynamic of the market.[47] This is another of those seemingly trivial replacements that is a tectonic shift, affecting a range of other principles and venues. Most importantly, equivalence is both the premise and the norm of exchange, while inequality is the premise and outcome of competition. Consequently, when the political rationality of neoliberalism is fully realized, when market principles are extended to every sphere, inequality becomes legitimate, even normative, in every sphere.

Although Foucault himself does not explore the point, this is a knife cut across the body of liberal democracy, where the enshrinement of equality in the rule and application of law is the promise of the social contract. Competition as the central principle of market rationality also means political subjects lose guarantees of protection by the liberal state. Competition yields winners and losers; capital succeeds by destroying or cannibalizing other capitals. Hence, when market competition becomes generalized as a social and political principle, some will triumph and some will die...as a matter of social and political principle.

Human capital replaces labor. Commensurate with neoliberal reason's replacement of exchange by competition and equality by inequality, human capital replaces labor in neoliberal reason.[48] When competition becomes the market's root principle, all market actors are rendered as capitals, rather than as producers, sellers, workers, clients or consumers. As capitals, every subject is rendered as entrepreneurial, no matter how small, impoverished, or without resources, and every aspect of human existence is produced as an entrepreneurial one.[49] "The individual's life itself—with his relationships to private property...with his family, household, insurance, and retirement—must make him into a sort of permanent and multiple enterprise."[50]

The transformation of labor into human capital and of workers into entrepreneurs competing with other entrepreneurs obviously obscures the visibility and iterability of class to an even greater degree than classical liberalism does. It also eliminates the basis for alienation and exploitation as Marx conceived them. And it vanquishes the rationale for unions, consumer groups, or other forms of economic solidarity apart from cartels. Also important, although not part of Foucault's concern, when neoliberal political rationality is complete, when there is only *homo oeconomicus* in every sphere and the domain of the political itself is rendered in economic terms, the figuration of human beings as human capitals eliminates the basis of a democratic citizenry, namely a demos concerned with and asserting its political sovereignty.

Entrepreneurship replaces production. From the replacement of exchange by competition as the market's fundamental value and from the establishment of economic subjects as human capital, it follows that an emphasis on entrepreneurship and productivity replaces an emphasis on commodities and consumption. Productivity is prioritized over product; enterprise is prioritized over consumption or

satisfaction. An enterprise society is not about trucking and bartering things (exchange), nor is it based on desires or appetites for things
(consumption). It is economic in an entirely different sense. Foucault
puts it this way:

> What is sought is not a society subject to the commodity effect but…to
> the dynamic of competition. Not a super-market society but an enterprise
> society. The *homo oeconomicus* sought after is not the man of exchange or
> man the consumer; he is the man of enterprise and production…. The
> art of government programmed by the ordoliberals around the 1930s,
> and which has now become the program of most governments in capital-
> ist countries involves…obtaining a society that is…oriented toward the
> multiplicity and differentiation of enterprises.[51]

Later in this chapter, I will argue that the early neoliberal figure of
enterprise and production has already been superseded by yet another
version of h*omo oeconomicus*, one built on an investment portfolio
model in which (human) capital appreciation replaces production.[52]
This is an implication of the overtaking of productive by finance capital and of profit rooted in productivity by economic rents yielded by
financialization. For now, however, we need to grasp Foucault's point
about enterprise as the orientation and activity of human capital and of
society as a whole. As a subject becomes a field of enterprises, society
is oriented "toward the multiplicity and differentiation of enterprises,"
rather than toward the exchange of commodities.[53] Foucault adds that
multiplying "the enterprise form within the social body is what is at
stake in neoliberal policy" and what makes neoliberalism much more
than a set of economic policies.[54] Rather, "it is a matter of making the
market, competition, and so the enterprise, into what could be called
the formative power of society."[55]

The economization and tacticalization of law. Governing *for* the market means that sovereignty and law become supports for competition,
rather than rights.[56] (In Chapter 5, I will argue that rights themselves

can undergo economization through neoliberal jurisprudence.) The rule of law is not set aside by neoliberalism, but instrumentalized for its purposes, on the one hand, and proliferated in complexity and detail, on the other. An entrepreneurial society, Foucault says, multiplies friction and hence multiplies laws and expands juridicature.[57] However, rule of law for neoliberal rationality is formal, rather than substantive: "The rule of law and *l'état de droit* formalize the action of government as a provider of rules for an economic game in which the only players...must be individuals...or enterprises."[58] Thus, neoliberal law is the opposite of planning. It facilitates the economic game, but does not direct or contain it.[59]

The market as truth. Neoliberalism involves an intensification of the market as a site of "veridiction," Foucault's coinage for the production and circulation of truths that are established, rather than foundational, but, importantly, govern. The economy had already become aligned with truth in classical liberalism when economical government became good government and economical behavior, as Weber reminds us, comported with serving (a Protestant) God. But with neoliberalism, the market becomes *the*, rather than *a* site of veridiction *and* becomes so for every arena and type of human activity. The market is generalized as a form of reason, or as Foucault puts it: "American neoliberalism involves generalizing [the economic form of the market] through the social body and including the whole of the social system not usually conducted through or sanctioned by monetary exchanges."[60] Thus, market principles frame every sphere and activity, from mothering to mating, from learning to criminality, from planning one's family to planning one's death.

The veridiction of the market has two dimensions in neoliberal reason: the market is itself true and also represents the true form of all activity. Rational actors accept these truths, thus accept "reality; conversely, those who act according to other principles are not simply irrational, but refuse "reality." Insofar as rational-choice theory expresses this equation and becomes the hegemonic model for social-science knowledge, it represents a further development of what Herbert Marcuse termed the "closing of the political universe"—the erasure of intelligible, legitimate alternatives to economic rationality.

Responsibilizing the state. The state and *raison d'état* conform to the veridiction of the market in precise ways. As we have already seen, economic metrics govern the institutions and practices of the state, and the state itself is legitimated by economic growth.[61] "The economy produces legitimacy for the state that is its guarantor."[62] The state must support the economy, organizing its conditions and facilitating its growth, and is thereby made responsible for the economy without being able to predict, control, or offset its effects. Hence, far more than a campaign mantra, "It's the economy, stupid!" defines political life in the neoliberal state.

While the state facilitates capital, it does not intervene at the level of exchange (access, opportunity), distribution (income inequality) or collateral damages (ecological, social, political). This aspect of neoliberalism is significant for understanding why the growing imbrication of the state with capital today does not generate the kind of legitimacy crisis predicted by 1970s Marxist state theorists— Jürgen Habermas, Claus Offe, Nicos Poulantzas, Ralph Miliband, among others.[63] The state is not neutral with regard to capital, nor, however, does it compensate for the infelicities or damages of capital.[64] The neoliberal state may act openly as a capitalist state and on behalf of capital because economic growth is its *raison d'état*, and capital appreciation is the presumed engine of growth. Whether this remains true in the era of financialization is taken up later in this chapter.

Political consensus replaces individuation and political contestation. Finally, in neoliberal reason, political integration and consensus replace the atomization and individuation of classical liberalism.[65] This is a brief and underdeveloped theme in Foucault's lectures, but anticipates what will eventually be explicitly achieved through neoliberal governance from the 1990s forward. Here is Foucault's account of what he understands as German postwar neoliberal rationality:

> the economic freedom that...[it] is the role of [the state] to guarantee and maintain, produces something more...than a legal legitimization; it produces a permanent consensus of all those who may appear as agents within these economic processes, as investors, workers, employers, and trade unions. All these economic partners produce a consensus, which is a political consensus, inasmuch as they accept this economic game of freedom.[66]

Foucault is not quite able to bring this claim about integration and consensus into a complete argument, but places markers for such an argument. He notes that "the economically free market binds and manifests political bonds" and that the "production of well-being by economic growth will produce a circuit going from the economic institution to the population's overall adherence to its regime and system."[67] These two claims open the problem that we will need to examine closely: How are neoliberal free-market principles administered in such a way as to bind the population to them politically and to the regime as a whole? How does this particular kind of governance through freedom take place?

The foregoing distillation of Foucault's account of neoliberal reason into brief principles does not do justice to his subtle interpretations of texts, debates, and historical events and to his discovery of connections among them. For that, there is no substitute for reading the lectures. My aim has been to bring forth key elements of this articulation of neoliberalism as a form of normative reason remaking state, society, and subject, generating social policy, positing truth and a theory of law. Where others saw only economic policy, Foucault discerned a revolutionary and comprehensive political rationality, one that drew on classical liberal language and concerns while inverting many of liberalism's purposes and channels of accountability.

However, in part because this research is incomplete, in part because it was undertaken before neoliberalism became hegemonic, in part because there have been so many new developments in capital and in neoliberalism since Foucault's research, and in part because of Foucault's own relative indifference to the problematic now being addressed in this book, there are some features of Foucault's account that require revision or must be jettisoned. We turn now to these problematizations of Foucault's neoliberalism.

NEOLIBERALISM IN THE AGE OF FINANCIALIZATION AND GOVERNANCE

Consider just a few of the contemporary features of neoliberal formations of the subject, state, social and economic, that did not exist or were minute aspects of the landscape Foucault analyzed, yet are significant today.

1) The rise of finance capital, the financialization of everything, and the importance of debt and derivatives in shaping the economy and political reason as well as transforming neoliberal rationality itself—its formulation of markets, subjects, and rational action. Consider, for example, the way that financialization has altered the figure of human capital from an ensemble of enterprises to a portfolio of investments. This transformation also replaces the classical figure of *homo oeconomicus* driven by interest with one driven by (human) capital appreciation.

2) The possibility that economic growth, as the only goal of the state for the economy and the only imperative of the economy, has been augmented through financialization by the aspiration for competitive positioning and a strong bond and credit rating.

3) The crises precipitated by finance capital, not only episodic meltdowns and bankruptcies of firms, cities, and nations, but the permanent joblessness and recessionary conditions produced by the growing

replacement of productive with financial activity across the economy. (While the financial sector now accounts for just under 9 percent of total GDP in the United States, it comprises over 30 percent of all corporate profits; before 2009, this figure exceeded 40 percent.).[68]

4) The austerity politics ensuing from these crises and the transformation of neoliberal rationality that such politics entail, from limitless to constrained, from freedom to sacrifice.

5) The marketization and outsourcing of the state (which Foucault called its "governmentalization") and the financialization of the state itself, which together make the state supremely vulnerable to the movements and crises of finance capital. Financialization also spurs the state to develop derivative markets of its own in everything from terror prediction to student loans and mortgages.

6) The rise of "governance," the meshing of political and business lexicons through which neoliberal reason is disseminated; the antipathy of governance to politics; and the displacement of the rule of law with instruments of governance such as benchmarks, guidelines, buyins, and best practices.

7) The transformation of economic actors and action by governance such that teamwork, responsibilization, and stakeholder consensus replace individual interest; the shift, in short from a neoliberal discourse of free subjects to a discourse featuring more explicitly governed, "responsibilized," and managed subjects.

8) The way that governance integrates self-investing and responsibilized human capital into the project of a growing economy, further mitigating the importance of individual "interests" and freedom.

9) As elements of this governance, the combination of devolved authority and responsibilization of the subject, which together intensify the effect of *"omnes et singulatim"*—all and each—power exercised through massification and isolation.

10) The way these features of governance and human capital generate a citizen who is both integrated into and identified with the project

of the economic health of a nation, a citizen who can be legitimately shed or sacrificed when necessary, especially in the context of austerity politics.

11) The way that "too big to fail" has as its complement "too small to protect": where there are only capitals and competition among them, not only will some win while others lose (inequality and competition unto death replaces equality and commitment to protect life), but some will be rescued and resuscitated, while others will be cast off or left to perish (owners of small farms and small businesses, those with underwater mortgages, indebted and unemployed college graduates). Combined with the relentless attack on publics and what Foucault called "society," an attack that has dismantled public institutions and political spaces, this alters the principle of "inclusion of all" that Foucault describes in his lectures as a novel feature of neoliberalism. Everyone is still rendered as human capital, but the protections he imagined extended to all have vanished.

12) Especially post-9/11, the way that neoliberal reason has intersected with securitization—their mutual legitimation of each other and collaborative bracketing of law, democratic principle, and social welfare in favor of other metrics, including those of efficacy, control, and an advantageous economic climate.[69]

There are many more features of neoliberalism that Foucault did not and could not anticipate, including its grinding of gears between the national, postnational, and global; the importance of transnational institutions to governance and regulation; and the socialization of risk accompanying the privatization of gain. Foucault's neoliberalism is notably statecentric, not governed by transnational or global institutions, and construes the relations between state, economy, and civil society in national terms. The purpose of the list above is simply to identify the elements in his depiction of neoliberalism that matter most to the argument of this book. Most will be taken up in greater detail in coming chapters.

PROBLEMS IN FOUCAULT'S FRAMING OF NEOLIBERALISM

In addition to updating Foucault's theory of neoliberal political rationality in light of the developments listed above, I will be questioning and supplementing several elements of Foucault's account. These include his formulation of the political, his argument that *homo oeconomicus* originated in the seventeenth century, his odd neglect of capital as a form of domination, and above all, his eclipse of the effect of neoliberalism on constitutional democracy and the democratic imaginary. Chapter 3 is largely devoted to telling a different story about the ascendance of *homo oeconomicus* than the one he offers in the lectures. Here, I simply want to prepare the way for that story with some general problematizations.

Insofar as Foucault's investigation and analysis of neoliberalism *is* driven by a concern with the birth of biopolitics,[70] by shifts from sovereignty to governmentality, and by reformations of liberalism, these coordinates are insufficient for capturing what neoliberalism has done to social life, culture, subjectivity, and, above all, politics. This points to a broader limitation in Foucault's work, which we might call his "formulation of the political," a formulation that is largely limited to the (ironically, state-centered) terms of "sovereignty" and "juridicism."

To put this slightly differently, in these lectures, when Foucault speaks of the governing of the modern subject, he speaks in an oddly confining liberal idiom. Governing emanates from the state and always works on the population and the subject—sometimes on the population through the subject, sometimes on the subject through managing the population. Whether Foucault is discussing biopower or discipline, law or sovereign edict, subjects are governed or resist being governed *as* individual subjects or as disciplinary bodies. There is no *political* body, no demos acting in concert (even episodically) or expressing aspirational sovereignty; there are few social forces from below and no shared powers of rule or shared struggles for freedom.

These absences are a perennial limitation of Foucault's work for political theory, but they are especially significant in the neoliberalism lectures. The individual is freed or freed to be governed, and government is the extent of the domain of the political. So there are subjects—produced, governed, and resisting—but not *citizens* in Foucault's genealogies and theories of government, governmentality, and biopolitics.

As a result, Foucault does not draw his account of neoliberal reason into a reflection on its intersection with or effect on democratic political life and citizenship. The remaking, corrosion, and transformation of these domains is ignored in his analysis, and resistance, if it appears at all, happens in other forms and venues. Again, put sharply, Foucault's coordinates of analysis do not permit him to ask: What effects does neoliberal rationality have on democracy, including on democratic principles, institutions, values, expressions, coalitions, and forces? Above all, what is the effect of this rationality on a democratic imaginary? What does it do to the very idea of the demos in popular sovereignty? To the values of political autonomy, political freedom, citizen voice, justice and equality?

This ellipsis in Foucault's thought is worthy of reflection—why is it there, and what are its ramifications?—and is considered further in the following chapter. However, it is also worth pondering in relation to a second major constraint in his thought, the one produced by his notorious late-1970s antagonism to Marxism. As I have already suggested, there is a sustained critique of Marxism running across these lectures, encompassing Marxist epistemology, historiography, and economic and political analysis.[71] Foucault offers a critique of the "logic of capital" in Marx's thought and of Marxist logics more generally. He holds the absence of a Marxist theory of government responsible for what he characterizes as a derivative and deeply impoverished political rationality in actually existing socialist states.[72]

The wholesale refusal of Marxist categories, logics, and historiography allows Foucault to bring forth undertheorized aspects of the emergence of political economy and permits a novel staging of the relationships between liberalism, the state, the economy, and the modern subject. However, this refusal also has its costs, especially in taking the measure of the unique dominations entailed in neoliberalism. Thus, Foucault's seemingly light judgments against neoliberalism pertain not only to his admirable commitment to excavating the novelties that only a genealogical curiosity can discover and not only to the fact that neoliberalism had not yet become hegemonic or fused with discourses that would integrate business, economy, and governance as well as the individual into national economic aims. Rather, Foucault averted his glance from capital itself as a historical and social force. Appearing with striking infrequency in these lectures, when capital is mentioned, it is usually to heap scorn on the idea that it follows necessary logics or entails a system of domination.[73]

However, capital and capitalism are not reducible to an order of reason. While Foucault is surely correct that "in the last analysis, we must produce truth as we must produce wealth, indeed we must produce truth in order to produce wealth in the first place," neither the imperatives nor the effects of capital can be wholly ascribed to capitalism as a regime of truth.[74] As Max Weber, Karl Polanyi, and not only Foucault remind us, capital requires certain truths to get under way at all, and as ideology critique reminds us, capital circulates certain truths to sustain its power as well as its legitimacy, or better, to sustain its legitimacy as power. Marx himself could not dispense with the role of fetishism and reification in securing the production and reproduction of capital. But none of this helps us grasp the imperatives that issue from the systemic drives of capitalism—the imperative of cheapening labor and expanding markets, the imperative of economic growth, the imperative of constant renovations in production (and now in financial instruments) to generate profit, and so forth. Certainly, neoliberalism ushers in a new order of economic reason, a new governing rationality, new modes and venues of commodification, and of course, new features of capitalism and new kinds of capital—from sharing economies to Bitcoin, from derivatives to human capital—but its systematic imperatives cannot be reduced to any of these things. These imperatives can be radically refashioned and reorganized (as financialization itself makes clear), and they are not matters of instinct or of hydraulics, yet they are fundamental life drives no less fierce than those of a living being.

To be very clear, my argument is not that there is only one capitalism, that capitalism exists or operates independently of discourse, or that capitalism has unified and unifying logics. It is simply that capitalism has drives that no discourse can deny . . . to grow, to reduce input costs, to search out new venues of profit, and to generate new markets, even as the form, practices, and venues for these drives are infinitely diverse and operate discursively. Moreover, capital itself (along with, but not reducible to the specific form of reason advancing, organizing, and generating new possibilities with it) always gives shape to human worlds—relations, arrangements, subject production—in excess of its economic operations and circulations and in excess of its aims: this is the power of its world making that Marx depicted so poetically in the *Manifesto* and attempted to systematize in the *German Ideology*. Capital, and not only the articulation of it in economic reason and governance, dominates the human beings and human worlds it organizes. If this aspect is omitted in the theorization of neoliberalism, which is what occurs in these lectures (partly because Foucault is seeking to trace a political rationality and not aiming to describe a form of capitalism, but also because of his profound antagonism toward Marxism at this point in his life), we will not grasp the intricate dynamics between the political rationality and the economic constraints, and we will also not grasp the extent and depth of neoliberalism's power in making this world and unfreedom within it.

Here is another way to see this: Foucault is clearly intrigued by the "freedom" that liberalism and neoliberalism promise. He knows we can be governed through such freedom, but refuses the Marxist point that what is being named as freedom elides and even discursively inverts crucial powers of domination. He rejects the early Marx's thesis that bourgeois freedom, a "great progress," is nevertheless compromised by alienation from and domination by humanly generated powers, powers we only navigate and do not control. He rejects the later Marx's argument that freedom in the realm of exchange sits atop a basement of exploitation and domination in the realm of production. The point here is not to correct Foucault with Marx, but to bring forward certain dimensions of Marx's analysis of capitalism that would have to be welded to Foucault's appreciation of neoliberal reason to generate a rich account of neoliberal dedemocratization.

Foucault's relative indifference to democracy and to capital constitutes the major limitations in his framework for my specific purposes. However, there are also several minor limitations that will be relevant to the work of the coming chapters. At the end of lecture 11, Foucault suggests that economics is a science "lateral to the art of governing," that it cannot be "the science *of* government." This seems importantly wrong today. The claim relates in part to his belief that economics is separated off from civil society, again, an implicit quarrel with Marx. It relates as well to his acceptance of the neoliberal claim that the economy constitutes the limit of government for liberalism and neoliberalism, that it must not be touched because it cannot be known. But it also relates to the fact that he did not anticipate the ways that the sciences of economics, business, and politics would be merged through rational choice, formal modeling, and above all, the language of administrative governance. When the expressly and intentionally antipolitical language of governance, discussed at length in Chapter 4, becomes the lingua franca of the state, corporations, schools, nonprofits, indeed, of all public and private enterprise, economics has become the science of government.

There is also Foucault's argument that *homo oeconomicus* is a creature of interest, one who from the seventeenth century forward has upstaged without fully vanquishing *homo juridicus* and *homo legalis*. According to Foucault, the two modern figures who, apart and together, pose the problem of governmentality are the subject of interest and the subject of right. This, too, will be contested in ensuing chapters. I will suggest that with the ascendency of neoliberalism, interest has ceased to anchor or characterize *homo oeconomicus* and also that Foucault ignores *homo politicus* in modern thought and practice. *Homo politicus*, I will argue in the next chapter, is not captured by the subject of right or by *homo legalis*. Yet it has persisted through most of modernity and has only recently been displaced by the specifically neoliberal formulation of *homo oeconomicus* as human capital, a creature for whom interest is no longer the proper designation. More generally, I will be arguing that Foucault was surprisingly unimaginative about the implications of the neoliberal refashioning of the subject as human capital. As humans become capital for themselves, but also for others, for a firm or a state, their investment value, rather than their productivity, becomes paramount; moral autonomy and hence the basis of sovereign individuality vanishes; and the space and meaning of political citizenship shrink.

These are among the critical concerns about Foucault's work bearing on the effort to theorize neoliberalism's undoing of democracy and a democratic imaginary. On the one hand, Foucault offers a crucial articulation of neoliberalism as a political rationality and a profound appreciation of all that it entailed apart from economic policy. On the other hand, there are limitations and anachronisms in the Collège de France lectures associated with the time, conditions, and intellectual temperament animating them. Moreover, I am seeking to think with, against, and apart from Foucault on subjects that would frankly not have interested him or to which he would have objected, including democracy, citizenship, and histories of political thought. Such heterodox practices of engagement are what I understand critical theory to be and to be for.

CHAPTER THREE

Revising Foucault:
Homo Politicus and *Homo Oeconomicus*

It is a commonplace today that market values are crowding out all others and that vulnerable, precious, or sacred things, including democracy itself, are being increasingly and inappropriately subjected to markets. This lament, along with analyses of its sources and trajectory, is sounded routinely in both popular and academic discourse.[1] In this chapter, I offer a theoretical exploration of a specific facet of this phenomenon: how the neoliberal triumph of *homo oeconomicus* as the exhaustive figure of the human is undermining democratic practices and a democratic imaginary by vanquishing the subject that governs itself through moral autonomy and governs with others through popular sovereignty. The argument is that economic values have not simply supersaturated the political or become predominant over the political. Rather, a neoliberal iteration of *homo oeconomicus* is extinguishing the agent, the idiom, and the domains through which democracy—any variety of democracy—materializes.

Homo oeconomicus has long been the subject of critical analysis. There is a diverse scholarly literature on its origins,[2] on its changing morphology,[3] and on its problematic ontologization and universalization.[4] There are many critiques of the *Weltanschauung* ushered in by its growing prominence in modernity, including concern with the ways that it reduces the human, disenchants the world, and forecloses alternative values.[5] These various studies and analyses contribute to my argument, but none capture it. While it is important to understand who and what this creature is, how and when it comes into being in Western history and thought, and the differences in its historical iterations, my aim is to grasp how it finally vanquishes other figurations and interpellations of the human and with what consequences. How does *homo oeconomicus* triumph over these other figures to become normative in every sphere? And what is its precise shape, comportment, and contents when this occurs? Who is *homo oeconomicus* at the moment of its triumph?

This chapter pursues these questions first through briefly engaging Foucault's theorization of *homo oeconomicus* in his Collège de France lectures on neoliberalism, second through reflecting on the changing morphology and positioning of *homo oeconomicus* and *homo politicus* in the history of Western political thought, then through brief reflections on the gender of contemporary *homo oeconomicus*, and finally through an argument about its dissemination via an order of normative reason and a governing rationality built on that order.

FOUCAULT'S *HOMO OECONOMICUS*

In the 1978–79 Collège de France lectures, Foucault describes a shift in *homo oeconomicus* from classical economic liberalism to neoliberalism wherein an image of man as a creature of needs satisfied through exchange gives way to an image of man as an entrepreneur of himself.[6] "The characteristic feature of the classical conception of *homo oeconomicus*," Foucault says, "is the partner of exchange and the theory of utility based on a problematic of needs."[7] We each come to the market to offer what we have (labor or goods) in exchange for what we need. By contrast, neoliberal man comes to the market, as Foucault puts it, "being for himself his own capital, his own producer, the source of his earnings."[8] Whether he is selling, making, or consuming, he is investing in himself and producing his own satisfaction.

Competition, not exchange, structures the relation among capitals, and capital appreciation through investment structures the relation of any capital entity to itself.

Foucault's recognition of the shifting conceptions of the economy in general and of economic man in particular are extremely helpful in understanding the distinctiveness of neoliberal conceptualizations of both. However, as I will explain shortly, there are some missing features in his account that keep him from taking this recognition toward an appreciation of its consequences for contemporary political life and political subjects.

What is *homo oeconomicus*? To say that it figures man as fundamentally driven and oriented by economic concerns begs two crucial questions. First, there is the question of *homo oeconomicus*'s constitutive outside. Every image of man is defined against other possibilities—thus, the idea of man as fundamentally economic is drawn against the idea of him as fundamentally political, loving, religious, ethical, social, moral, tribal, or something else. Even when one image becomes hegemonic, it carves itself against a range of other possibilities—tacitly arguing with them, keeping them at bay, or subordinating them. So it is not enough to know that humans are economic in their drives and motivations—we must know what this means we are *not*, and especially what has been sent packing, what we are *adamantly* not.

The second question begged by the simple answer pertains to the form and contents imputed to the economic. That is, what *homo oeconomicus* is depends upon how the economy is conceived and positioned vis à vis other spheres of life, other logics, other systems of meaning, other fields of activity.[9] Timothy Mitchell reminds us in *Rule of Experts* that "the economy," a noun with a definite article, a noun naming an objective domain, rather than a process or practice, came into being only in the 1940s and 1950s.[10] Prior to this time, "economy" (without the article) referred to seeking a desired end with the least possible expenditure of means, closer to our notion of efficiency or thriftiness today. (A trace lingers in our language, as when we say "that's a very economical method" or refer to "economizing" in our expenditures or to "economy class" on an airplane.) Thus, when coupled with the adjective, "political," Mitchell argues, "economy" identified a particular mode of governing community affairs, not a structure of production and exchange and not the domain of the market or the sphere of material life. In fact, it is only when the definite article is slipped in that "the economy" is cast as a self-contained structure, one in which wealth generation becomes its own autonomous sphere.[11] Compare this with the etymological root of economy, *oikos*, which identified for the ancient Greeks the space/place of the household, not material life as such, not the market, and not the economy.

In short, the identification and reification of "the economy" as a distinct object is recent, and that recency influences what we mean and what we hear when we say "*homo oeconomicus*." Indeed, appreciation of this recency could also reorient our hearing of phrases like "the markets are jumpy" or "unhappy" or "reacting to fears about Spanish debt." It also provides perspective on what's unfolding now: Although we continue to refer to "the" economy—its activity, health, growth rates, predicaments—this usage is becoming almost anachronistic as the boundaries of the economic erode through the neoliberal dissemination of market metrics to all other spheres of life and human activity, a process that Koray Çalışkan and Michel Callon name "economization."[12] This suggests that *the* economy, far from being a transhistorical category, may have been a brief twentieth-century event. Who or what, then, is *homo oeconomicus* across the ages? Surely a very protean character.

Conceptualization of the economic and of the character taken to be shaped in its image thus requires attention to its historicity and its constitutive opposition or adjacency to other orbits of activity. It also requires specification of its central dynamics, characteristics, and actors. Is economic life fundamentally characterized, as Smith had it, through division of labor and exchange, or as Marx renders it, through class relations of capital and labor?[13] Is it, as for Ricardo, an operation of distribution?[14] Or as for Malthus, a work in and on demography?[15] Or is it, as Keynes insisted, rooted in the problem of employment and the marginal efficiency of capital, or as later macroeconomists would argue, a vast mechanism of social dynamism and integration?[16] Or is economic life, as various neoliberalisms would have it, best defined as a market of competing capital entities, large and small?[17] The particular ways in which the economic is constructed and conceived—its foundations, constitutive elements and dynamics—also determine how subjects within it are cast, for example, as labor or labor power, as commodities or creatures of exchange, as consumers, clients, entrepreneurs, or self-investing human capital.

Who and what *homo oeconomicus* is, what drives and rewards him, what context he operates in, his relation to self and others, depends on the casting of economic life in any particular time and place. While Foucault is alert to this problem (after all, we learned to think like this from him), there are two important respects in which he fails to follow out its full implications in the lectures on neoliberalism. First, across the classical and neoliberal schemas, Foucault sustains as a constant the notion that *homo oeconomicus* is a man of interest, or as he puts it, "a subject of interest within a totality which eludes him and which nevertheless founds the rationality of his egoistic choices."[18] According to Foucault, what "characterizes *homo oeconomicus*" is that he is driven by interest and his "action has a multiplying and beneficial value through the intensification of interest."[19] As I will be arguing, I do not think "interest" adequately captures the ethos or subjectivity of the contemporary neoliberal subject; this subject is so profoundly integrated into and hence subordinated to the supervening goal of macroeconomic growth that its own well-being is easily sacrificed to these larger purposes.

Moreover, the idea and practice of responsibilization—forcing the subject to become a responsible self-investor and self-provider—reconfigures the correct comportment of the subject from one naturally driven by satisfying interests to one forced to engage in a particular form of self-sustenance that meshes with the morality of the state and the health of the economy.[20] Thus, neoliberalism differs from classical economic liberalism not only in that there ceases to be what Smith formulated as an "invisible hand" forging a common good out of individual, self-interested actions,[21] and not only because the naturalism is replaced by constructivism, although both of these are the case. Equally important, reconciling individual with national or other collective interests is no longer the contemporary problem understood to be solved by markets. Instead, the notion of individuals naturally pursuing their interests has been replaced with the production through governance of responsibilized citizens who appropriately self-invest in a context of macroeconomic vicissitudes and needs that make all of these investments into practices of speculation. *Homo oeconomicus* is made, not born, and operates in a context replete with risk, contingency, and potentially violent changes, from burst bubbles and capital or currency meltdowns to wholesale industry dissolution. Put differently, rather than each individual pursuing his or her own interest and unwittingly generating collective benefit, today, it is the project of macroeconomic growth and credit enhancement to which neoliberal individuals are tethered and with which their existence as human capital must align if they are to thrive. When individuals, firms, or industries constitute a drag on this good, rather than a contribution to it, they may be legitimately cast off or reconfigured—through downsizing, furloughs, outsourcing, benefits cuts, mandatory job shares, or offshore production relocation. At this point, the throne of interest has vanished and at the extreme is replaced with the throne of sacrifice.[22]

In short, *homo oeconomicus* today may no longer have interest at its heart, indeed, may no longer have a heart at all, the implications of which we will pursue shortly. This is one important way that Foucault's story falls short: treating interest as this character's essential and transhistorical drive keeps us from seeing important implications of the shift from a classical liberal to a neoliberal formation, from Adam Smith and Jeremy Bentham to Gary Becker.

The second limit in Foucault's articulation of the novel dimensions of the contemporary neoliberal subject pertains to that subject's break with crucial strains of Western humanism. Despite his identification of the morphological shifts in *homo oeconomicus* over three centuries, Foucault fails to register its specific eclipse of *homo politicus* in the contemporary era. In the Collège de France lectures, he refers to the continued presence of *homo juridicus* or *homo legalis* and to the sustained heterogeneous existence of these two figures with *homo oeconomicus*. So for Foucault, modern citizenship features a double persona, juridical-legal, on the one hand, economic on the other. There is, he says, "the subject of interest" and "the subject of right," with the former always "overflowing" the latter, irreducible to it, and subject to a completely different logic and form of governance.[23] The "subject of right," *homo juridicus*, is derived from what Foucault calls the "totalizing unity of the juridical sovereign" and comes into being through specified limits on that sovereign. In other words, *homo juridicus* is a creature derived or deduced from state sovereignty, not from imagined primary drives or capacities in the human being—it bears no parallel with the primary drives of *homo oeconomicus*. *Homo juridicus* arises from the constituting power of sovereignty, its production of certain kinds of subjects, and the specification of the relation between these subjects and itself as one in which each has some rights.[24] "Liberalism," Foucault says, "acquired its modern shape precisely with the formulation of this essential incompatibility between the non-totalizable multiplicity of economic subjects of interest and the totalizing unity of the juridical sovereign."[25]

For Foucault, then, there is a triangle in modern liberalism whose three angles are sovereignty (state), economy, and subject;

the problematic relating them is who rules, who limits what power, who has what jurisdiction, who or what is knowable and touchable by whom, and who is not.[26] The key elements of this problematic are limits, rules, knowledge, knowability, and interventions, and its constitutive tensions are despotism versus the rule of law, limits on the sovereign versus individual freedom, sovereign knowledge and rule versus the "critique of governmental reason" presented by the neoliberal economy.

Certainly, this schema of the constitutive tensions in liberal governmentality is interesting and fruitful. But it is also flat and highly behavioral. What is missing in this picture (apart from changing configurations of the family-individual relation, which would foreground gender), is the creature we may call *homo politicus*, the creature animated by and for the realization of popular sovereignty as well as its own individual sovereignty, the creature who made the French and American Revolutions and whom the American Constitution bears forth, but also the creature we know as the sovereign individual who governs himself. Perhaps Foucault never really took this creature seriously, or perhaps Foucault saw him knocked off the stage very early in modernity—by the sovereign, by the economy, or even earlier by the church. Or perhaps Foucault saw him as only an episodic, rather than routine character in the triangle of modern governmentality that he outlined. Still, it is strange that sovereignty for Foucault remains so closely allied to the state and never circulates through the people—it's almost as if he forgot to cut off the king's head in political theory.

In any event, *homo politicus* is not a character in Foucault's story, which is consequential both for understanding what is at stake in the ascendency of neoliberal reason and for the prospects of contesting its table of values. The remainder of this chapter aims to redress this absence. I will be suggesting that *homo politicus*, however anemic, has existed side by side with *homo oeconomicus* through much of modernity and that the shape and contents of both are continuously changing, in part, but not only through their relation to one another. I will also argue that *homo politicus* is the most important casualty of the ascendance of neoliberal reason, above all because its democratic form would be the chief weapon against such reason's instantiation as a governing rationality, the resource for opposing it with another set of claims and another vision of existence. There is not only a "subject of right and a subject of interest," as Foucault would have it, but a subject of politics, a demotic subject, which cannot be reduced to right, interest, individual security, or individual advantage, although of course these features everywhere dapple its landscape and language in modernity.[27] This subject, *homo politicus*, forms the substance and legitimacy of whatever democracy might mean beyond securing the individual provisioning of individual ends; this "beyond" includes political equality and freedom, representation, popular sovereignty, and deliberation and judgment about the public good and the common. Only toward the end of the twentieth century did *homo oeconomicus* (in its distinctly neoliberal iteration) finally get the better of *homo politicus*, usurping its territory, terms, and objects both in the figure of the human and the polity. If this process were to become complete, if *homo politicus* were really vanquished, it would darken the globe against all possibilities of democratic or other just futures.

THE CHANGING MORPHOLOGY OF *HOMO OECONOMICUS* AND *HOMO POLITICUS*

In the beginning, there was *homo politicus*: man was "by nature an animal intended to live in a polis."[28] The ancient ascription of a political nature to man did not refer, as is often thought today, to the human will to power or connivance, but to living together in a deliberately governed fashion, to self-rule in a settled association that comprises yet exceeds basic needs, and to the location of human freedom and human perfectibility in political life. As Aristotle tells it, the phenomenon of the polis itself—internally complex and externally diverse across various instantiations—features the many ways in which human beings are distinguished from beasts and gods. There we realize and develop our distinctive capacities for association, speech, law, action, moral judgment, and ethics. Thus, our political nature issues from the distinctly human capacities of, on the one hand, moral reflection, deliberation, and expression and on the other, of generating multiple forms of association. Moral reflection and association making—these are the qualities that generate our politicalness. The two are related by Aristotle himself insofar as linguistically conveyed moral judgments permit humans to order and govern their associations—from the family to the state—according to deliberations about the good.[29] They are also related by their contribution to "self-sufficiency": as creatures who are mutually dependent, humans who live in a polis can enjoy justice, as well as the capacity to pursue the "good life," that is, life that engages distinctly human capacities and exceeds concern with mere survival.[30]

Aristotle's conviction that man is by nature a political animal who, with his equals, "rules and is ruled in turn," is complicated without being undone by his account of political man's prerequisites—slavery and private property in the *oikos*. Infamously naturalizing slavery as an instrument of acquisition (*chrematistic*), Aristotle discerns and embraces a certain instrumentalism that could easily get out of hand. Both master and subordinates risk becoming wholly defined by relations that could permit the generation of household wealth to become its own end. Much of book 1 of *The Politics* can be read as the formulation of a moral hedge against this danger, one that moves strenuously against *homo oeconomicus*, essentially designating him unnatural and perverse. Here is how this goes.

For Aristotle, the household features both relations of rule and relations of production. Thus, it has both an ethical-political and an economic dimension, and although Aristotle carefully aligns the two, he devotes more attention to the former than to the latter. The relations of authority, pedagogy, and rule between citizens and their wives, children, and slaves are carefully specified in ways that establish them as beneficial to both rulers and ruled. Even the slave, accounted as a piece of the master's "animate property" and a household "instrument," is benefitted by the master's rule, just as the body is benefitted by rule of the soul. Aristotle also develops the norms of *chrematistic* in accord with nature and provides a naturalistic ontology as well for the relations of household, village, and polis, or, put differently, between "the economic" and "the political."

While the household has both a moral function, entailing the proper exercise of authority over inferiors, and an economic function, provisioning for itself, the latter is both limited by the former and limited in general. Governing must always tend to the good of the governed, *and* wealth is never to become its own end. Rather, as Aristotle says, "there is a bound fixed [for the property needed by the art of household management]. All the instruments needed by all the arts are limited, both in number and size, by the requirements of the arts they serve."[31] Aristotle goes on to criticize as "unnatural" wealth that is accumulated for its own sake and above all, usury.[32] He sharply distinguishes the aims and ethos of household provisioning or need satisfaction from the world of market exchange, even as the two might be practically imbricated.[33] Aristotle tries to separate the two practices of *chrematistic* not only according to what they are for, but according to *where* they occur—in the household or the market—although again, they cannot be practically separated in this fashion; lacking self-sufficiency, most households must participate in markets to some degree, which is why the village is part of the teleological development toward the polis.

So what will keep households from becoming scenes of wealth accumulation and familial self-interest (Plato's worry in the *Republic*), rather than need satisfaction? What will keep propertied citizens oriented toward *chrematistic* as an order of need satisfaction prerequisite to the good life, rather than as an end in itself? In short, what will keep *homo oeconomicus* from emerging? Aristotle's first move on this front is to favor barter over market relations, because barter hews to need, while markets veer toward gain. However, even for need provision, Aristotle recognizes the inevitability of currency-based exchange arising from trade across distances.[34] So he reaches for other ways to cap the impulses generated by the presence of the market. One of these is moral, the other ontological.

The moral tactic is this: acknowledging that involvement with exchange for profit can easily incite the desire for wealth for its own sake, Aristotle denotes this practice "unnatural" precisely because of its foundation in currency and exchange, rather than in use and need, and because "the gain in which it results is not naturally made [from plants and animals] but is made at the expense of other men."[35] The unnaturalness of money, profit, and the derivation of wealth from trade make them morally inferior to the household's concern with "furnishing subsistence" to itself. It is easy to see in this moral depredation of the man of exchange an effort to contain and constrict economic desire, to maintain its subordination to the purpose of provision (use value) so that it doesn't develop its own energies and ends.

The other leash that Aristotle places on acquisitive impulses involves ontologically separating the concerns of the propertied citizen from *chrematistic* in the marketplace.

> The [natural] form of the art of acquisition is connected with the management of the household; but the other form is a matter only of retail trade, and it is concerned only with getting a fund of money, and that only by the method of conducting the exchange of commodities. This latter form may be held to turn on the power of currency; for currency is the starting-point, as it is also the goal, of exchange. It is a further point of difference that the wealth produced by this latter form of the art of acquisition is unlimited.[36]

Aristotle goes on to specify the difference between household *chrematistic* and its retail or market form as the difference between anxiety about livelihood versus well-being, accumulation versus sustenance, physical enjoyments versus providing for the "good life."[37] By the end of this discussion, he leaves no doubt that while the objects, activity, and even personnel may be the same, the two realms are opposite: one is natural, the other unnatural; one is morally high, the other is morally debased; one is necessary, the other is unnecessary; and above all, one is limited, and the other is unlimited.[38] "The acquisition of wealth by the art of household management (as contrasted with the art of acquisition in its retail form) *has* a limit; and the object of that art is not an unlimited amount of wealth."[39] Thus, while the leisure generated by household *chrematistic* is essential to the ethical and political life of man, cultivation of this prerequisite is sharply contained by its purpose.

In sum, more than simply theorizing the nature of man as political, Aristotle works assiduously at preventing *homo oeconomicus* from coming into being and designates such a creature "unnatural" and "perverse." If the problem Aristotle struggles against—the proximity of household acquisition to other kinds—is one he creates for himself by defending private property, families, and slavery against Plato's move to abolish them, it is a problem he meets directly. The formulation of man as fundamentally political—meant to live in the polis, share in its rule, deliberate about proper actions and just relations in every sphere of life—is the foundation for handling this problem. Man is political because he is a language-using, moral, and associational creature who utilizes these capacities to govern himself with others. Even during the long centuries between antiquity and modernity, when these very capacities became suffused with the project of serving God, man continued to be defined by them.[40]

Homo politicus is often thought to have withered in the seventeenth century as interest, especially in property and things, became paramount, and then to have died in the eighteenth, as the growth of capitalism and its overtaking of public life reduced us to what C. B. MacPherson famously characterized as possessive individualists, "proprietors of our own person or capacities, owing nothing to society for them," with society largely reduced to "relations of exchange between proprietors."[41] This is the story, as Foucault would say in another context, that we tell ourselves, and indeed, it is told by thinkers ranging from Rousseau and Marx to Hannah Arendt, from Antonio Gramsci to Jürgen Habermas, from Leo Strauss to Sheldon S. Wolin.

Certainly Adam Smith's *Wealth of Nations* marks a radical transmogrification of the "being meant for political association" described in the first book of Aristotle's *Politics*. In Smith's 1776 work, human distinctiveness from the gods and the beasts rests in our unique propensity to make deals, which Smith also casts as generating the division of labor, a division itself at the foundation of all society and civilization. For Smith, it is not action, speech, moral reasoning, deliberation, or the capacity for association-making that signals our singularity, but marketeering; it is not collective political self-determination that serves as the basis and sign of civilized existence, but wealth production generated by the division of labor.[42] Marx specifies the matter further: labor itself, not only its division, distinguishes us as a species and creates the world.[43] Thus, the story seems to hold up: in intellectual and practical life, *homo oeconomicus* has displaced *homo politicus*. Aristotle has been inverted, if not buried.

However, if we take our cue from Foucault's appreciation of polyvalent discourses and heterogeneous histories, the emergence of *homo oeconomicus* may not mean that *homo politicus* vanishes or even becomes subordinate. Indeed, if we return to Smith, we can see that when he first introduces our trucking and bartering propensities, he is careful to stipulate marketeering as but one quality of being human. Nor is it primary and unmediated. Rather, Smith rests this quality in our capacity for language, deliberation, calculation, and a certain self-sovereignty in an intensely interdependent world. Immediately after introducing the propensity to truck, barter, and exchange, Smith says that it is less likely an "original principle" of human nature than "the necessary consequence of the faculties of reason and speech" and of our complex and singular species interdependence.[44] Language and calculation facilitate deal making, itself animated by our intense need for one another. We bargain, he says, to provide advantage to others in meeting our own needs, something neither required nor possible from the more autarkic creatures of the animal world, something dependent upon a degree of knowledge, calculation, and relationality unavailable to other animals. In short, while *homo oeconomicus* certainly operates according to interest for Smith, the form of interest is neither primordial nor unhistorical. Arising from need amid interdependence, interest is facilitated by language and reason and generates relations of mutual benefit through exchange. Far from a creature of naked interest, Adam Smith's *homo oeconomicus* is premised on and saturated with deliberation, self-direction, and restraint, all basic ingredients of sovereignty. Moreover, as readers of his *Theory of Moral Sentiments* know well, self-interest is hardly an exclusive or even central node in his account of human nature.[45]

If we return again to Timothy Mitchell's point that in its origins, "political economy" referred to (economical) governing of the polity, rather than to the politics or powers of economic life, then the rise of political economy in the eighteenth century remains compatible with a presumed sovereignty of the political over the economic. It permits the sustained primacy of the political both in the state and in man, the state's miniature—these twin sovereignties being modernity's continuation of the ancient city-soul homology. In fact, Smith's brief for laissez-faire is premised on the notion that the state may choose its relation to economic activity in the society emerging from the marketeering side of humans; it could lean in as a mercantilist or stand back as a proper capitalist state, but there is no question about what is sovereign.

To put the point another way, as both man and state are becoming increasingly concerned with productivity, wages, and wealth, both are becoming economical in their governing, but this does not yet make them economic in identity and form. The prominence of man's *economic* features in modern thought and practice reconfigures without extinguishing his *political* features—again, these include deliberation, belonging, aspirational sovereignty, concern with the common and with one's relation to justice in the common. This is evident enough in the fact that eighteenth-century, nineteenth-century, and twentieth-century quests for political emancipation, enfranchisement, equality, and, in more radical moments, substantive popular sovereignty, cannot have emerged from *homo oeconomicus* and are not formulated in economic language. Of course, class interests contour and intersect political claims, but *homo politicus* has not been supplanted by the image of man as a speck of capital.

Alertness to the persistence of *homo politicus*, however thinned through modernity, places much of early modern and modern political thought under a different light from that of Foucault's discussions of classical liberalism in the Collège de France lectures. It highlights, for example, the intensely political quality of life in Locke's state of nature before property is introduced. In this early condition, as Locke tells the story in the *Second Treatise*, we are not mere self-preservationists, but responsible for discerning, judging, and executing the law of nature on behalf of the common.[46] Before the social contract, we have in our own hands, and as part of our moral obligation to God and one another, the powers of executing and enforcing natural law in the name of communal justice and preservation. These markedly political powers and this markedly political orientation are what we will eventually confer to political institutions when we enter the social contract. Of course, this primordial politicalness in Locke's state of nature is dampened by the intensification of individual interest that property introduces into that state. However, this politicalness never fades completely from the project of making the social contract or from its purpose and legitimacy.[47] Far from giving us a figure of man as relentlessly driven by individual interest, Locke features the strain between that drive and *homo politicus*, even the direct danger posed to *homo politicus* by the rise of *homo oeconomicus*, a tension that Rousseau would make explicit.

Indeed for Rousseau, we are free, sovereign, and self-legislating only when we join with others to set the terms by which we live together.[48] Those who remain slaves to instinct or to individual interest forsake both freedom and humanness as they surrender this sovereignty over themselves. For Rousseau, humans are the only creatures capable of generating complex orders of domination from their needs, of enslaving themselves by giving free rein to *homo oeconomicus*, by letting it overtake their personalities, social relations, and politics: this is the essence of Rousseau's critique of emerging liberalism. Thus, for Rousseau the deliberate and fierce cultivation of *homo politicus* (and it is most definitely not *homo juridicus* or *homo legalis*) is the only antidote to this peril. *Homo politicus*—understood as self-sovereign through collective sovereignty—must literally subdue the creature of self-interest and self-absorption. Otherwise, we not only fall into egoism, narcissism, and superficiality, but are dominated by the social relations and regimes generated by unbridled interest. Although Rousseau's distinctive critique of modernity and liberalism places him outside the mainstream, the opposition he articulates between a regime of interest and a regime of popular sovereignty and freedom is sustained as a tension in the centuries of thought that follow.

The Hegelian subject, for example, is consummated through the universality of the state and political life, rather than through the particularity of civil society and ethical life.[49] Political, rather than interest-bearing freedom, freedom linked to equality, mutual recognition, and identification in belonging—this is how man is realized and perfected for Hegel. The importance of *homo politicus* in modern political thought explains as well Marx's obsession in his early writings with the unrealized figure of sovereign political man and with his critique of the compromised status of political man in constitutional democracy.[50] It helps us understand why, as Marx struggles with the Hegelians and the fictions of the bourgeois state, his concern initially is not with class inequality or exploitation but with what he takes to be the illusory freedom and thin notion of citizenship and belonging tendered by bourgeois constitutionalism. Similarly his critique of the French Revolution pertains to its failure to realize the quest for "Liberté, Égalité, Fraternité" animating it.[51] In his assessment of "political emancipation"—the formal enfranchisement of heretofore excluded portions of humanity—he finds the politically emancipated individual to be isolated and impotent, subject to powers beyond its control that have lost their political names. For Marx, modern man is both a ghostly sovereign and is ghosted by his own alienated political powers, which come to dominate him in the powers of the state and economy.[52]

The lingering presence of *homo politicus* appears even in Bentham's calculating utilitarian subject, the subject so often hailed as an early prototype of the neoliberal subject. Bentham introduces the utilitarian subject as a little sovereign, albeit one yanked about by those "masters within," pleasure and pain, which means our individual *raison d'état* is not wide open for content or meaning, but necessarily serves these masters.[53] Yes, Benthamite subjects are bound by interests, but it is their politicalness—their aim to procure for, gratify, and secure themselves—that contrasts with the contemporary neoliberal subject and that also permits utility to slide so easily in Bentham from a principle of individual conduct to a principle of government.

John Stuart Mill, too, formulates us as little sovereigns choosing our means and ends; the essence of humanity rests in making these choices. Consequently, in *On Liberty*, the key question is where to draw the proper line between state and individual sovereignty, public law and private choice.[54] This is a political question about a political boundary, one that implicates jurisdiction, legislation, norms, punishments, and above all, spheres of action. For Bentham and Mill, in other words, the subject may weigh the costs and benefits of each end and action and may be regulated or even coerced by the state to increase productive capacities and orientation. But the subject is not circulating or fungible human capital instrumentalized by itself, society, economy, or the state. Rather, it is a miniature sovereign, with a range of possible ends. If, in this moment of political theory, the state is receding as a destination for our equality, freedom, and orientation toward public life, if it is being reconfigured as a behavioral or what Foucault will call a "biopolitical" agent for managing populations and their desires, *homo politicus* still lingers in the subject's relation to itself. Its trace is apparent in our complex achievement of the rationality required for self-sovereignty, including being master of our desires, rather than slave to them, as well as resisting social and state interference in our life choices.

Nor does Mill the political economist proffer either a descriptive or a normative account of *homo oeconomicus*. On the contrary, in his little essay "On the Definition of Political Economy and the Method of Investigation Proper to It," Mill makes clear that humans are multifaceted beings and, even in the economic realm (which "does not treat of the whole of man's nature...nor of the whole conduct of man in society"), we may be driven as much by the desire for leisure or for procreation as by the desire for wealth.[55] Perhaps most importantly, Mill insists that political economy "makes entire abstraction of every other human passion or motive" and thus operates with a fictional subject, one necessary "to obtain the power of either predicting or controlling the effect [of certain causes]," but fictional all the same.[56] Indeed, highlighting the irony of contemporary treatments of Mill as a founder of *homo oeconomicus*, Mill writes, "no political economist was ever so absurd as to suppose that mankind are really [driven] solely [by] the desire for wealth."[57]

Freud is often understood by political theorists as having imbued utilitarianism with psychic complexity: The id-driven pleasure principle leads us toward gratifying our desires in an unmediated way, while the superego's successful incorporation of the reality principle bridles and redirects the drives, even limits ego gratification in the name of the laboring and productive body. Repressed and redirected, original self-interest is never cancelled, but is contoured through repression and sublimation, which makes it more pacific, less self-destructive, and more productive. Still, don't foundational libidinal drives and psychic economies that reroute without eliminating them mean that Freud places interest at the heart of civilized man? Without rebutting this wholesale, recall that Freud's most sustained and chilling figure for humans in civilization is not bridled animals, but "conquered cities." The superego, he says in *Civilization and Its Discontents*, obtains mastery of our dangerous desires by weakening, disarming, and watching over them "like a garrison in a conquered city."[58] The homology is the classic one between soul and city; the figure of man and his psyche is relentlessly political. Moreover, the utterance occurs in a text that opens by analogizing the psyche with the city of Rome: both hold their truth under layers of ruins, reconstruction, and contemporary activity. Above all, both are troubled and troubling projects of sovereignty.

This has been a long way of making my point, an overview at once too involved with the history of political theory and too superficial in its treatment of it. The point could be compressed this way: *Homo oeconomicus* certainly ascends and expands its dominion in Euro-Atlantic modernity, but *homo politicus* remains alive and important through this time, as well—full of demands and expectations, the seat of political sovereignty, freedom, and legitimacy. If Rousseau is nearly alone in boldly reasserting this creature's dominance in social contract theory, *homo politicus* is hardly absent from others' accounts. Nor is it aptly captured by what Foucault calls *"homo juridicus"* or *"homo legalis,"* both of whom are too bound to law and rights to capture the political ethos and demands at stake.[59] This means that the vanquishing of *homo politicus* by contemporary neoliberal rationality, the insistence that there are only rational market actors in every sphere of human existence, is novel, indeed, revolutionary, in the history of the West. Before considering the implications of this event in more detail, I want to inquire briefly into the *homo* in *homo oeconomicus*—does it include or exclude women? This is not a broad inquiry into the gendered, racialized, or colonial character of neoliberal capitalism, but a more narrow one into the discursive status of feminized family labor entailed in the neoliberal displacement of *homo politicus* by *homo oeconomicus*. Does *homo oeconomicus* have a gender? Does human capital? Is there a *femina domestica* invisibly striating or supplementing these figures, or are wives and mothers also comprised by them?[60]

THE GENDER OF *HOMO OECONOMICUS*

Historically, even when its masculinity was not explicitly asserted and women's exclusion from the category was not overt, *homo politicus* from Aristotle through Kant and Hegel assumed a masculinist comportment and sphere of activity. Whether stipulated as participating in rule of the common (Aristotle), as paralleling military *virtu* (Machiavelli), as manly measure and fortitude (Weber), or simply as autonomy, rationality, and self-sovereignty (the moderns), *homo politicus* was almost always and expressly male.[61] Thus, as Joan Scott reminds us, French revolutionary feminists were decried as monstrous not just for their demands, but for the very fact of acting politically, just as nineteenth-century and twentieth-century bids for female suffrage were widely reviled as unnatural, as well as unnecessary.[62]

But what of *homo oeconomicus*? Prominent modern and contemporary economists rarely gender this creature, and when they occasionally glance in the direction of sexual difference, it is generally to argue or imply that physiology is irrelevant to the form, though not to the content of rationally choosing market animals. Adam Smith's market creature, Gary Becker's human capital, quotidian rational choosers—none of these are specified as male or presumed gendered, even as neoliberals recognize the possibility of gender-specific attributes on which certain kinds of human capital may be built, for example, football players or haute couture models. Indeed, the putatively generic character of rational choice and the putative advantages for all of a gendered division of labor between family and marketplace are the skillfully twinned arguments animating Becker's remarkable book, *A Treatise on the Family.*

However, feminists know well that when scholars presume their subject has no gender, this is far from the last word on the matter. *Homo oeconomicus* is no exception. There are a number of dimensions to its gender and hence a number of effects of its recent ascendency and dissemination. We begin with Margaret Thatcher, who, in the course of her campaign to neoliberalize Britain in the 1980s, infamously declared: "There is no such thing as society. There are only individual men and women...and their families." Our concern is with the ellipsis, which is hardly Thatcher's alone, but rather a routine neoliberal stumble over the relation of its basic unit of analysis, the individual, to what it takes as a basic unit of society, the family. In fact, Thatcher's stumble closely echoes one by Milton Friedman three decades earlier: "As liberals," he wrote in *Capitalism and Freedom*, "we take freedom of the individual, or perhaps the family, as our ultimate goal in judging social arrangements."[63] Again it is the "or perhaps," the uncertainty, that interests us. Later in the work, Friedman asserts: "The ultimate operative unit in our society is the family, not the individual."[64]

The fundamental incoherence here is obvious enough: if the family is the ultimate operative unit, the site of freedom, and the perspective from which we judge social arrangements, then the individual cannot be, and vice versa. One way to explain this incoherence is that it is ideo-logically driven: neoliberals who are also conservatives are inclined to ontologize the individual, the heterosexual nuclear family, *and* sexual difference. They seek to root each in nature, rather than in power, and do not want the family held responsible for gendering individuals or generating social inequalities. They naturalize the family as they natu-ralize the free individual and seek to conjoin and reconcile them with-out worrying over the logic that would or would not achieve this.

Another way to explain the incoherence is through the gender sub-ordination it tacitly presumes: the individual freedom iterated by neo-liberals is not compromised by or in the family because it pertains only to those who freely come and go from them into the domain of mar-ket freedom, not those who perform unwaged work or activity within them. The story being told, in other words, is not from the perspective of families as ensembles of generic individuals, but from a social posi-tioning long associated with male heads of households. The stumble, then, occurs precisely because this perspective is disavowed, even as it is assumed.

Such explanations, however, offer only an account of why the oscil-lation between individual and family occurs and do not address what it effects when neoliberalism becomes a governing rationality. What does the oscillation between individual and family achieve semiot-ically when *homo oeconomicus* is figured as human capital and van-quishes all other images of the human? Here, we have to ask about the relation of the afterthought to the main object of Thatcher's sentence. Conceptually and rhetorically, what is the work done by the phrase after the ellipsis in the assertion that "there are only individual men and women...and their families"? Is the family being positioned as a backdrop, as a possession, or as an extension of the individual? Is it an alternative way of describing the individual—its fuller or enlarged form? Or is it an association to which the individual and its conduct is subsumed? Is the family something that *homo oeconomicus* "has" or "is"? Does the family belong to it, or it to the family? Or does the family alchemically comprise the individual? Does neoliberalism position the family as part of the market, adjacent to it, or as a nonmarket sphere that can nevertheless be "economized" in Çalışkan and Callon's sense, that is, ordered by and refracted through economic reason?

A second set of questions arises here about what holds families or societies together in neoliberal regimes. When neoliberal reason casts each human, positively and normatively, across every domain of existence, as self-investing entrepreneurial capital, responsible for itself and striving to appreciate its value vis à vis other capital entities, how does this comport with the need-based, explicitly interdependent, affective, and frequently sacrificial domain of family relations? How is the family taken to cohere from elements of self-investing human capital? How is it even possible to think its "freedom" or "interests" when it is neither corporate nor individual? Gary Becker draws on the notion of "psychic income" to explain the mother who sacrifices for her children and suffers economic privations for her "natural" commitment to caregiving.[65] But Becker leaves fundamentally untouched the question of what holds families together, given the lack of social stickiness in human capital itself. When there is only *homo oeconomicus*, and when that figure is relentlessly committed to appreciating its own individual value, how does the family, not to mention the larger social order, cohere?

This question, along with the wish to account for motivations and investments—love, loyalty, community—that exceed interest and self-enhancement, are the starting points for critics of rational-choice economics such as Deirdre McCloskey, Annette Baier, Carol Rose, Julie Nelson, and Paula England.[66] Each argues that there is no possibility of families or societies cohering, let alone functioning within what McCloskey calls the "Hobbes paradigm" of unsocial and unsocialized human beings motivated only by calculations of competitive positioning and survival.[67] These critics are joined by others who, while not explicitly concerned with gender, favor the *homo oeconomicus* of Smith over that of Hobbes or Bentham.[68] Despite Smith's popular reputation for reducing man to a creature of interest, such critics suggest, Smith painted a more complex portrait of human conduct, needs, and virtues, even within economic life. McCloskey compresses the critique of contemporary *homo oeconomicus*, which she claims is based on Hobbesian and Benthamite man, this way: "Smith's project was an ethical one. Bentham derailed it and brought economists to think only of *P*, Prudence. If economics is going to get serious about being a "positive" science...and not amount merely to a chaos of precise ideas, it needs to be back to Smith's project of seeing Prudence within a system of virtues, and vices, for a commercial society."[69]

Taken together, these critiques suggest that one way of approaching neoliberal *homo oeconomicus* is to reveal it as a misrepresentation, one that disavows all that sustains it and all human arrangements. In this approach, *homo oeconomicus* reduced to human capital is false: it fails to feature the conduct that binds families and societies and is also falsely autonomous—shorn of needs and dependencies. Thus, the feminist economic critique finds in the Thatcher ellipsis a neoliberal repetition of the old story—that of the liberal subject portrayed from a masculinist, bourgeois viewpoint, one nourished by sources and qualities themselves not featured in the story. Only performatively male members of a gendered sexual division of labor can even pretend to the kind of autonomy this subject requires; to bind the familial and social order and to provision the needs that this subject disavows, others (whether paid or unpaid domestic workers) must be oriented differently, toward what Deirdre McCloskey calls "virtue ethics," what Joan Tronto calls "care work," and what sociologist Paula England names "soluble," rather than "separative" selves.[70]

However, our family-individual conundrum—the question of whether the family or the individual is the proper unit of analysis for a human world conceived as competing units of self-subsistent capital—is not yet resolved. We are not simply dealing with an *analytic* elision or disavowal in liberal and neoliberal formulations of human nature. Rather, we are dealing with a world made and governed by this elision and disavowal. There are two ways to think about the neoliberal figure of the human whose self-care and self-investment cannot be obtained within its own terms, that is, who is dependent upon invisible practices and unnamed others. One is that neoliberalism makes a mistake, that *homo oeconomicus* is both more multidimensional and more dependent upon human noncapital entities (that is, women) than this ontology suggests. There is some bite to this critique, but it is not a radical bite. We have yet to ask what kind of gendered order is produced and reproduced when this rationality prevails, when the activity of individual human capital appreciation becomes the ubiquitously governing norm, when through responsibilization, privatization, and dismantled infrastructure, along with the dissemination of neoliberal metrics to every sphere of existence, this bad ontology becomes the governing truth of the Euro-Atlantic world today. What happens, in short, when we are dealing not merely with an absurd and false account of human motives and conduct, a misrepresentation of who we are and what sustains us, but with the production of the "real" through this depiction of human purposes, conduct, and ends? What happens when the indispensably necessary ethos and labors highlighted by McCloskey, Tronto, and England are both disqualified and trod underfoot as *homo oeconomicus* becomes the real in every sense of the word?

When *homo oeconomicus* becomes normative across all spheres, and responsibilization and appreciation of human capital become *the* governing truth of public life, social life, work life, welfare, education, and the family, there are two possibilities for those positioned as women in the sexual division of labor that neoliberal orders continue to depend upon and reproduce. Either women align their own conduct with this truth, becoming *homo oeconomicus*, in which case the world becomes uninhabitable, or women's activities and bearing as *femina domestica* remain the unavowed glue for a world whose governing principle cannot hold it together, in which case women occupy their old place as unacknowledged props and supplements to masculinist liberal subjects. As provisioners of care for others in households, neighborhoods, schools, and workplaces, women disproportionately remain the invisible infrastructure for all developing, mature, and worn-out human capital—children, adults, disabled, and elderly. Generally uncoerced, yet essential, this provision and responsibility get theoretically and ideologically tucked into what are assumed as preferences issuing naturally from sexual difference, especially from women's distinct contribution to biological reproduction. It is formulated, in short, as an effect of nature, not of power.[71]

This conclusion is old news insofar as it resonates with forty years of feminist critiques of liberalism and capitalism. The question, then, is whether theoretically and politically invisible gender subordination is intensified or fundamentally altered by neoliberalism. Does the ascendency of *homo oeconomicus* and its specific formulation as human capital gender contemporary social arrangements more intensively or differently than its liberal democratic capitalist predecessor?

I think the answer is that gender subordination is both intensified and fundamentally altered.[72] The intensification occurs through the shrinking, privatization, and/or dismantling of public infrastructure supporting families, children, and retirees. Such infrastructure includes, but is not limited to affordable, quality early childhood and afterschool programs, summer camps, physical and mental health care, education, public transportation, neighborhood parks and recreation centers, public pensions, senior centers, and social security. When these public provisions are eliminated or privatized, the work and/or the cost of supplying them is returned to individuals, disproportionately to women. Put another way, "responsibilization" in the context of privatizing public goods uniquely penalizes women to the extent that they remain disproportionately responsible for those who cannot be responsible for themselves. In this respect, familialism is an essential requirement, rather than an incidental feature of the neo-liberal privatization of public goods and services.

So that is how liberalism's old gender problem is intensified by neo-liberalism. How is it transformed by a political-economic rationality featuring only competing capitals, large and small? When there is only capital (human, corporate, finance), what disappears analytically is the already liminal labor of the household, the extension of this labor as increasingly indispensable volunteer labor in schools and communities in the context of public disinvestment, and the gendered division of labor *between* market and household. Now divested of a place in language, visually and discursively absent from public consciousness, these forces shaping women's lives are intensified by privatizing formerly public goods and sheering benefits from part-time labor in which women are disproportionately employed. Thus, even as, in the United States, the numbers of women in the paid labor force approach those of men and as women now obtain more education than men after high school, because women remain disproportionately responsible for care work of all kinds, they earn less than 80 percent of what their male counterparts earn and are radically underrepresented at the top of all professions. The language of responsibilized, individualized human capital cannot metabolize, let alone explain this combination of effects. Instead, one more often hears accounts like those of economist Lawrence Summers who, as Harvard's president, speculated that the gender gap in academic science was best explained by differences in "innate abilities."[73]

Put another way, while neoliberal *homo oeconomicus* is both gendered and gendering in its ascendency and dissemination, this is illegible within its own terms. The persistent responsibility of women for provisioning care of every sort, in and out of the household, means that women both *require* the visible social infrastructure that neoliberalism aims to dismantle through privatization and *are* the invisible infrastructure sustaining a world of putatively self-investing human capitals. Thus, the figure of *homo oeconomicus* is not simply illusory or ideological in its disavowal of the persons and practices that make and sustain human life. Rather, when *homo oeconomicus* becomes the governing truth, when it organizes law, conduct, policy, and everyday arrangements, the burdens upon and the invisibility of those excluded persons and practices are intensified.[74]

Our attention to the Thatcher ellipsis reveals that neoliberalism's unit of analysis, the generic individual who becomes responsibilized human capital, is, unsurprisingly, socially male and masculinist within a persistently gendered economic ontology and division of labor. This is so regardless of whether men are "stay-at-home fathers," women are single or childfree, or families are queer. From this perspective, families belong to such individuals and are not held to generate or gender them, position them differentially in the market, or burden them outside the market. With only competing and value-enhancing human capital in the frame, complex and persistent gender inequality is attributed to sexual difference, an effect that neoliberalism takes for a cause. Consequently, an impoverished single mother is framed to fail in the project of becoming a responsibilized neoliberal subject, especially in the contexts of the kinds of austerities imposed by the budget "sequester" in the United States or by the European Union bailouts in Southern Europe. More than failure, the freedom tendered by neoliberal rationality (freedom from state regulation and need provision) is literally inverted into new forms of gender subordination as women remain chief providers of unremunerated and undersupported care work outside the market *and* are increasingly solo income streams for themselves and their families.

THE VANQUISHING OF *HOMO POLITICUS* BY *HOMO OECONOMICUS*

Perversely, it would seem, but precisely because *homo politicus* in its popular-sovereignty variant is today less gendered than *homo oeco-*

nomicus ever was, we now return to the more general question: What are the implications of the neoliberal vanquishing of *homo politicus* by *homo oeconomicus*? While *homo politicus* is obviously slimmed in modern liberal democracies, it is only through the ascendency of neoliberal reason that the citizen-subject converts from a political to an economic being and that the state is remade from one founded in juridical sovereignty to one modeled on a firm. As neoliberalism submits all spheres of life to economization, the effect is not simply to narrow the functions of state and citizen or to enlarge the sphere of economically defined freedom at the expense of common investment in public life and public goods. Rather, it is to attenuate radically the exercise of freedom in the social and political spheres. This is the central paradox, perhaps even the central ruse, of neoliberal governance: the neoliberal revolution takes place in the name of freedom—free markets, free countries, free men—but tears up freedom's grounding in sovereignty for states and subjects alike. States are subordinated to the market, govern for the market, and gain or lose legitimacy according to the market's vicissitudes; states also are caught in the parting ways of capital's drive for accumulation and the imperative of national economic growth. Subjects, liberated for the pursuit of their own enhancement of human capital, emancipated from all concerns with and regulation by the social, the political, the common, or the collective, are inserted into the norms and imperatives of market conduct and integrated into the purposes of the firm, industry, region, nation, or postnational constellation to which their survival is tethered. In a ghostly repetition of the ironic "double freedom" that Marx designated as the prerequisite of feudal subjects becoming proletarianized at the dawn of capitalism (freedom from ownership of the means of production and freedom to sell their labor power), a new double freedom—from the state and from all other values—permits market-instrumental rationality to become the dominant rationality organizing and constraining the life of the neoliberal subject. This is also, of course, the significance of economic models and methods spreading across the social sciences, becoming notably dominant in political science, but gaining ground in anthropology and sociology, as well. Across politics, culture, and society and hence across the disciplines that study them, there is only *homo oeconomicus.*

As long as *homo politicus* was also on the liberal democratic stage, freedom conceived minimally as self-rule and more robustly as participation in rule by the demos was fundamental to political legitimacy. But when citizenship loses its distinctly political morphology and with it the mantle of sovereignty, it loses not only its orientation toward the public and toward values enshrined by, say, constitutions, it also ceases to carry the Kantian autonomy underpinning individual sovereignty. Here we must remember the fundamental liberal democratic promise since Locke, that popular and individual sovereignty secure one another. Put the other way around, *homo politicus* in modernity is simultaneously rooted in individual sovereignty and signals the promise of social, political, and legal respect for it. When *homo politicus* fades and the figure of human capital takes its place, no longer is each entitled to "pursue his own good in his own way," as Mill famously put the matter. No longer is there an open question of what one wants from life or how one might wish to craft the self. Human capitals, like all other capitals, are constrained by markets in both inputs and outputs to comport themselves in ways that will outperform the competition and to align themselves with good assessments about where those markets may be going. Moreover, regardless of how disciplined and responsibilized it is, market flux and contingencies can swiftly bring it to a dark fate.[75]

The hegemony of *homo oeconomicus* and the neoliberal "economization" of the political transform both state and citizen as both are converted, in identity and conduct, from figures of political sovereignty to figures of financialized firms. This conversion in turn effects two significant reorientations: on the one hand, it reorients the subject's relation to itself and its freedom. Rather than a creature of power and interest, the self becomes capital to be invested in, enhanced according to specified criteria and norms as well as available inputs. On the other hand, this conversion reorients the relationship of the state to the citizen. No longer are citizens *most importantly* constituent elements of sovereignty, members of publics, or even bearers of rights.[76] Rather, as human capital, they may contribute to or be a drag on economic growth; they may be invested in or divested from depending on their potential for GDP enhancement.

It is difficult to overstate the significance of these two reorientations—that of the subject to itself and of the state to the citizen. Of course, they entail the dramatic curtailment of public values, public goods, and popular participation in political life. Obviously, too, governance according to market metrics supplants classical liberal political criteria (justice, citizen protection, balancing diverse interests) with concerns with economic growth, competitive positioning, and credit rating. But as already suggested, these reorientations also entail an existential disappearance of freedom from the world, precisely the kind of individual and collaborative freedom associated with *homo politicus* for self-rule and rule with others. Moreover, the subject that is human capital for itself and the state is at persistent risk of redundancy and abandonment.[77] As human capital, the subject is at once in charge of itself, responsible for itself, and yet a potentially dispensable element of the whole. This is yet another way in which the social contract is turning inside out.

Foucault was alert to this possibility; he described *homo oeconomicus* as "someone…eminently governable…the correlate of a governmentality…determined according to the principle of economy."[78] But he did not fathom the extreme to which this governability could go in a neoliberal regime, an extreme expressed through the formula of maximum governance through maximum individual freedom. In place of the liberal promise to secure the politically autonomous and sovereign subject, the neoliberal subject is granted no guarantee of life (on the contrary, in markets, some must die for others to live), and is so tethered to economic ends as to be potentially sacrificible to them.

Weber depicted capitalism as originally fashioned from the combination of an ascetic ethic, multifold separations (*inter alia*, between owners and producers, production and exchange) and an instrumental rationality wielded for efficient production of wealth. The irony, indeed, tragedy of capitalism for Weber is that this original project of human mastery, even freedom, culminates in a machinery of unprecedented human domination imprisoning "Man" in an iron cage. Like bureaucracy, capitalism begins as an instrument but metamorphoses into a system with its own ends, constraining all actors to serve those ends.

Weber's account appears quaint now: neoliberal rationality builds much more than a cage from which plaintive creatures peer out at unobtainable freedom. So also is Marx's depiction of capitalism—vampire-like, exploitative, alienating, inegalitarian, duplicitous, profit-driven, compulsively expanding, fetishistic, and desacralizing of every precious value, relation and endeavor—inadequate to what neoliberal rationality has wrought. If Marx's analysis remains unequaled in in its account of capitalism's power, imperatives, brutality and world-making capacities, this analysis also presumed subjects who yearned for emancipation and had at hand a political idiom of justice—unrealized principles of democracy—through which to demand it. These subjects and principles can be presumed no longer.

Put slightly differently, Weber and Marx assume a political exterior and subjective interior that is disharmonious with capitalism—political life featuring at least the promise of freedom, equality and popular sovereignty and a figure of subjective personhood bound to ideals of worth, dignity, self-direction, even soulfulness. It is precisely such an exterior and interior that neoliberal reason's configuration of states, citizens and souls in the image of *homo oeconomicus*, and elimination of *homo politicus*, threaten to extinguish.

DISSEMINATING
NEOLIBERAL REASON

CHAPTER FOUR

Political Rationality and Governance

"Political rationality" or "governing rationality" are the terms Foucault used for apprehending, among other things, the way that neoliberalism comes to govern as a normative form of reason. Foucault's idea, underdeveloped in theory, although extensively explored in his genealogies and lectures, is that political actions, regimes, violence, and everyday practices ought neither to be understood as simply emanating from the intentions of rulers or participants nor, on the other hand, as driven by either material conditions or ideology. Rather, he uses the term "political rationality" to identify the governing form of normative reason that, as Mitchell Dean formulates it, is both "anterior to political action and a condition of it."[1] Political rationality is thus a specific development of Foucault's long-standing insistence that truth, knowledge, and forms of reason are never outside of power relations. Power itself does not exist either as raw domination or in a material substratum of existence independent of thought and language. Rather, power always governs or acts as part of a regime of truth that is itself generative of power, yet not identical with its exercise. Moreover, power always brings into being the subjects and orders that it may be seen only to organize or to rule. Political reason, on the other hand, is not timeless or universal, but always comes in a particular form, secures and circulates specific norms, and posits particular subjects and relations.

The idea of political rationality appears to be Foucault's effort to harness and develop these precepts for understanding how societies and populations may be ruled intensively, yet indirectly, how states and other institutions may themselves be brought into being and into certain orientations, and how several different and potentially colliding forms of reason (or what Foucault often calls "games") may be combined in the practices of states and citizens. Political rationality is not an instrument of governmental practice, but rather the condition of possibility and legitimacy of its instruments, the field of normative reason from which governing is forged. As Mitchell Dean puts the point in reverse, "Political rationality is a condition of governmental practice, but as a practice, government relies on means irreducible to this rationality."[2] In William Callison's words, political rationality must be understood as *constitutive*, "as subject-constituting (e.g. '*homo oeconomicus*'), as object-constituting (e.g. 'the population'), as the condition of a particular socio-political assemblage of forces."[3]

Political rationality is thus the term Foucault uses to capture the conditions, legitimacy, and dissemination of a particular regime of power-knowledge that centers on the truths organizing it and the world it brings into being. But which truths? Not those that it carries on the surface—not, for example, liberty, equality, and universality, or even *raison d'état*, or a free market, or the rule of law. Rather, for Foucault, political rationalities posit ontological qualities and relations of citizens, laws, rights, economy, society, and states—qualities and relations inhering in orders of reason such as liberalism, Christianity, Roman law, and so on, which may combine awkwardly, but nonetheless all become salient parts of that by which worlds are ordered, humans act, and governments rule.

Political rationality came late and sparely in Foucault's work, and it may be helpful to distinguish it from better-known terms in his lexicon. "Political rationality" is not equivalent to "discourse," although rationalities surely generate and operate by means of discourses. Synoptically, "discourse" may be specified as an order or ensemble of normative speech acts that constitute a particular field and subjects within it; in discourses, norm and deviation are the means by which subjects and objects in any field are made, arranged, represented, judged, and conducted. Discourses, when they become dominant, always circulate a truth and become a kind of common sense, but Foucault's primary emphasis in theorizing discourse is on norms and normalization. However, a governing rationality, while operating discursively, exceeds this emphasis to capture the way a normative order of reason comes to legitimately govern as well as structure life and activity as a whole. Thus, "at stake in neoliberalism is nothing more, nor less, than the *form of our existence*—the way in which we are led to conduct ourselves, to relate to others and to ourselves."[4] No discourse governs society as a whole, and it is also not quite right to say that discourses "govern." Rather, for Foucault, there are many and sometimes conflicting discourses circulating in a modern social order, each of which constructs certain fields of knowledge, identity, and action, for example, discourses of sexuality, education, immigration, multiculturalism, security, nature, or rights. A political rationality, such as neoliberalism, is that by which we are ubiquitously governed even as there will also be discourses crosscutting and incompletely contoured or controlled by such a rationality.

Political rationality is also not the same thing as "governmentality," Foucault's term for an important historical shift in the operation and orientation of the state and political power in modernity. This is a shift away from sovereignty and its signature—"do this, or die"—to what Foucault calls governing through "the conduct of conduct"—"this is how you live." Put differently, governmentality represents a shift away from the power of command and punishment targeting particular subjects and toward the power of conducting and compelling populations "at a distance." Foucault does indeed speak of neoliberalism as a "new programming of liberal governmentality"—it changes the way the liberal state reasons, self-represents, and governs and it also changes the state-economy relation. But these changes mark something apart from the political rationality of neoliberalism. Political rationality does not originate or emanate from the state, although it circulates through the state, organizes it, and conditions its actions.

Political rationality also differs from a normative form of reason, although the former emanates from and is suffused with the latter. Neoliberalism might have remained only a form of reason generated by Ordoliberalism and the Chicago School, without ever becoming a political rationality. Indeed, this seemed its likely fate at midcentury, although Foucault (and Daniel Stedman Jones, in his history of neoliberal thought) insist that postwar Germany was already organized by it.[5] Political rationality could be said to signify the *becoming actual* of a specific normative form of reason; it designates such a form as both a historical force generating and relating specific kinds of subject, society, and state and as establishing an order of truth by which conduct is both governed and measured.

Foucault's formulation of political rationality would appear to draw on the early Frankfurt School, which in turn drew on the work of Max Weber. Weber famously distinguishes two types of rational action: value rational (*wertrational*) and instrumentally rational (*zweckrational*).[6] The rationality in the first does not pertain to the rational quality of the value itself, but to the "self-conscious formulation of the ultimate values governing the action"—their being chosen through the actor's deliberation, rather than derived from authority, tradition, or affect. Thus, value-rational action permits us to choose a value such as peace, equality, or wealth accumulation. Value-rational action may, but need not be animated or constrained by the chosen value in the selection of means to achieve the value.

Instrumentally rational action may pertain only to the means for obtaining a particular value, or it may saturate the action completely.[7]

Either way, the only value animating it is efficiency (minimization of costs) in obtaining an end; it consists of pure calculation. Put differently, instrumentally rational action may serve an end selected through value rationality, but instrumentally rational action itself does not carry the value, and in this important respect, the means are distinct from the end. Weber also suggests that from the perspective of instrumental rationality, "value-rationality is always irrational," a matter that will be important shortly.[8] Instrumental rationality is efficient and powerful, more so than any other kind of rationality, Weber says, precisely because it is not freighted or constrained by anything apart from obtaining an end.

In the process that Weber calls "rationalization," rational action comes to displace all other forms, those springing from faith, tradition, affect, fealty to a leader, or any other prerational or nonrational source.[9] But this displacement is only the beginning of rationalization, which does not really get underway until instrumental rationality takes over everything, displacing even value-rational action. Initially only a means, instrumental reason becomes a force of its own in the world and dissolves other values with that force. For Weber, capitalism and bureaucracy are each examples of this. Each system begins as a means—for wealth generation and for administration—but both break out of harness to become unprecedented systems of domination and automatic reproduction, placing humanity in "an iron cage."[10] Both become formations of power and rationality that cease to be instruments of our existence and instead become forces of history unto themselves—governing, dominating, fashioning human beings and worlds in every way. This is one strain of thinking about rationality from which Foucault appears to draw in formulating neoliberalism as a political rationality.

The second strain comes from Theodor Adorno, Max Horkheimer, and especially Herbert Marcuse, who themselves developed and radicalized Weber's appreciation of differentiated forms of rationality, along with the potential of instrumental rationality to be a governing force of its own. For reasons of space and complexity, I want to bracket Adorno and Horkheimer's *Dialectic of Enlightenment* to focus instead on Marcuse's *One-Dimensional Man*. In that work, Marcuse argues that instrumental reason in the twentieth century had become suffused with the norms and imperatives of capitalism to generate a rationality that saturated society and secured capitalism in ways Marx and Marxism could not fathom or explain. Thus, in place of a Marxist notion of bourgeois ideology in workplaces, schools, and the state, Marcuse traces the specific rationalities with which modern capitalism saturates and governs the world and the human. "Technological rationality has become political rationality" and produces "a comfortable, smooth, reasonable, democratic unfreedom...in advanced industrial civilization."[11] This rationality comprises a technological, instrumental, and above all positivist form of reason that extends from advertising to analytic philosophy, from the methods of the social sciences to psychology, leisure, and consumption.[12] This is the second strain of thought which Foucault would seem to be developing for his own formulation of political rationality.

While Foucault appears to draw on both Weber and the early Frankfurt School for the idea of neoliberalism as a political rationality, neither source is adequate to his purposes, and both contain limitations. The anti-Marxism animating Weber's theory of rationalization makes instrumental rationality into something of its own engine and force field, an alternative to dialectics, materialism, or capitalism, but flying above any geopolitical or historical location. On the other hand, the Marxism animating Marcuse's theory of rationality establishes bourgeois instrumental rationality (and one-dimensional society) as emanating from capitalism, hence not something that could give capitalism itself a new form. Foucault's innovation in conceiving neoliberalism as a political rationality lies in sliding between this Scylla and Charybdis, this continued face-off between idealist and materialist engines of history. For Foucault, political rationalities are world-changing, hegemonic orders of normative reason, generative of subjects, markets, states, law, jurisprudence, and their relations. Political rationalities are always historically contingent, rather than necessary or teleological; however, once ascendant, they will govern as if they are complete and true until or unless challenged by another political rationality.

Still another way of framing what Foucault is doing with neoliberalism as a political rationality would have him tracking how an economic rationality becomes a governing (or political) one, giving new shape and orientation to the state, but also governing subjects themselves and every institution on the landscape: schools, hospitals, prisons, families, human rights organizations, nonprofits, social welfare agencies, youth culture, and more. That said, political rationality is not itself an instrument of governing, but rather the condition of possibility and legitimacy of its instruments, the field of normative reason from which instruments and techniques such as those discussed in this chapter are forged.

In the Collège de France lectures on neoliberalism, Foucault uses the descriptor "political rationality" rather infrequently. More often, he speaks of neoliberalism as "governmental reason," "governmentality," "governmental rationality," or "economic rationality." Above all, he identifies it as "a new programming of liberal governmentality," a reformulation of the relations between state, economy, and subject posited and produced by liberalism.[13] Thus, I am pressing much more from the formulation of neoliberalism as a political rationality than Foucault did. Moreover, in seeking to extend some of his unfinished lines of thinking here, I do not pretend to do so in ways he would have approved. The aim is not to complete a Foucauldian theory of neoliberal political rationality, but to offer a generative and useful theorization of our times.

GOVERNANCE

To understand how neoliberalism becomes a governing political rationality, we need to examine a set of developments in formulations and
practices of governance. Over the past two decades, the term "governance" has acquired an increasingly central place in politics, business,
public agencies, NGOs, and nonprofits, along with the social sciences
that study them, including sociology, economics, political science, business, anthropology, and education and social welfare schools. Governance is not identical with or exclusive to neoliberalism; it was no part
of the neoliberal imaginary set out by Milton Friedman or F. A. Hayek
and had little place in neoliberal transformations in Latin America or
South Asia in the 1970s and 1980s. However, as it matured and con-
verged with neoliberalism, governance has become neoliberalism's
primary administrative form, the political modality through which it
creates environments, structures constraints and incentives, and hence
conducts subjects. Contemporary neoliberalism is unthinkable without
governance. It is also key to securing accession to the "economization"
of all areas of life, the process that Foucault, drawing on Becker, equates
with "accepting reality" and "reacting to reality in a non-random way."[14]
The challenge, then, is to grasp the convergence of the ascendance of
governance and neoliberal reason as intertwined and synergistic, yet
short of inevitable and unified. Governance is not only or by nature
neoliberal, but neoliberalism has both mobilized and increasingly saturated its formulations and development. This chapter focuses on that
mobilization and saturation to articulate the importance of governance
in disseminating neoliberal rationality across contemporary existence
and in transforming the nature and meaning of the political.

There is no settled definition of governance, and scholars differ
significantly in their understanding and use of it.[15] Some emphasize
the departure it signifies from the centrality of the state in organizing
society and human conduct. Others use it to indicate novel processes

of governing. Still others highlight the new norms it circulates. Fifteen years ago, R. A. W. Rhodes already had identified at least six distinct uses of governance: "As the minimal state, as corporate governance, as the new public management, as 'good governance', as a socio-cybernetic system, as self-organizing networks."[16] However, almost all scholars and definitions converge on the idea that governance signifies a transformation from governing through hierarchically organized command and control—in corporations, states, and nonprofit agencies alike—to governing that is networked, integrated, cooperative, partnered, disseminated, and at least partly self-organized. As Rhodes suggests, it is "governing without Government," as well as a practice born from "hollowing out the state," and is hence well suited to the practical dissemination of neoliberal reason, even if it was born in part for other purposes and projects.[17]

We begin with a telling lexical phenomenon. "Governance" is often used interchangeably with both "governing" and "managing" across a range of institutions—political, economic, educational, profit, non-profit, service, and production industries. This interchangeability and promiscuity suggest that governance comprises and indexes an important fusion of political and business practices, both at the level of administration and at the level of providing goods and services. In fact, although its genealogy is contested, some insist that "the concept comes from the business world" and refers originally "to a mode of managing complex businesses in which vertical hierarchy gives way to a more horizontal, even egalitarian arrangement."[18]

The emergence and use of the concept of governance across a range of venues and endeavors signals a dissolving distinction between state, business, nonprofit, and NGO endeavors—not simply the emergence of public-private partnerships (themselves an important feature of governance), but of significantly altered orientations and identities of each as everything comes to comport increasingly with a business model and business metrics. "New Public Management" (NPM), born in the 1980s in Britain, epitomizes this: its explicit aim was to transfer private-sector management methods to public services and to employ economic techniques such as incentivization, entrepreneurialism, outsourcing, and competition for public goods and services.[19] Thus, "governance," and especially "good governance," signals not only different metrics from those used to measure the charge and legitimacy of liberal democratic states, but a specific relationship between power and its constituencies and, in the case of politics, a specific relationship between the state, civil society, and markets.

Formal analyses of government and governance tend to explain the difference between them as that between institutions (government) and process (governance): "*Government* often refers to the governing body itself, while *governance* refers to the act of governing. So members of a government are engaged in governance."[20] But why is the term "governance" needed (and needed only recently) as a substitute or supplement for the active verb "to govern"? Why does the act of governing need to be consolidated into a noun, and what is the significance of that conversion? What continuous process of power, detached from agents of execution or enforcement, does it signify?

We might put the problem as a proposition: "Governance" signifies a specific mode of governing that is evacuated of agents and institutionalized in processes, norms, and practices. According to social theorist Thomas Lemke, "governance involves a shift in the analytical and theoretical focus from institutions to processes of rule." Lemke adds that governance "announces the eclipse or erosion of state sovereignty"[21] Importantly, this emphasis on process over sources or institutions is not restricted to methodology. Rather, as we will see in the discussions of devolution, responsibilization, and best practices, much of the normative and constitutive power of governance occurs through and in processes that bear no reference to agents. At this point, it would seem that the term "governance" expresses a good deal more than the "act of governing."

The United Nation's account of "good governance" confirms this and adds another twist. There, "governance" is described as "the process of decision-making and the process by which decisions are implemented or not."[22] It notes further that governance involves formal as well as informal actors and structures—these include the media, the military, corporations, organized crime, and political parties, among others.[23] Thus, as an analytical term, "governance" signifies the decentering of the state and other centers of rule and tracks in its place the specifically modern dispersal of socially organizing powers throughout the order and of powers "conducting" and not only constraining or overtly regulating the subject.[24] As Elizabeth Meehan argues, the attention to governance in scholarship today arises from a Foucauldian understanding (acknowledged or not) of power as "dispersed and relational." But again, the shift is not only methodological. Governance differs from governing, according to Meehan, in that it arises from "a lack of capacity by governments, acting alone, to effect desired changes" today. [25] Meehan enumerates a historically specific set of developments that generated the supplanting of government with governance where the latter is understood as engaging and mobilizing a variety of nonstate actors: "Europeanization [in place of nation-state sovereignty], devolution, pressures on the welfare state and new political cultures."[26] These and other developments incite new arrangements and practices that include sharing public power among different tiers of regulation, privatizing the provision of utilities and services, and above all, increasing reliance on partnerships, networks, and novel forms of connection and communication about policy design and delivery. Together, these signal a decrease in the centralized and hierarchical exercise of public power, what is often called the older "command and control" model by governance theorists.

At this point, it becomes clear that "governance" carries both a positive and a normative valence: while it identifies and works with what is often specified as the specifically modern dispersion of power, it affirms the advantages of this dispersal and the importance of exploiting it effectively. Similarly, while acknowledging the historicity of the emergence of governance, many of its theorists also make a tacitly universal and transhistorical claim about power, insisting that it always was dispersed, shared, soft, and not only emanating from the center in the form of rule and command. (This tension is to be found in Foucault's own account of political power, an account that vacillates between being historically specific and using the present as a critical vantage point for revising our more general understandings of power—its elements, operations, circulation, terminal points, and so forth. Appreciation of this vacillation is the only way to make sense of Foucault's critique of the sovereign model of power, which is simultaneously an argument about the nature of power generally and about political power in high-modern as opposed to premodern and early modern Europe.)

Already it is evident that governance marks more than a shift in tone, emphasis, and arrangements; rather, a whole conceptualization and practice of power and administration is at stake, one that reconceives relations between the market, the state, and the citizenry, reconceives the operation of power and rule, and as such, reconceives democracy. Lester Salamon sums up the major shifts this way.

Governance focuses on tools or instruments for achieving ends, rather than preoccupation with specific agencies or programs through which purposes are pursued.[27]

Governance replaces the opposition or tension between government and the private sector (sovereign and market relations) with collaboration and complementarity. Governance emphasizes the importance of each sector doing what it does best and the importance of partnerships across these differences.[28]

Governance replaces hierarchical, top-down mandates and enforcement with horizontal networks of invested stakeholders pursuing a common end.[29]

And governance replaces "command and control" with negotiation and persuasion.[30] Effective governors create incentives for desired outcomes and negotiate over goals, even those that public action is to serve. Governance also replaces orders with orchestration, enforcement with benchmarks and inspection, and mandates with mobilization and activation.[31]

Above all, governance reconceives the political as a field of management or administration and reconceives the public realm as "a domain of strategies, techniques and procedures through which different forces and groups attempt to render their programs operable."[32] Thus, when governance becomes a substitution for government, it carries with it a very specific model of public life and politics. Note what does *not* appear in Meehan's account of the public realm: deliberation about justice and other common goods, contestation over values and purposes, struggles over power, pursuit of visions for the good for the whole. Rather, public life is reduced to problem solving and program implementation, a casting that brackets or eliminates politics, conflict, and deliberation about common values or ends. Indeed, when this narrowing of public life is combined with the strong emphasis of governance on consensus, a hostility to politics becomes palpable. As problem solving replaces deliberation about social conditions and possible political futures, as consensus replaces contestation among diverse perspectives, political life is emptied of what theorists such as Machiavelli took to be its heart and the index of its health: robust expressions of different political positions and desires. For Machiavelli, such expressions were the very essence of political liberty and also prevented the differences and the energies inherent in the political body from becoming toxic.[33]

Similarly, the predilection of governance for devolution, decentralization, and public-private partnerships transforms political struggles over national purposes and resources into local administrative practices that receive as given both the resource constraints and the aims they are handed. These new practices themselves recast the very meaning and understanding of democracy, even as they promise to deliver more of it. According to Meehan, devolution and decentralization are "synonymous with democratization in the sense of inaugurating a 'new politics' of participation, partnership and inclusion" for problem solving.[34]

What has happened here? Inclusion and participation as indices of democracy have been separated off from the powers and the unbounded field of deliberation that would make them meaningful as terms of shared rule. Put another way, while inclusion and participation are certainly important elements of democracy, to be more than empty signifiers, they must be accompanied by modest control over setting parameters and constraints and by the capacity to decide fundamental values and directions. Absent these, they cannot be said to be democratic any more than providing a death row inmate with choices about the method of execution offers the inmate freedom. Rather, this is the language of democracy used against the demos.

Thus, governance fundamentally reconceptualizes democracy as distinct or divorced from politics and economics: democracy becomes purely procedural and is detached from the powers that would give it substance and meaning as a form of rule. Democracy defined as inclusion, participation, partnership, and teamwork in problem solving is also absent all concern with justice and the designation of purposes, along with pluralistic struggles over these things. As power vanishes and ends become givens in the way problems are specified, democracy becomes divested of politics, defined either as the handling of power or as struggle over common fundamentals or goals. Thus, democracy reformulated by governance means that participants are integrated into the process of benchmarking, consensus building, policy making, and implementation. Civic participation is reduced to "buy-in."

Not only democracy, but contestation about the nature of justice itself is displaced by contemporary norms of good governance and

by the move to align governance with problem solving. Most definitions of good governance include the following elements: participation, consensus, accountability, effectiveness, efficiency, equitability,
inclusiveness, and following the rule of law.[35] Thus, while governance
analytically describes decentered and devolved power, as a policy
term, governance aims to substitute consensus-oriented policy formation and implementation for the overt exercise of authority and power
through law and policing. It is a short step from this reorientation of
democracy into problem solving and consensus to a set of additional
replacements fundamental to the meaning and operation of governance today: "stakeholders" replace interest groups or classes, "guidelines" replace law, "facilitation" replaces regulation, "standards" and
"codes of conduct" disseminated by a range of agencies and institutions replace overt policing and other forms of coercion.[36] Together,
these replacements also vanquish a vocabulary of power, and hence
power's visibility, from the lives and venues that governance organizes
and directs.

I have already hinted that the emphasis placed on problem solving and consensus by the concept of governance downplays to the
point of disavowing structural stratifications in economy and society that could produce different political stakes and positions, as well
as normative conflicts over the good. Emphasizing "stakeholder consultation" and "multiparty cooperation," the aim is to produce and
implement practical solutions for technically defined problems. In
neoliberal governance, however, such integration and consensus
does not collectivize responsibility. On the contrary, contemporary
neoliberal governance operates through isolating and entrepreneurializing responsible units and individuals, through devolving authority, decision making, and the implementation of policies and norms
of conduct. These are the processes that make individuals and other
small units in workplaces responsible for themselves while binding them to the powers and project of the whole. Integration and

individuation, cooperation without collectivization—neoliberal governance is a supreme instance of *omnus et singulatim*, the gathering and separating, amassing and isolating that Foucault identified as the signature of modern governmentality.[37]

The discourse and practice of governance depoliticizes its own deployment and field of application on several fronts. As governance "responsibilizes" each element in its orbit, it eliminates from view the stratification and disparate positions of these elements—the powers producing, arranging, and relating them. Governance also disavows the powers *it* circulates, the norms it advances, the conflicts it suppresses or dispatches. As it promulgates a market emphasis on "what works," it eliminates from discussion politically, ethically, or otherwise normatively inflected dimensions of policy, aiming to supersede politics with practical, technical approaches to problems. Governance also draws from business an emphasis on integrating disparate elements (of a firm) into a harmonized set of ends, an integration that also presumes the fungibility and dispensability of each element, the legitimacy of casting them off or replacing them as needed. Thus does the "economization of the political" entailed in neoliberal governance weld citizens to a common enterprise while backgrounding (at best) the classic principles of equality, political autonomy, universality, or even the paternalistic protectiveness proffered by the classical liberal or welfare state.

As William Walters notes, the embrace, if not the very idea of governance in politics emerges from a postideological claim—"the end of history"—to be pragmatic and solutions oriented; it features dialogue, inclusion, and consensus, rather than power, conflict, or opposition.[38] Governance aims to supersede the antagonisms and partisanship of realpolitik and democracy alike; the press toward consensus-driven managerial solutions to problems has as its opposite partisan maneuvering or brokering of policy, interest-group pluralism, and of course, class conflict and struggle. As governance becomes the "lingua franca of both the political and business establishments," ostensibly neutral, yet norm-laden notions such as best practices circulate across a range of public institutions, knowledge domains, warfare, and welfare.[39] We will consider best practices in more detail shortly.

In sum, governance disseminates a depoliticizing epistemology, ontology, and set of practices. Soft, inclusive, and technical in orientation, governance buries contestable norms and structural striations (such as class), as well as the norms and exclusions circulated by its procedures and decisions. It integrates subjects into the purposes and trajectories of the nations, firms, universities, or other entities employing it. In public life, governance displaces liberal democratic-justice concerns with technical formulations of problems, questions of right with questions of efficiency, even questions of legality with those of efficacy. In the workplace, governance displaces the lateral solidarities of unions and worker consciousness and the politics of struggle with hierarchically organized "teams," multiparty cooperation, individual responsibility, and antipolitics. Governance is also a key mechanism of the "responsibilization" policies and practices that make individual agency and self-reliance (regardless of means, social position, or contingencies) the site of survival and virtue and for the economization of domains and conduct through best practices and the metrics of benchmarking, points to which we now turn.

DEVOLUTION AND RESPONSIBILIZATION

Neoliberal governance stresses the devolution of authority as part of its formal antipathy to centralized state power and as part of its emphasis on problem solving achieved by stakeholders. But devolved power and responsibility are not equivalent to thoroughgoing decentralization and local empowerment. Devolution frequently means that large-scale problems, such as recessions, finance-capital crises, unemployment, or environmental problems, as well as fiscal crises of the state, are sent down the pipeline to small and weak units unable to cope with them technically, politically, or financially. Thus, state funding cuts in education or mental health devolve responsibility for these undertakings to municipalities, which in turn devolve them to individual schools or agencies, which devolve them to individual departments, which then have something called "decision-making authority," absent, of course, the resources to exercise this ghostly autonomy and sovereignty.

In this way, devolution also sets in motion certain neoliberal reforms via incentivization, rather than mandate. For example, several years ago, my university system devolved responsibility for paying employee benefits to individual academic departments. This tiny change effects a wholesale transformation of the university by incentivizing departments to hire ever-larger numbers of part-time academic and office staff who, when working less than 50 percent time, do not qualify for benefits at all. Thus does a flexibilized, unprotected and poorly paid labor force come to replace one enjoying modest security of employment, along with provisions for health, disability, and retirement. Nowhere was this intention decreed or mandated. Rather, when devolution of authority to ever smaller and weaker units is combined with seeding competition among them and aimed at "entrepreneurializing" them, the result is a mode of governance that political scientist Joe Soss describes as "at once muscular in its normative enforcement and diffuse in its organization."[40]

Neoliberal devolution of authority is related to, but differs from responsibilization, which sociologist Ronen Shamir describes as a "moralization of economic action that accompanies the economization of the political."[41] Devolution sends decision making and resource provision down the pipeline of power and authority. Responsibilization, on the other hand, especially as a social policy, is the moral burdening of the entity at the end of the pipeline. Responsibilization tasks the worker, student, consumer, or indigent person with discerning and undertaking the correct strategies of self-investment and entrepreneurship for thriving and surviving; it is in this regard a manifestation of human capitalization. As it discursively denigrates dependency and practically negates collective provisioning for existence, responsibilization solicits the individual as the only relevant and wholly accountable actor. Governance—with its emphasis on consensus, antipolitics, and the integration of individualized efforts into harmonized ends—facilitates both the practice and the legitimacy of responsibilization. As Shamir argues, "while obedience had been the practical master-key of top-down bureaucracies, responsibility is the practical master-key of governance."[42]

The new form of power orchestrating the conduct of subjects—and the importance of governance in activating this power—is apparent in the grammar used to describe and enact it. The ugly words "flexibilization" and "responsibilization" have their roots in human capacities associated with modest autonomy. To be flexible or responsible is to have capacities for adaptation or accountability that, as Nietzsche and not only Kant remind us, are nominative signs of sovereignty: only a moral agent understood as willing its actions can bear responsibility for itself. But when the act of being responsible is linguistically converted into the administered condition of being *responsibilized*, it departs from the domain of agency and instead governs the subject through an external moral injunction—through demands emanating from an invisible elsewhere. The word "responsibilization" takes a step further this move from a substance-based adjective to a process-based transitive verb, shifting it from an individual capacity to a governance project. Responsibilization signals a *regime* in which the singular human capacity for responsibility is deployed to constitute and govern subjects and through which their conduct is organized and measured, remaking and reorienting them for a neoliberal order. Again, governance facilitates and imposes responsibilization, but the powers orchestrating this process are nowhere in discursive sight, a disappearing act that is both generic to neoliberalism and particular to responsibilization itself.

Responsibilization is not an inherent entailment of devolution; there are decidedly more empowering and more democratic potentials for devolved decision making. Demands for local authority and decision making, it is well to remember, may emanate from both the Right and the Left, from anarchists or from religious fundamentalists. However, when conjoined, devolution and responsibilization produce an order in which the social *effects* of power—constructed and governed subjects—appear as morally burdened agents. Through this bundling of agency and blame, the individual is doubly responsibilized: it is expected to fend for itself (and blamed for its failure to thrive) *and* expected to act for the well-being of the economy (and blamed for *its* failure to thrive). Not only, then, are Greek workers, French pensioners, California and Michigan public employees, American Social Security recipients, British university students, European new immigrants, and public goods as a whole made to appear as thieving dependents operating in the old world of entitlement, rather than self-care, they are blamed for sinking states into debt, thwarting growth, and bringing the global economy to the brink of ruin. Perhaps most importantly, even when they are not blamed, even when they have comported properly with the norms of responsibilization, austerity measures taken in the name of macroeconomic health may legitimately devastate their livelihoods or lives.

Thus, responsibilized individuals are required to provide for themselves in the context of powers and contingencies radically limiting their ability to do so. But devolution and responsibilization also make individuals expendable and unprotected. This turn in neoliberal political rationality signals more than the dismantling of welfare-state logic or even that of the liberal social contract: once more, it expresses its precise inversion.

BENCHMARKING AND BEST PRACTICES

Like devolution and responsibilization, best practices today appear in a vast range of sites and institutions—private firms of every kind, social services, police forces, schools, military counterinsurgency operations, government agencies, hospitals, stock brokerages, laboratories, and consultancies—and they concern everything from greening an operation to downsizing or outsourcing one. Social scientists now use the term unblinkingly to describe research methodology, with the effect of eliding the political stakes in methodological choices, even ending methodological debate altogether. University administrations use the language of best practices to implement reorganizations and cuts with enormous implications for student access, staff positions, and education itself, to discuss the policing of demonstrations, and to prepare "rollouts" of new information systems and/or benefits policies.[43] Philip Mirowski describes a consulting service called Family/360 that, for a price, provides tailored best practices for parents to help them "create more positive family memories for [their] children."[44] Legislation introduced to prohibit the use of live animals (pigs and goats) in U.S. armed forces combat training was named the BEST Practices Act (the Battlefield Excellence through Superior Training Practices Act).[45] An independent association of funeral homes runs a competition for best practices by funeral homes that awards the winner an iPad Air.[46]

While best practices are promiscuous across research protocols, service agencies, industries, investment strategies, policing, and more, equally striking is their traffic across these and thus their effect in reconfiguring policing, education, military, and social-service activity through a business model. Best practices "entail a never-ending loop" between researchers and practitioners and between diverse endeavors and institutions—firms, families, factories, schools, government, NGOs.[47] Dissimulation of the normative work they do is achieved in part by this ostensibly generic applicability, by their emergence from the combination of consensus and objective research, and by their formally neutral status as practices, rather than purposes or missions. Best practices can be effectively contested only by postulating better practices, not by objecting to what they promulgate. Formally, they are nonnormative, pure means, "exemplary behaviors modeled into processes." But this is only the surface of the matter.

The ubiquitous concept of best practices and its close cousin and predecessor, "benchmarking," are exemplary of many features of neoliberal governance—its emphasis on soft power, antipolitics, buy-ins, consensus, teamwork, market metrics, and rejection of external regulation, command, partisan interest, and ideology. And it represents both an instance and an instrument of marketizing previously nonmarketized spheres, agencies, industries, or activities. Here is how this goes.

Emerging from the private sector in the early 1980s, but taken up soon after in the public, nonprofit, and NGO worlds, best practices and benchmarking embody a distinctive fusion of business, political, and knowledge concerns and an easy translatability across various spheres and "industries" in generating and applying governance techniques.[48] To unfamiliar ears, "benchmarking" may sound like a fancy word for goal setting, but its meaning is rather different. Benchmarking refers to the practice of a firm or agency undertaking internal reforms on the basis of studying and then importing the practices of other, more successful firms or agencies. In other words, benchmarks are set by industry leaders, and benchmarking represents the process of nonleaders understanding, distilling, and then implementing the practices that make those leaders successful.[49]

Benchmarking dispenses with history as a form of knowledge—how an organization or firm has traditionally or recently done things is irrelevant to how it should do them and must be the first thing jettisoned in a benchmarking process. Benchmarking also dispenses with the belief that different industries or sectors have practices and norms necessarily specific to them. A key premise of benchmarking is that best practices can be exported from one industry or sector to another and that some of the most valuable reforms will happen by creatively adapting practices in one field to another. (Histories of benchmarking cite the famous midcentury trips to the United States by Japanese businessmen bent on studying a wide range of industries with the assumption that "methods found in seemingly unrelated industries could provide a competitive advantage.")[50]

The presumed interchangeability of processes and practices across industries and sectors and the consolidation of best practices out of many different sources have several important implications for neoliberal rationality's dissemination of economic metrics everywhere, its generation of the basic contours and features of human capital, and its subsumption of formerly public institutions into enterprise. First, in benchmarking, practices are separated from products. Productivity, cost effectiveness, or consumer satisfaction are understood to inhere in practices with little respect to what is being produced, generated, or delivered. This permits private-sector practices to move readily into the public sector; it allows, for example, educational or health care institutions to be transformed by practices developed in the airline or computer industries.

Second, the reason practices are separable from products and are transferable is that the ultimate end of every organization is presumed to be the same: competitive advantage in a marketplace. As one benchmarking expert puts the matter, "benchmarking is a positive, proactive, structured process which leads to changing operations and eventually attaining superior performance and a competitive advantage."[51] Benchmarking works because "solving ordinary business problems, conducting management battles and surviving in the market place are all forms of war, fought by the same rules [know your enemy and know yourself]."[52] While benchmarking manuals for the nonprofit and public sectors may issue cautions about organizations importing "unproven ideas" with great expenditures and "minimal fiscal returns as a result," the issue is not one of borrowing from a sector with different purposes from one's own.[53] Rather, the problem is mistaking untested "promising practices" for "Best Practices."[54] Thus, one scholar of benchmarking notes that "as educational institutions have been focusing more and more on quality related issues," they are wisely employing benchmarking because "educational institutions tend to have quite similar core competence areas, that is, educating the customer to her needs."[55]

The third implication of benchmarking's presumptive isolation of practices builds on the first two: if practices can be separated from products precisely because every organization is presumed to be driven by the aim of succeeding in a competitive marketplace, the employment of benchmarking and best practices themselves challenge or simply wither other aims in nonprofit institutions by marketizing their cultures. Extractable in principle only, best practices bring with them the ends and values with which they are imbricated; by the experts' own accounts, these are market values. Meanwhile, the aims they replace could include those of educating citizens and developing human beings with those of meeting investor or consumer demand in a university; or those of vitalizing democracy or securing the health of the indigent with those of compressing costs in municipal agencies; or those of producing food sovereignty, war recovery, sustainable resource use or access to the arts with those of branding and competitive positioning for nonprofits and NGOs. Of course best practices are selected and tailored for specific features or challenges of an operation—customer service, employee-driven product innovation, downsizing, management restructuring, outsourcing—but the criterion for a best practice is its help in achieving competitive advantage. Competition, which neoliberal reason features as the essential, but constructed principle of markets, is installed by best practices wherever they are imported.

The contemporary ubiquitousness and promiscuity of best practices thus simultaneously indexes and facilitates neoliberal economization of heretofore nonmarketized spheres and activities. Public educational, artistic, civic, and other kinds of human endeavor are dissolved into a marketized medium through the circulation of best practices across private and public sectors. Consequently, many public and nonprofit institutions, from charities to universities, find themselves in a kind of mission drift today, disoriented by practices adopted from the profit sector that subtly recalibrate their goals and constituencies, along with their structures and processes. Mission drift, however, is only one way in which governance through best practices has altered public entities and public life. As I suggested at the beginning of this discussion, best practices stand for value-free technical knowledge validated by experience and consensus, where the alternative is not only tradition or mandate, but partisanship and contestation over purposes, values, and ends. Best practices connote both expertise and neutrality; they emerge from and cite research, as well as frame it. Their authority and legitimacy is corroborated through replacing rigid rules and top-down commands with organically gestated procedures validated by experience and success. In all of these ways, they are not merely claiming to be unpolitical, but constitute an antipolitics and thereby construct a particular image of the political. From the epistemological standpoint of best practices, politics appears as a combination of dicta or commands where there should be expertise, as particular interests or debate about ends where there should be teamwork for a goal, as partisanship where there should be neutrality and objectivity in both knowledge and practice, as provincialism where there should be the open doors and the lingua franca of the market.

While best practices are intended to displace and replace politics in whatever domain they govern, they do not ignore issues such as ethics or workplace harmony or inclusion. Thus, one online encyclopedia of market terms defines "Best Practices" as "a set of guidelines, ethics or ideas that represent the most efficient or prudent course of action."[56] Another best practices site offers this account:

> Best Practices are often exemplary behaviors modeled into processes. Conceptually, Best Practices are *ethical, legal, fair, replicable and applicable to anyone within an organization*; therefore they are Good Practices. However, they are not only good practices…they are Best Practices because their implementation aims at improving an organization's performance through additional *accountability, compliance, transparency and risk control*. A best practice is a technique, method, process, activity or incentive which has proven to be most effective in providing a certain outcome…. In order to survive the volatile market conditions and the tough competition dominating it, organizations from all industries have started adopting the Best Practices of their respective fields.[57]

On its face, this passage is gibberish—a gossamer net of high ethical values wafted over a bottom line of market success. However, it is gibberish bearing significance. These two definitions suggest that best practices aim to maximize competitive advantage without cheating—they represent a steroidally charged form of Weberian instrumental rationality wrapped in Aristotelian ethics and Kantian legal rectitude. So why the wrapping? In bundling together concerns with legality, transparency, accountability, ethics, and competitiveness and at least formally attending to each, best practices represent more than the suffusion of the public sphere with market metrics. They also represent the opposite, namely, the absorption of public or political concerns into markets and consequently the elimination of the need for legal, political, or ethical interference from the state or any other source. In combining ethics, fairness, legality, efficiency, and maximized outcomes in a competitive environment, best practices at once substitute for conventional government regulation, stand as a critique of it (preferring appropriate and tailored guidelines and standards over generic laws and commands), and represent paramount concern with business outcomes wherever such regulations might appear.

In short, best practices represent not merely the intimacy, but the consolidation of government, business, and knowledge endeavors into a market episteme that subtly banishes nonmarket values and aims. As best practices imbricate the formerly distinct purposes and ends of business, government, and knowledge in neoliberal regimes, they neuter or deflect normative challenges to neoliberal reason precisely through this imbrication. How do you contest a winning practice that claims (by virtue of being only a practice) value neutrality? How would you do so in the name of a (nonmarket) value or purpose that the practice spurns or does not recognize? It is through carrying market values while claiming only to be techniques that best practices promulgate certain norms and foreclose arguments about norms and ends. The bind here makes clear how best practices exemplify more broadly the soft power of governance, its focus on problem solving through team-based and consensus-based efforts, which exclude nonmarket concerns, protocols, metrics, and constituencies.

While best practices may be "set forth by an authority, such as a governing body or management," they embody precisely the consensus-developed directives with which neoliberal governance more generally aims to replace law, policing, punishment, and top-down directives. At the same time, best practices may incite or instigate certain legal reforms that would permit closer comportment between the law and business interests, and they also may entail or generate certain legal and ethical workarounds. Thus, while best practices often operate as replacements for law and regulation (not to mention for religion, tradition, or other forms of deliberation), while they are neoliberalism's alternative to the state that it officially abjures, proof that we can be both ethical and efficient without external interference, they can also be the Trojan horse through which law and the political order it secures may be transformed for and by neoliberal reason.

An example from the neoliberalization of post-Saddam Iraq will make this clear.

BEST PRACTICES IN TWENTY-FIRST-CENTURY IRAQI AGRICULTURE

In 2003, months after Saddam Hussein was toppled, Paul Bremer, the American-appointed head of the Coalition Provisional Authority, declared Iraq "open for business" and spelled out a set of 100 orders that came to be known as the Bremer Orders.[58] These mandated selling off several hundred state-run enterprises, permitting full ownership rights of Iraqi businesses by foreign firms and full repatriation of profits to foreign firms, opening Iraq's banks to foreign ownership and control, and eliminating tariffs—in short, making Iraq a new playground of world finance and investment. At the same time, the Bremer Orders restricted labor and throttled back public goods and services. They outlawed strikes and eliminated the right to unionize in most sectors, mandated a regressive flat tax on income, lowered the corporate rate to a flat 15 percent, and eliminated taxes on profits repatriated to foreign-owned businesses.

Many of these orders were in violation of the Geneva and Hague Conventions concerning war, occupation, and international relations, which mandate that an occupying power must guard, rather than sell off the assets of the occupied country. But if illegal under international law, the orders could be implemented by a sovereign Iraqi government. To that end, an interim government was appointed by the United States in late 2003 and was pressed to ratify the orders when it was pronounced "sovereign" in 2004. And lest future elected governments not be so pliable, one order declares that no elected Iraqi government will have the power to alter them.[59]

The Bremer Orders and the U.S.-dominated state under construction that ratified and executed them obviously exemplify a host of neoliberal features: the use of a calamity ("shock doctrine") to impose neoliberal reforms; the elimination of public ownership and welfare; the reduction of taxes and tariffs; the extensive use of the state to structure market competition through inequality; the breakup of labor and popular solidarities; the creation of ideal conditions for global finance and investment capital. Yet the orders, defined as "binding instructions or directives to the Iraqi people that create penal consequences or have a direct bearing on the way Iraqis are regulated, including changes to Iraqi law,"[60] would seem to be at odds with the idea of the soft power of governance and best practices we have been considering as the mode through which neoliberal rationality is disseminated. As William Engdahl notes, the orders had the shape of "do it or die."[61] But what we will see on close inspection is the importance of law in codifying and disseminating best practices, on one side, and the role of best practices in generating law and policy, on the other. The orders emanated from neoliberal understandings of best practices *and* set them in motion. Law can be mobilized to structure competition and facilitate capital accumulation, but also to codify and animate best practices in lieu of violence or commands. Close inspection of one Bremer order vividly illustrates this concatenation of effects.

Bremer Order 81, the "Patent, Industrial Design, Undisclosed Information, Integrated Circuits and Plant Variety Law," includes a prohibition against "the re-use of crop seeds of protected varieties."[62] Why a law against seed saving and reuse? The protected varieties named in the order refer to genetically modified seed produced by Monsanto, Dow, DuPont, and other agribusiness giants, and at first blush, the prohibition seems mainly designed to protect the intellectual property rights of these firms—farmers cannot just buy the seed once and then pirate its offspring: ruthless, perhaps, but hardly unethical or uncommon. And hardly relevant to best practices. However, the story only begins with the letter of the law.

Monsanto and other large seed corporations are selling a package around the world that is transforming agriculture: the package includes patented, genetically modified seed and the fertilizers and pesticides that go with it.[63] With the promise of giant crop yields and an end to struggling with pests, the agribusiness giants aim to convert farmers across the developing world from "traditional" to "modern" techniques, materials, *and* markets.

Since at least 8000 B.C. Iraqi farmers have successfully grown wheat without this package in what is known today as the Fertile Crescent. Over the centuries, farmers cultivated the range of varieties essential to crop sustainability by saving seeds from thriving wheat plants one year and planting and cross-pollinating them with seeds of different strengths the following year. By using such practices, the crop continually improves and diversifies, partly through selection by experienced farmers, partly through plant evolution, partly through open pollination conducted by winds, insects, and animals. As late as 2002, writes ecologist Jeremy Smith, the Federal Accounting Office "estimated that 97 percent of Iraqi farmers" engaged in these practices, with the consequence "that there are now over 200,000 known varieties of wheat in the world."[64]

For millennia, Fertile Crescent farmers informally shared and traded seeds at harvest and planting time. In the twentieth century, they shifted to storing and retrieving seed from a national seed bank, located, alas, in Abu Ghraib, where the entire bank vanished after the bombings and occupation. This calamity, following war and episodes of draught since 1991 and combined with the embargo by the United States and United Kingdom that limited access to agricultural equipment, caused Iraqi wheat production to drop dramatically and become unable to sustain the population for the first time in centuries.[65] The production crisis opened the door for the agribusiness giants to move in: the seed bank destroyed, the harvest yield dramatically down due to natural disaster and years of war, Iraqi farmers were vulnerable, desperate, exploitable. They needed seed, and agribusiness-backed relief efforts were there to provide it.

Bremer Order 81 sealed the farmer's permanent dependence on the agribusiness giants.

The U.S. government handout of genetically modified seed in 2004 was like offering heroin to a desperate single mother out of a job, facing eviction, and despairing of the future. Not only did it promise relief, but the first bag was free. It permanently attached the recipient to the supplier, and the addiction was deadly—to sustainable Iraqi farming, Iraqi self-sufficiency, and even the farmers themselves.

As the ink dried on the Bremer Orders, the U.S. Agency for International Development began delivering thousands of tons of wheat seed to the Iraq Agricultural Ministry, which distributed it at little or no cost to Iraqi farmers.[66] An Arizona agriresearch firm, the World Wide Wheat Company, provided thousands more bags of free seed.[67] These donations were combined with demonstration plots, run by Texas A&M for USAID and aimed at teaching Iraqi farmers how to grow the new high-yield crops. Thousands of farmers were lured into the new agricultural techniques, which also required the use of specialized fungicides, pesticides, and herbicides. Free seed, the promise of soaring production levels, and their teachers' insistence that the uniform crops and accompanying chemicals represented modernity, wealth, and the future—together, these transformed centuries of Iraqi agriculture almost overnight. Bremer Order 81 secured that transformation. Prohibited from saving seeds of protected varieties, Iraqi farmers are now permanently bound to their foreign dealers, whose seed is ubiquitous in their fields, intermixed with all the heritage seed. Organic, diversified, low-cost, ecologically sustainable wheat production in Iraq is finished.[68]

Half the free wheat seeds distributed in post-Saddam Iraq were for bread wheat; the other half was for pasta wheat, and pasta is no part of the Iraqi diet.[69] Thus, in addition to making Iraqi farmers dependent on giant corporations whose seeds, licensing, and chemicals they must now purchase annually (and for which state subsidies are available, while other farm subsidies were eliminated), they were being transformed from multicrop local food providers into monocrop participants in global import-export markets.[70] Today, Iraqi farmers generate profits for Monsanto by supplying pasta to Texas school cafeterias, while Iraq has become an importer of staples formerly grown on its own soil.

There is more to this heartbreaking story of the destruction of thousands of years of sustainable agriculture and of what some activists call "food sovereignty," but let us fast-forward to one possible future. A similar experiment took place in India in the 1990s.[71] Tens of thousands of farmers were lured into using genetically modified cotton seed by village-to-village agribusiness representatives promising bigger crops with export potential, something especially important at a time when neoliberal reforms were eliminating government price supports and subsidies for cotton production. Farmers were abetted in the transition by the availability of large bank loans to purchase seed and the needed pesticides, fungicides, and herbicides. Like the Iraqis, Indian cotton farmers were not only adopting new agricultural technologies, but becoming fully integrated into world markets and debt finance.

The problem is that farming in general is uniquely vulnerable to fluctuations in nature, such as draughts and floods, and farming for export is also vulnerable to fluctuations in world markets. One bad year with either can leave debt-burdened farmers without the means to repay loans, which means bad credit, which means the inability to borrow more (or borrowing at scandalous rates), which means the inability to plant and thus recoup losses. This is what happened in India a decade ago, pushing cotton farmers into an ever-deepening hole of debt.[72] The result? An epidemic of farmer suicides (at least twenty thousand at this point), often committed by drinking a bottle of RoundUp®, the Monsanto-produced herbicide that kills everything except Monsanto's genetically modified seed.[73]

Certainly, Monsanto did not intend the calamity in India. Bremer Order 81 does not aim for it in Iraq, either. Rather the order promulgates a set of best practices—"techniques, methods, processes, activities or incentives proven to be most effective in providing a certain outcome"—that promote modernization of farming techniques, high-yield monocrop production, integration into the world economy, and development of export capacity in the context of free trade, all while securing a favorable climate for agribusiness. Order 81 explicitly identifies each of these goals in its preamble. Here are relevant excerpts from that preamble:

> *Acknowledging* the Governing Council's desire to bring about significant change to the Iraqi intellectual property system as necessary to improve the economic condition of the people of Iraq,
>
> *Determined* to improve the conditions of life, technical skills, and opportunities for all Iraqis and to fight unemployment with its associated deleterious effect on public security,
>
> *Recognizing* that companies, lenders and entrepreneurs require a fair, efficient and predictable environment for protection of their intellectual property,
>
> *Recognizing* the demonstrated interest of the Iraqi Governing Council to become a full member in the international trading system, known as the World Trade Organization...
>
> *Acting* in a manner consistent with the Report of the Secretary General to the Security Council...concerning the need for the development of Iraq and its transition from a non-transparent centrally planned economy to a free market economy characterized by sustainable economic growth through the establishment of a dynamic private sector, and the need to enact institutional and legal reforms to give it effect.[74]

An improved investment climate in Iraq, its integration into world trade, elimination of its nontransparent state ownership and planning in favor of private enterprise—these are the "outcomes" that Bremer

Order 81 aims to achieve. What Nancy Scola calls the "legal tweak" that effectively ended seed saving was the reform required to bring them about.[75] Casting itself as the opposite of regulation, this order launched the practices that would integrate Iraqi farming and farmers into the global order, an integration achieved by eliminating, on the one hand, nonmonetary trade, local sourcing, and traditional techniques and by generating, on the other, dependence on large foreign corporations, on fertilizers and pesticides, on debt financing, and on global export and important markets. The legal tweak instigates these best practices but, like the Protestant ethic Weber deemed crucial to inaugurating capitalism, its importance falls away once the machinery is in motion.[76] Thus, Order 81 epitomizes the neoliberal mobilization of law not to repress or to punish, but to structure competition and effect "the conduct of conduct." It alters one tiny practice (seed saving) to inaugurate the convergent purposes of Iraqi economic growth, protection of corporate intellectual property, and Iraqi participation in world trade and finance.

Consider again Order 81's preamble. It includes the goals of improving the life conditions, technical skills, opportunities, and public security of Iraqis; producing a desirable environment for companies, banks, and entrepreneurs; integrating Iraq into the international trading system; and creating a dynamic free and transparent market economy. The preamble exemplifies the coming together in governance of veridiction with objectivity, expertise with consensus, need fulfillment with competitive advantage. It exemplifies as well how best practices presume a common goal, rather than appearing to favor the interest of one party over another or even acknowledging divergent interests. As they neutralize or obscure contested or conflicting ends, best practices codify existing market norms and features as the reality principle. Thus, while it is certainly possible to imagine more ecologically, economically, and socially sustainable practices for Iraqi agriculture, these would be at odds with global markets and competition, intellectual property rights, and new financing conventions, not to mention modernized agricultural techniques. Farming practices that are organic, biodiverse, small scale, cooperative, free of debt financing, and aimed at generating "food sovereignty" for the nation might be sensible from the perspective of how Iraqi wheat production could draw on past knowledge, materials, and techniques for a sustainable future. But insofar as they would make Iraq an outlier in the global economy, they could not qualify as best practices.

Also visible in this story is the specific meshing of state and business aims through neoliberal governance, a meshing that exceeds the interlocking directorates or quid pro quo arrangements familiar from past iterations of capitalism. The project of the state is to facilitate economic growth and a strong investment climate, not the well-being of a particular sector or people, and the project of capital is to generate such growth, though it also absorbs into itself the broader purposes and ethics previously provisioned elsewhere. And so a series of historical transpositions unfolds in neoliberal governance: business devotes itself to local development as government devotes itself to global positioning; governments negotiate contracts as firms become educators; government concerns itself with the investment climate, business concerns itself with ethics; government prioritizes economic growth, credit ratings, and global economic positioning while business represents the interests of the needy or underserved.

Order 81 is reputed to have been drafted by Monsanto and emerges from the Bush administration's close ties to agribusiness (and the extensive presence in the Bush cabinet of those ties), yet these facts are almost beside the point. The orders expressed and executed Bremer's purpose in Iraq, which was not to democratize it, but to neoliberalize it. In this regard, even more significant than Monsanto's direct influence is that the orders fostering economic deregulation, privatization, and the structuring of competition *preceded* the building of democratic institutions; orders first, then constitutions, parliaments, councils, elections, and civil liberties. It is also noteworthy that the provisional government authorizing them, whose members were handpicked by the Bremer team and subject in all their actions to Bremer's veto, consisted only of those who supported the U.S. occupation. In turn, this government proposed a process for ratifying the permanent constitution that excluded all political parties not supporting the occupation.[77] Again, this could be read as the direct and heavy hand of the United States in making Iraq a playground for international capital and especially for U.S. corporations, ranging from Halliburton to Monsanto. More important, however, are the ways in which these moves represent distinctive features of neoliberal governance: while states operating on a business model will eschew *excessive* uses of violence or extraconstitutional conduct, they are also not about to enfranchise competing or oppositional interests, cede control, or prioritize justice and welfare over investment climate and economic growth.[78] This fundamental shift in state purposes and legitimacy is more important than the question of precisely which politicians, corporations, and banks are in bed with one another. That old model could easily be charged with corruption. Neoliberal governance facilitates a more open-handed and effective fusion of political and economic power, one that largely eliminates the scandal of corruption as it erases differences in goals and governance between states and capital, indeed, as the best practices circulating between them perform this erasure.[79]

CHAPTER FIVE

Law and Legal Reason

In his Collège de France lectures, Foucault argues that "the juridical brings form to the economic" in neoliberal rationality, a remark some have cast as his Weberian reversal of what he takes to be a Marxist historiography in which law is presumed to derive from and mirror modes of production.[1] Certainly, the discussion in chapter 4 of the Bremer regime in Iraq comports with Foucault's argument: neoliberalizing Iraq required a plethora of large and small legal reforms even before a state could be (re)built. Chile under Augusto Pinochet and the "Chicago Boys" after the overthrow of Salvador Allende offers another obvious example. On the one hand, law was mobilized to privatize state industries, seduce foreign ownership and investment, secure profit retention, and reduce trade restrictions. On the other hand, popular assemblies and Left parties were outlawed, strikes were criminalized, unions banned.

However, this chapter takes Foucault's point about law's role in neoliberalization further than he did: law and legal reasoning not only give form to the economic, but economize new spheres and practices. In this way, law becomes a medium for disseminating neoliberal rationality beyond the economy, including to constitutive elements of democratic life. More than simply securing the rights of capital and structuring competition, neoliberal juridical reason recasts political rights, citizenship, and the field of democracy itself in an economic register; in doing so, it disintegrates the very idea of the demos. Legal reasoning thus complements governance practices as a means by which democratic political life and imaginaries are undone. Before pursuing this argument, it is important to mark the ways that dedemocratization through neoliberalized law transpires at the more analytically familiar level, that of legal reforms that strengthen the political hand of capital and weaken associations of citizens, workers, and consumers.[2] In addition to the Chilean and Iraqi examples mentioned above, consider these four American legal decisions from 2010–11.

In January 2010, in *Citizens United v. Federal Election Commission*, the Supreme Court ruled against government bans on corporate contributions to super PACS, political action committees formed to support a candidate outside the auspices of her or his campaign. Calling such bans an abridgement of free speech and giving corporations the standing of persons with an unqualified right to political speech, the ruling permits corporate money to overwhelm the election process.[3]

In April 2011, another Supreme Court decision, *AT&T Mobility LLC v. Concepcion*, permitted corporations to end-run class-action suits, forcing disgruntled consumers to enter into individual arbitration, instead. Class-action suits have long been crucial instruments of worker and consumer resistance to discriminatory, deceptive, or fraudulent corporate behavior, from underpaying and overcharging to polluting or violating health and safety laws.[4] These have now been effectively neutered. Since the decision, lower court judges have cited the law more than one hundred times to turn back class-action lawsuits, vindicating Vanderbilt University law professor Brian Fitzpatrick's claim that it was not merely favorable to business but "a game-changer."[5]

In June 2011, following a series of state and federal legislative actions limiting the powers of organized labor, the Wisconsin Supreme Court upheld a state law gutting the collective-bargaining power of public unions. (Wages may still be negotiated, but work conditions and benefits may not.)[6] The state supreme court decision, upheld in federal appeals court in 2013, is a death blow to organized labor in the public sector.[7]

Also in June 2011, in *Wal-Mart Stores, Inc. v. Dukes et al*, the largest employment-discrimination case in history, the Supreme Court turned back a class-action suit against Wal-Mart in which 1.5 million women sought back pay for gender discrimination. The court rejected the standing of the women as a class, arguing that nothing bound together the millions of discrete employment decisions producing across-the-board lower pay for Wal-Mart's female workers.[8]

More is at stake in these four decisions than support for capital in the name of freedom. Rather, an important remaking of the demos is taking place. The first decision permits large corporations to finance elections, the ultimate icon of popular sovereignty in neoliberal democracy. The second eliminates the primary legal means by which consumers or workers band together to fight corporate abuses. The third and fourth join a string of recent laws constricting the capacity of public-sector and private-sector workers to act in concert. Together, these decisions assault every level of organized popular power and collective consciousness in the United States: citizens, consumers, workers. When these kinds of assaults on collective consciousness and action are combined with neoliberalism's displacement of democratic values in ordinary political discourse, with dramatic disinvestment in public education, and with the governance-based substitution of efficacy for accountability in economic and political policy, the result is not simply the erosion of popular power, but its elimination from a democratic political imaginary. It is in that imaginary that democracy becomes delinked from organized popular power and that these forms of identity and the political energy they represent disappear, generating the "changing of the heart and soul" that Margaret Thatcher identified as fundamental to the success of the neoliberal project.[9] More than merely being abandoned, legal supports for popular power are discursively identified in neoliberal reason as unacceptable blockades in a (mythical) free market, parallel to the ways that welfare provisions such as health care and Social Security, and even public services and public institutions come to be coded as socialist and cast as market democracy's antithesis.

How, though, does the legal assault on social solidarities and identities couple in its effects with those of neoliberal governance to replace such identities with that of human capital? How is neoliberal law not only diminishing democratic organizations and energies, but erasing democratic subjects and their instruments of power? Certain legal enactments abet this process, but the work also happens through legal reasoning that draws on and disseminates neoliberal rationality as common sense. Thus, along with intensifying inequalities by unleashing capital or restraining labor, and along with dismantling popular associations and solidarities, there is a third important operation to track in law's contribution to neoliberal dedemocratization: its economization of political fields, activities, subjects, rights, and purposes. The remainder of this chapter examines this economization in the 2010 U.S. Supreme Court decision *Citizens United v. Federal Election Commission.*

Building on two Supreme Court decisions from the 1970s, *Buckley v. Valeo* and *First National Bank of Boston v. Bellotti*, to undo a century of campaign-finance regulation, *Citizens United* is often taken to emblematize the radical neoliberal turn of the Roberts Court.[10] The majority opinion in *Citizens United,* authored by Justice Kennedy, permits corporate money to flood American elections by lifting restrictions on corporate expenditures for all types of electoral communications. *Citizens United* overturns previous regulations concerning the time, place, and amount of corporate spending in elections, arguing these are unconstitutional limits on free-speech rights to which corporations, as "fictional persons," are entitled and from which the citizenry also benefits.

Certainly, the *Citizens United* decision expresses neoliberal values in an obvious way. It erases the distinction between fictitious (corporate) and natural (human) persons in allocating free-speech rights; it subverts legislative and popular efforts at limiting corporate influence in politics; and it overturns previous Supreme Court rulings aimed at modestly restricting the power of money in politics. *Citizens United*, however, represents more than the ideological favoring of wealth, deregulation, and corporations by the court. And it represents more than the unleashing of market forces in politics or the elimination of a crucial membrane between politics and markets.[11] Rather, it is a chapter in the far-reaching neoliberalization of politics, mobilizing law and even the Constitution for the relentless remaking of political life with market values, not merely by market forces.

In one of the most analytically astute critical commentaries on *Citizens United*, legal scholar Timothy Kuhner terms the decision "neoliberal jurisprudence" insofar as it applies neoclassical economic theory to the political sphere, analogizes that sphere to the market, and ultimately undoes what he calls the boundary between democracy and capitalism, "two different systems that belong to two different spheres."[12] Kuhner is certainly correct, yet still understates the accomplishment of the decision. The reasoning in *Citizens United* exceeds analogizing democracy to the market and applying neoclassical economic principles to First Amendment cases.[13] Rather, in what Foucault identified as the signature move of neoliberal rationality, the decision recasts formerly noneconomic spheres *as* markets at the level of principles, norms, and subjects. It remakes the political sphere as a market and remakes *homo politicus* as *homo oeconomicus*—in the political sphere, individuals, corporations, and other associations are all operating to enhance their competitive positioning and capital value. Moreover, it replaces the distinctively political valences of rights, equality, liberty, access, autonomy, fairness, the state, and the public with economic valences of these terms. Thus, more than merely unleashing market forces into democratic life, or embedding and advancing a procorporate and antipopular viewpoint, or even applying neoclassical economic principles to the interpretation of rights and the space of politics, *Citizens United* advances neoliberal rationality's signature economization of law and politics. It is not merely bad jurisprudence, but a force in remaking the concept and practices of democracy.

In the majority opinion, Justice Kennedy argues that campaign finance regulations concerning corporate electioneering bear upon a First Amendment right that ought neither to be limited to natural persons nor apportioned differently among them. "All speakers," he declares simply, "use money amassed from the economic marketplace to fund their speech, and the First Amendment protects the resulting speech."[14] Restrictions on speech ought not to pertain to differential resources or differential capacity for influence, he adds, and First Amendment standards must always prioritize "protecting rather than stifling speech."[15] Hence, Justice Kennedy concludes, there is no justification for limiting spending on campaign ads by corporations; such restrictions represent both inappropriate governmental intervention in the free market of ideas and discrimination against certain speakers on the basis of status or content.

That is the reasoning, at once simple and radical in its jettisoning of more than a century of law aimed at mitigating the potentially overwhelming power of corporate wealth in electoral politics. But what makes this reasoning possible? What new common sense does it draw upon and what transformations of the Constitution and political life does it enact?

SPEECH IS LIKE CAPITAL

Writing for the majority in *Citizens United*, Justice Kennedy sets out to emancipate speech from the webs of regulation and censorship by which he claims it is currently discouraged or worse. "First Amendment freedoms need breathing space to survive," he quotes approvingly from Chief Justice Roberts's opinion in an earlier case.[16] "As additional rules are created for regulating political speech," Kennedy adds, "any speech arguably within their reach is chilled."[17] Depicting the Federal Election Commission as generating "onerous restrictions" that "function as the equivalent of prior restraint" and largely reducing it to the business of censorship,[18] Kennedy underscores the danger represented by this government agency, a danger that it is the task of the court to hold off:

> When the FEC issues advisory opinions that prohibit speech, "many persons, rather than undertake the considerable burden (and sometimes risk) of vindicating their rights through case-by-case litigation, will choose simply to abstain from protected speech — harming not only themselves but society as a whole, which is deprived of an uninhibited marketplace of ideas." *Virginia v. Hicks, 539 U.S. 113, 119* [citation omitted]. Consequently, "the censor's determination may in practice be final." *Freedman, supra* at 58.

At times, Kennedy raises the pitch in *Citizens United* to depict limits on corporate funding of PAC ads as "an outright ban on speech";[19] at other times, he casts them merely as inappropriate government intervention and bureaucratic weightiness.[20] But beneath all the hyperbole about government's chilling of corporate speech is a crucial rhetorical move: the figuring of speech as analogous to capital in "the political marketplace." On the one hand, government intervention is featured throughout the opinion as harmful to the marketplace of ideas that speech generates.[21] Government restrictions damage freedom of speech just as they damage all freedoms. On the other hand, the unfettered *accumulation and circulation* of speech is cast as an unqualified good, essential to "the right of citizens to inquire…hear… speak…and use information to reach consensus [itself] a precondition to enlightened self-government and a necessary means to protect it."[22] Not merely corporate rights, then, but democracy as a whole is at stake in the move to deregulate speech. Importantly, however, democracy is here conceived as a marketplace whose goods—ideas, opinions, and ultimately, votes—are generated by speech, just as the economic market features goods generated by capital. In other words, at the very moment that Justice Kennedy deems disproportionate wealth irrelevant to the equal rights exercised in this marketplace and the utilitarian maximization these rights generate, speech itself acquires the status of capital, and a premium is placed on its unrestricted sources and unimpeded flow.

What is significant about rendering speech as capital? Economization of the political occurs not through the mere *application* of market principles to nonmarket fields, but through the *conversion* of political processes, subjects, categories, and principles to economic ones. This is the conversion that occurs on every page of the Kennedy opinion. If everything in the world is a market, and neoliberal markets consist only of competing capitals large and small, and speech is the capital of the electoral market, then speech will necessarily share capital's attributes: it appreciates through calculated investment, and it advances the position of its bearer or owner. Put the other way around, once speech is rendered as the capital of the electoral marketplace, it is appropriately unrestricted and unregulated, fungible across actors and venues, and existing solely for the advancement or enhancement of its bearer's interests. The classic associations of political speech with freedom, conscience, deliberation, and persuasion are nowhere in sight.

How, precisely, is speech capital in the Kennedy opinion? How does it come to be figured in economic terms where its regulation or restriction appears as bad for its particular marketplace and where its monopolization by corporations appears as that which is good for all? The transmogrification of speech into capital occurs on a number of levels in Kennedy's account.

First, speech is like capital in its tendency to proliferate and circulate, to push past barriers, to circumvent laws and other restrictions, indeed, to spite efforts at intervention or suppression.[23] Speech is thus rendered as a force both natural and good, one that can be wrongly impeded and encumbered, but never quashed.

Second, persons are not merely producers, but consumers of speech, and government interference is a menace—wrong in principle and harmful in effect—at both ends. The marketplace of ideas, Kennedy repeats tirelessly, is what decides the value of speech claims. Every citizen must judge the content of speech for himself or herself; it cannot be a matter for government determination, just as government should not usurp other consumer choices.[24] In this discussion, Kennedy makes no mention of shared deliberation or judgment in politics or of voices that are unfunded and relatively powerless. He is focused on the wrong of government "command[ing] where a person may get his or her information or what distrusted source he or she may not hear, [using] censorship to control thought."[25] If speech generates goods consumed according to individual choice, government distorts this market by "banning the political speech of millions of associations of citizens" (that is, corporations) and by paternalistically limiting what consumers may know or consider. Again, if speech is the capital of the political marketplace, then we are politically free when it circulates freely. And it circulates freely only when corporations are not restricted in what speech they may fund or promulgate.

Third, Kennedy casts speech not as a medium for expression or dialogue, but rather as innovative and productive, just as capital is. There is "a creative dynamic inherent in the concept of free expression" that intersects in a lively way with "rapid changes in technology" to generate the public good.[26] This aspect of speech, Kennedy argues, specifically "counsel[s] against upholding a law that restricts political speech in certain media or by certain speakers."[27] Again, the dynamism, innovativeness, and generativity of speech, like that of all capital, is dampened by government intervention.

Fourth, and perhaps most important in establishing speech as the capital of the electoral marketplace, Kennedy sets the power of speech and the power of government in direct and zero-sum-game opposition to one another. Repeatedly across the lengthy opinion for the majority, he identifies speech with freedom and government with control, censorship, paternalism, and repression.[28] When free speech and government meet, it is to contest one another: the right of speech enshrined in the First Amendment, he argues, is "premised on mistrust of governmental power" and is "an essential mechanism of democracy [because] it is the means to hold officials accountable to the people."[29] Here are other variations on this theme in the opinion:

> The First Amendment was certainly not understood [by the framers] to condone the suppression of political speech in society's most salient media. It was understood as a response to the repression of speech.[30]

> When Government seeks to use its full power, including criminal law, to command where a person may get his or her information or what distrusted source he or she may not hear, it uses censorship to control thought.... The First Amendment confirms the freedom to think for ourselves.[31]

This reading of the First Amendment and of the purpose of political speech positions government and speech as warring forces parallel to those of government and capital in a neoliberal economy.

Justice Kennedy's opinion construes the First Amendment not as a human or civil right, but as a capital right. He aims to secure from regulation or interference not ideas, deliberation, or the integrity of the democratic political sphere, but an unimpeded flow (barrage) of speech. While retaining the language of rights and persons, he has effectively detached speech and speech rights from individuals, which facilitates the move to protect corporate speech rights. Thus, the problem with *Citizens* is not (as is often declared by critics of this decision) that corporations have been awarded the rights of individuals, but that individuals as rights-bearing participants in popular sovereignty disappear when speech flows obtain the status of capital flows and all actors are seeking to enhance the value of their capital.

For Kennedy, not only must both speech and capital circulate freely, the only enemy to such freedom is government. This formulation links all members of society and economy, from the poorest citizen to the richest corporation, as potential victims of government interference or censorship. As individuals and corporations are thus allied—even identified with one another in the perils they face—the distinctive power of corporate speech, more than glossed over, is converted into a cause. What must be fought are conditions in which "certain disfavored associations of citizens—those that have taken on the corporate form—are penalized" and prevented "from presenting both facts and opinions to the public," which is deprived of "knowledge and opinion vital to its function."[32]

In a rhetorically structured field in which there is only speech and its endangerment by government and in which the unimpeded flow of speech benefits all, while government intervention invariably targets and discriminates, significant differences among speakers disappear. Whether the speaker is a homeless woman or Exxon, speech is speech, just as capital is capital. This disavowal of stratification and power differentials in the field of analysis and action is a crucial feature of neoliberal rationality, precisely the feature that discursively erases distinctions between capital and labor, owners and producers, landlord and tenant, rich and poor. There is only capital, and whether it is human, corporate, financial, or derivative, whether it is tiny or giant, is irrelevant to both its normative conduct and its right to be free of interference. Similarly, in *Citizens United*, there is only speech, all of which has the same right, the same capacity to enrich the marketplace of ideas, the same capacity to be judged by the citizenry, and the same vulnerability to restriction or repression by government.

In sum, in Justice Kennedy's formulation, speech is *like* capital in its natural, irrepressible, dynamic, and creative nature; its market field of operations and circulation; its undifferentiated standing across diverse social agents; its generation of freedom through producer and consumer choice; its right to be free; and its wholesale antagonism to government regulation. As we will see, speech operates *as* capital to enhance the positioning of its bearer in what Kennedy calls the "political marketplace." This transformation of the meaning, character, purpose, and value of speech from a political to an economic register quite precisely expresses the unfolding of neoliberal rationality in a political and ethical sphere. It also facilitates arguments to lift restrictions on entering the speech marketplace, to eliminate regulations on operating within it, and to quash concerns with its internal distributions of power and effect. Once this economization is secured, to subject the marketplace in which speech operates to manufactured equality or redistribution is simply to make a Keynesian moral and technical error. If all markets are domains of natural equality founded on and fostered by unimpeded competition, government may facilitate entry and foster competition, but is otherwise an unwarranted intruder. Thus, Justice Kennedy opines, previous Supreme Court decisions that place limits on corporate speech interfere with the "open marketplace" of ideas protected by the First Amendment.[33]

MARKETS MULTIPLIED

Like the figuration of speech as capital, the multiplication of marketplaces is another index of the economization of law and politics achieved by *Citizens United*. Kennedy makes frequent allusions to marketplaces of speech and ideas, and, drawing from *Bellotti*, depicts electoral contests themselves as "political marketplaces."[34] According to Kennedy, the question before the court is whether winners in the economic marketplace may operate unimpeded in "the political marketplace."[35] This is how he construes the relevant precedents:

> Political speech is "indispensable to decisionmaking in a democracy, and this is no less true because the speech comes from a corporation rather than an individual." (*Bellotti*, 435 US at 777)…Austin sought to defend the antidistortion rationale as a means to prevent corporations from obtaining "'an unfair advantage in the political marketplace'" by using "'resources amassed in the economic marketplace.'" (494 US at 659) But Buckley rejected the premise that the Government has an interest "in equalizing the relative ability of individuals and groups to influence the outcome of elections." (424 US at 48) Buckley was specific in stating that "the skyrocketing cost of political campaigns" could not sustain the governmental prohibition. (424 US at 26) The First Amendment's protections do not depend on the speaker's "financial ability to engage in public discussion." (*Id.* at 14)[36]

Justice Kennedy acknowledges that if everything is a marketplace, those dominant in one will likely bring some of that power to another. Yet this does not justify government intervention to equalize marketplace positioning. Even if amassed wealth can be mobilized to influence election outcomes, marketplaces must be left free of government interference and practices of equalization. Markets, no matter how they overlap and affect one another in reinforcing power and powerlessness, must all be left to work on their own.

What has happened here? Democratic political speech, far from being a delicate, monopolizable, and corruptible medium for public persuasion becomes, in and as a marketplace, an unhindered capital right. Similarly, the political, far from being a field of highly specific powers through which common existence is negotiated, protected, or transformed, becomes, as a market, a field for advancing every kind of capital—human, corporate, financial, cultural. Both of these moves make perfect sense insofar as neoliberal rationality recognizes market conduct as the sole principle of action and market metrics as the sole measures for every sphere of human action. Importantly, the Kennedy opinion, more than merely drawing on this rationality, articulates it as a set of principles for interpreting the Constitution, construing democracy, and producing political life. Neoliberal rationality constitutes the hermeneutics through which constitutional principles are read and applied in *Citizens United* and in this way enacts the economization of politics through law.

STRICT SCRUTINY FOR CORPORATIONS

While Justice Kennedy marketizes every sphere, he also braids key strands of civil rights discourse into the opinion to bolster his argument for deregulating corporate speech in the political sphere. Here is how this goes.

In one of the most notorious parts of the decision, Justice Kennedy argues that construed as a person (or as an aggregate or association of persons), corporations straightforwardly share with all persons the right to speak in the political sphere. A corporation's potentially greater power to finance the broadcast of its speech is no more relevant to constriction of this right than are the greater buying capacities of the rich to constriction of their private-property rights. Equality, for neoliberals as for classical economic liberals, pertains to rights' distribution, not to the effects of rights' exercise.

Justice Kennedy also formulates corporate rights to political speech as bearing directly on citizen information gathering: "The right of citizens to inquire, to hear, to speak, and to use information to reach consensus is a precondition to enlightened self-government and a necessary means to protect it," and "for these reasons, political speech must prevail against laws that would suppress it, whether by design or inadvertence."[37] Thus, Kennedy aims to protect both corporate rights to speak and citizen rights to know; he argues that the latter are abridged when government intervenes in the marketplace of speech. Speech restrictions aimed at preventing the "distorting effects of immense aggregations of wealth" deprive, rather than protect citizens.[38] A viewpoint is suppressed, and voices from an essential quarter of society are lost:

> The censorship we now confront is vast in its reach. The Government has "muffled the voices that best represent the most significant segments of the economy." *McConnell, supra,* at 257–258. And "the electorate [has been] deprived of information, knowledge and opinion vital to its function." *CIO,* 335 US at 144. By suppressing the speech of manifold corporations, both for-profit and non-profit, the Government prevents their voices and viewpoints from reaching the public and advising voters on which persons or entities are hostile to their interests.[39]

Here is the added fillip: While corporate political speech may be especially valuable, it is the least likely to be protected, according to Justice Kennedy. Muzzled by previous Supreme Court decisions, burdened by government bureaucracy, suffering prejudice in ordinary political discourse, corporations emerge in the Kennedy opinion as beleaguered and victimized in their speech rights, hovering close to a suspect class. "Speech restrictions based on the identity of the speaker," he intones, "are all too often simply a means to control content."[40] And worse:

> Quite apart from the purpose or effect of regulating content, moreover, the Government may commit a constitutional wrong when by law it identifies certain preferred speakers. By taking the right to speak from some and giving it to others, the Government deprives the disadvantaged person or class of the right to use speech to strive to establish worth, standing, and respect for the speaker's voice. The Government may not by these means deprive the public and privilege to determine for itself what speech and speakers are worthy of consideration. The First Amendment protects speech and speaker, and the ideas that flow from each.[41]

In sum, government privileging of any speaking subject over any other is discrimination of the classic sort, making the deprivileged subject (corporations) into a disadvantaged person or class. Such discrimination is wrong on its face, but also deprives (him? it?) of the ability to use speech to articulate one's value in the world of speaking creatures. Thus a cycle of prejudice is perpetuated: corporations denied speech rights because of prejudice against them are in turn deprived of a means for overturning this prejudice and advancing their public worth. And again, when the government chooses "which speech is safe for public consumption," the public, too, is deprived of its right to exercise its judgment.[42] More than merely protecting speech, on this reading, the First Amendment protects the integrity of all parties—corporations, citizens, publics—and the value of speaking, listening, and judging.

We are now in a position to grasp how the civil rights language works as a supplement to the marketplace language. Corporations share with all persons free-speech rights in the political sphere. The decision in *Citizens United* aims to secure these rights for a historically disenfranchised class of persons so that this class of persons may freely compete in the political marketplace and so that all may benefit from this enriched competition. Two different strands from two different eras of minority discourse are mobilized on behalf of deregulating corporate electoral speech: the classic progressive equal-rights argument and the more recent all-are-enriched-by-diversity argument. Drawing on both to advance what Justice Stevens, in his dissent, notes that the public has never clamored for more of, namely, corporate influence in politics, Justice Kennedy positions the court as enfranchising not the powerful, but the disliked, unwanted, and historically excluded.[43] Removing the boot from the necks of this class of persons simultaneously advances the cause of universal rights and enriches the political marketplace of democracy.

RIGHTS VERSUS MARKETS

One effect of deploying rights discourse in this way is that the unimpeachable virtue of civil and political rights as instruments of resistance against discrimination and against state power obscures their own subversion by economization. The inclusive and egalitarian promise of political rights shrouds the fundamental dynamic of the marketplaces in which Kennedy is resituating them: competition in which the strong extinguish the weak. Corporate speech rights do not technically cancel the right of others to speak, but as Justice Stevens notes in his dissent, when corporations eat up the airwaves and drive up the price of media ads, views backed by less funding are driven out.[44] There is no limit to how many may enjoy speech rights in the abstract, but there are limits to how much speech may be bought and sold in a given venue at a given time. Submission of democratic politics to the market thus subverts equal rights to participation, or, put the other way around, when rights to political participation are marketized, political equality is the first casualty.

In his dissent, Justice Stevens refers to this development as trammeling the long-held constitutional principle of restricting "the speech of some in order to prevent a few from drowning out the many."[45] He rereads the very cases—*Austin, Bellotti, Buckley,* and *McConnell*—on which Kennedy rests his judgment and draws opposite conclusions. "Over the course of the past century Congress has demonstrated a recurrent need to regulate corporate participation in candidate elections," and the Supreme Court has appropriately vindicated this need.[46] Both branches of government limited and regulated "corporate electoral advocacy" to "preserve the integrity of the electoral process, prevent corruption, sustain the active, alert responsibility of the individual citizen, protect the expressive interests of shareholders, and preserve…the individual citizen's confidence in government."[47] Preventing the many from being drowned out by the few is precisely what legislatures and courts have historically understood as their task in preserving democracy. Such prevention, however, is squarely at odds with the economization of politics. It has no place in a market, where the most innovative, ambitious, and aggressive prevail, where this prevalence also equates their "voices" with "valuable expertise" in interpreting and shaping political life, and above all, where competitive positioning and consumer choices rather than equality and deliberation are at stake.[48]

CORRUPTION AND INFLUENCE

The thoroughgoing character of the economization of the political in *Citizens United* is also evident in Justice Kennedy's discussion of corruption. Kennedy raises the issue of corruption in order to dismiss its relevance to limiting corporate spending in elections: "influence over or access to elected officials does not mean that these officials are corrupt."[49] How is this remarkable sentence possible? Citing *Buckley*, he limits the meaning and existence of corruption to explicit quid pro quo arrangements—"dollars for political favors."[50] The classical definition of political corruption refers to the sustained bending of the public interest to private interests and identifies it as is a disease almost impossible to cure once it has settled into the body politic.[51] Such a meaning cannot be featured in neoliberal rationality, where there are only private interests, contracts, and deals and where there is no such thing as a body politic, public good, or political culture. Thus, while large corporations will obviously wield their financial might in the political sphere in pursuit of their own ends (consider, for example, investment banks writing the new finance regulations, pharmaceutical and insurance companies writing significant parts of Obamacare, or agribusiness developing intellectual property rights law for GMOs),[52] this does not qualify as bending the public interest to private interests because, on the one hand, neoliberalism eliminates the very idea of the public interest and, on the other, corporations now have standing as persons whose speech is public and "all can judge its content and purpose."[53]

Justice Kennedy also cites his own previous opinion in *McConnell* for this point, a passage that further illuminates the way neoliberal rationality transforms the meaning and operation of democratic terms. Here is Kennedy in *McConnell*:

> Favoritism and influence are not...avoidable in representative politics. It is in the nature of an elected representative to favor certain policies, and by necessary corollary, to favor the voters and contributors who support those policies. It is well understood that a substantial and legitimate reason, if not the only reason, to cast a vote for or to make a contribution to, one candidate over another is that the candidate will respond by producing those political outcomes the supporter favors. Democracy is premised on responsiveness.[54]

What exactly is Kennedy claiming about political influence in *McConnell* and reaffirming in *Citizens*? He begins with the simple point that elected representatives naturally favor voters and contributors who support the policies that the representative favors, but already this suggests that one elected to office is not representing a district or constituency, but rather "responds to" and "favors" the people and money corresponding to the positions she or he holds. And then Kennedy argues that the "only" reason to vote for or give money to a candidate is that the candidate "will respond" by producing the outcomes the voter or contributor desires. The verb and its tense are both crucial here, their importance underlined by Kennedy's concluding statement that "democracy is premised on responsiveness." Kennedy sets aside the conventional view that voters or contributors support candidates whose political positions align with their own to argue that political "representatives" will respond to support by producing the political outcomes supporters expect. Public service thus gains a new meaning as representatives literally stand to deliver the outcomes their support-ers purchase with votes and dollars.

As he equates voters with financial contributors, including cor-porate contributors, Kennedy may seem to be finessing a point that would be more tendentious if he spoke only of contributors. But the equation is actually crucial to the transformation of democracy that his words perform, the shift from representative to a purely market form. In his economic-contractarian account of political representa-tion premised on responsiveness, we all expect to get something from our investment, whether a campaign contribution or a vote. Elected officials are for making deals with, not for securing justice or national welfare, and not for addressing contemporary common challenges or preventing future common predicaments. If votes and money are the available currencies for these deals, big capital can enhance its own value and positioning by delivering votes, exactly what *Citizens United* facilitates.

There are still more inversions of meaning in Kennedy's dis-cussion of corruption and influence. Here is his formulation of the chain of influence from money to votes to political office: "The fact that a corporation, or any other speaker, is willing to spend money to try to persuade voters presupposes that the people have the ultimate influence over public officials." Again, how is this sentence possi-ble and what could it mean? Here is the full passage from which it is extracted: "The appearance of influence or access...will not cause the electorate to lose faith in our democracy. By definition, an inde-pendent expenditure is political speech presented to the electorate that is not coordinated with a candidate. The fact that a corporation, or any other speaker, is willing to spend money to try to persuade voters presupposes that the people have the ultimate influence over elected officials."[55]

Clearly, Justice Kennedy is flailing a bit: the first declarative is wild, especially insofar as it depends on the second, which repeats the formal conceit about the independence of PACS that no one believes. And the lack of logical entailment from one sentence to the next is almost painful. However, these strange stipulations and leaps of logic can also be explained by the radically new set of meanings for which the justice is reaching and for which a new idiom must be crafted. (Non corrupt) influence has now been redefined as responsiveness, narrowly stipulated as following the money. Corporately financed super PACS have been redefined as speech. Super PACS are by definition independent political speech, because they are not the direct voice of corporations or the political campaign: the super PAC is independent of each by virtue of its distinct corporate persona. And if the purpose of super PACS is to enable corporate speech to persuade voters, it stands to (neoliberal economic) reason that voters must have the greatest influence over elected officials, otherwise, why would corporations bother persuading them, rather than moving to influence politicians directly? Thus, Justice Kennedy comforts himself, even with unlimited corporate funds working over the electorate, democracy remains intact because the point of the super PACs is not to influence the candidate directly, but to deliver votes, the source of "ultimate influence."

But in what sense is a vote identical with influence, especially as it has just been defined? That is, how do we square this passage with the previous one on favoritism and responsiveness? It would seem that Kennedy is now making a distinction between votes and financial contributions, a distinction he elided in the discussion of democracy as a system of responsiveness to both. If voters have the "ultimate influence," but corporations seek to persuade them via super PACS, has he not effectively confessed that voters are but a medium through which corporations wield their political influence? Has democracy become more than a scrubbing or a shield of legitimation for corporate domination?

Justice Kennedy, of course, spins the matter differently, returning us to the importance of corporate speech as an indispensable contribution to the democratic process, the people's deliberations, and sovereignty. He cites at length from a three-justice dissent in the 1957 decision to remand in *United States v. Automobile Workers*:

> Under our Constitution it is We The People who are sovereign. The people have the final say. The legislators are their spokesmen. The people determine through their votes the destiny of the nation. It is therefore important—vitally important—that all channels of communications be open to them during every election, that no point of view be restrained or barred, and that the people have access to the views of every group in the community.[56]

Thus, the 1957 dissent concludes, deeming "a particular group too powerful" is not a justification for withholding First Amendment rights from any group—labor or corporate.[57] So while corporations "speak" to persuade voters through whom they will influence politics, this persuasion is construed as voter information essential to popular sovereignty. A ruse? Or, again, a new way of conceiving democracy in which voters depend upon corporate points of view, corporations share free speech rights because speech itself is a form of capital, elections are political marketplaces where resource inequities are a given, political advertising is detached from either objective value or public interest, and the game of influence and even of quid pro quo is one in which everyone plays a part.

——————

The many inversions of democratic meaning in *Citizens United* suggest that this decision does far more than permit corporate funds to transform elections in the United States. In its insistence that the corporation must share in the rights of man, its heralding of corporate speech as vital to democracy, and its jettisoning of concerns with equality in access to or effects of political speech, certainly, the court licenses and legitimates unlimited corporate power in politics. But it also does something deeper and more significant: as it submits politics, rights, representation, and speech to economization, it subverts key components of liberal democracy—popular sovereignty, free elections, political freedom, and equality. Casting every actor and activity in market terms, it vanquishes the political meaning of citizenship and erases the crucial distinction between economic and political orders essential to the most modest version of popular sovereignty. It aggressively abandons the distinctively political valence and venue of democracy and turns its back on the fragility of democratic conditions and cultures. It supplants democratic political deliberation and voices with a formulation of speech as capital and free speech as an unhindered capital right. It reduces political knowledge and political participation to practices of individual or corporate capital enhancement achieved through broadcasting one's economic position as a political one. Rendering government regulation or limits as the enemy of freedom everywhere, the court blends flows of capital and speech into a single stream, sharing characteristics and rights against a common enemy: the regulatory state.

Each of these moves is novel in the history of democratic thought and practice. Each hollows out the practices and institutions of liberal democracy and scorches the ground of any other democratic form. Together, they threaten to extinguish a conception of democracy where this would matter.

CHAPTER SIX

Educating Human Capital

Each of you starts the next portion of your life's journey with the tremendous benefit of a Cornell education. I hope that you'll carry with you...a continuing commitment to build human capital so that more will have opportunities to pursue their dreams.

—President David Skorton, Cornell University,
  2014 commencement address

These are the disadvantages of a commercial spirit: The minds of men are contracted and rendered incapable of elevation. Education is despised, or at least neglected, and the heroic spirit is almost utterly extinguished. To remedy these defects would be an object worthy of serious attention.

—Adam Smith, *Lectures on Justice, Police, Revenue and Arms*

It is a commonplace that broadly accessible and affordable higher education is one of the great casualties of neoliberalism's ascendance in the Euro-Atlantic world.[1] This chapter is concerned with how this casualty in turn threatens democracy itself. Citizens cannot rule themselves, even if that means only thoughtfully choosing representatives or voting on referenda, let alone engaging in more direct practices of shared rule, without understanding the powers and problems they are engaging. Providing tools for such understanding has been a key premise of public secondary and higher education in the West over the past two centuries and has especially undergirded cultivation of a liberal arts curriculum in American universities. In recent years, this premise has given way to a formulation of education as primarily valuable to human capital development, where human capital is what the individual, the business world, and the state seek to enhance in order to maximize competitiveness.

Neoliberalism, I have argued throughout this book, is best understood not simply as economic policy, but as a governing rationality that disseminates market values and metrics to every sphere of life and construes the human itself exclusively as *homo oeconomicus.* Neoliberalism thus does not merely privatize—turn over to the market for individual production and consumption—what was formerly publicly supported and valued. Rather, it formulates everything, everywhere, in terms of capital investment and appreciation, including and especially humans themselves. Four related effects of this rationality bear on public higher education in the liberal arts.

First, *public goods* of any kind are increasingly difficult to speak of or secure. The market metrics contouring every dimension of human conduct and institutions make it daily more difficult to explain why universities, libraries, parks and natural reserves city services and elementary schools, even roads and sidewalks, are or should be publicly accessible and publicly provisioned. Why should the public fund and administer them? Why should everyone have free access to them? Why shouldn't their cost be borne only by those who "consume" them? It is already a symptom of the vanishing value and lexicon for public things that such questions today are generally converted to a different one, namely, the role of government versus the private sector for the provision of goods and services. In this conversion, government is not identified with the public, but only as an alternate market actor. Citizens, meanwhile, are rendered as investors or consumers, not as members of a democratic polity who share power and certain common goods, spaces, and experiences.

Second, *democracy* itself has been radically transformed by the dissemination of neoliberal rationality to every sphere, including politics and law. Thus, distinctly political meanings of "equality," "autonomy," and "freedom" are giving way to economic valences of these terms, and the distinctive value of popular sovereignty is receding as governance through expertise, market metrics, and best practices replaces justice-framed contestations over who we are, what we should be or become, what we should or should not do as a people. Democracies are conceived as requiring technically skilled human capital, not educated participants in public life and common rule.

Third, *subjects*, including citizen subjects, are configured by the market metrics of our time as self-investing human capital. Human capital is not driven by its interests, as was *homo oeconomicus* of yore. Nor is the classical liberal subject free to make its life and choose its values at will. Rather, human capital is constrained to self-invest in ways that contribute to its appreciation or at least prevent its depreciation; this includes titrating inputs such as education, predicting and adjusting to changing markets in vocations, housing, health, and retirement, and organizing its dating, mating, creative, and leisure practices in value-enhancing ways. Human capital is distinctly not concerned with acquiring the knowledge and experience needed for intelligent democratic citizenship.

Fourth, *knowledge, thought, and training* are valued and desired almost exclusively for their contribution to capital enhancement. This does not reduce to a desire only for technical knowledges and skills. Many professions today—from law to engineering to medicine—require analytical capacities, communications skills, multilingualism, artistic creativity, inventiveness, even close reading abilities. However, knowledge is not sought for purposes apart from capital enhancement, whether that capital is human, corporate, or financial. It is not sought for developing the capacities of citizens, sustaining culture, knowing the world, or envisioning and crafting different ways of life in common. Rather, it is sought for "positive ROI"—return on investment—one of the leading metrics the Obama administration proposes to use in rating colleges for would-be consumers of higher education.[2]

DEMOCRACY

"Democracy" is the name of a political form in which the whole of the people rule the polity and hence themselves. How this is best achieved and through what complementary economic, social, cultural, and theological conditions and practices is contestable and historically variable. Consequently, there are many theories and modalities of democracy—direct, representative, liberal, socialist, libertarian, republican, social, anarchic, plebiscite, and more. At a minimum, however, democracy requires that the people authorize their own laws and major political decisions, whether directly or through elected representatives, and also that they share modestly in other, nonlegal powers governing their lives. Anything less means the people do not rule.

In addition to basic principles, democracy has certain conditions without which it cannot be even minimally nourished or sustained. Democracy does not require absolute social and economic equality, but it cannot withstand large and fixed extremes of wealth and poverty, because these undermine the work of legislating in common. As Jean-Jacques Rousseau insisted, when such extremes prevail, shared values vanish, and class powers and resentments become decisive, making the act of combining to rule together impossible.[3] Precisely such extremes have been generated in the United States over the past thirty years through neoliberal deregulation and the dismantling of public institutions that served modest redistributive functions and advanced equal opportunity over inherited privilege.[4]

If democracy does not require absolute equality, but cannot survive its opposite, the same is true of an educated citizenry. Democracy may not demand universal political participation, but it cannot survive the people's wholesale ignorance of the forces shaping their lives and limning their future. A citizenry left to its (manipulated) interests and passions, especially in an epoch of unprecedentedly complex powers, inevitably comes to be governed by what Alexis de Tocqueville termed the "gentle despotism" of these powers, even as it continues to travel under the sign of democracy and imagine itself "free."[5] At the same time, neoliberal rationality reduces the meaning of freedom and autonomy to unimpeded market behavior and the meaning of citizenship to mere enfranchisement. This evisceration of robust norms of democracy is accompanied by unprecedented challenges to democratization, including complex forms and novel concentrations of economic and political power, sophisticated marketing and theatricality in politics, corporately owned media, and a historically unparalleled glut of information and opinion that, again, produces an illusion of knowledge, freedom, and even participation in the face of their opposites. The dramatic thinning of key democratic values coupled with this intensification of nondemocratic forces and conditions threatens to replace self-rule with a polity in which the people are pawns of every kind of modern power.

In short, the essential *conditions* of democratic existence remain these: limited extremes of concentrated wealth and poverty, orientation toward citizenship as a practice of considering the public good, and citizens modestly discerning about the ways of power, history, representation, and justice. Each of these conditions is severely challenged by neoliberal rationality and policy. Indeed, limits on wealth and poverty and educated citizens oriented toward problems of public life are left in the dust by neoliberal values, governance, and the dismantled social state.

These same elements of democracy are at the heart of the crises besetting public universities today. Growing and increasingly legitimate socioeconomic inequalities and abandonment of the project of educating a public for citizenship are at once cause and effect of public divestment from universities and public universities' departure from a mission of providing broad liberal arts education to the many. Put the other way around, curtailed access to public universities, along with their changing mission and content, reflects and intensifies contemporary dedemocratizing tendencies in Euro-Atlantic nation-states generally and the United States in particular. These are the circuitries probed in this chapter.

PUBLIC HIGHER EDUCATION

The North American twentieth century, for all its ghastly episodes and wrong turns, retroactively appears as something of a golden age for public higher education. This is not to say that higher education in this period realized perfection or was absent the usual cruel exclusions from Western humanism, only that its values and practices were vastly superior to those preceding and succeeding it. Beginning in the interwar period and reaching its pinnacle in the 1960s, this age promised not merely literacy, but liberal arts to the masses. It also featured cultivation of a professoriat, and a professional class more generally, from the widest class basis in human history. And it was a time in which a broad, if not deep college education—one inclusive of the arts, letters, and sciences—became an essential element of middle-class membership.[6] No mere instrument for economic advancement, higher education in the liberal arts was the door through which descendants of workers, immigrants, and slaves entered onto the main stage of the society to whose wings they were historically consigned. A basic familiarity with Western history, thought, literature, art, social analysis, and science was integral to middle-class belonging, in many ways more important than a specific profession or income.

Today, this status for liberal arts education is eroding from all sides: cultural values spurn it, capital is not interested in it, debt-burdened families anxious about the future do not demand it, neoliberal rationality does not index it, and, of course, states no longer invest in it. According to popular wisdom, the liberal arts are passé, the protected ivory tower is an expensive and outmoded relic, and the more the university remakes itself through and for the market, the better off everyone—except overpaid, underworked tenured faculty—will be. Skills for twenty-first-century jobs provided by an instructional staff itself organized by market metrics ought to replace the patently anachronistic conceits and trappings of university life and content. This is the story told by both insiders and outsiders to academe, by earnest liberal reformers, by reactionary attacks on "tenured radicals," by the for-profit colleges, by many of the new rich.[7] But what are the implications, for an ostensibly democratic people, of jettisoning a broad and deep university education in favor of job training? What kind of world will be made through conceptions and practices of postsecondary education that reduce students to future human capital, citizens to manipulable consumers, and the public to GDP? Above all, what does such a transformation in the education of the many mean for the promise of popular sovereignty, as well as for the practices of liberty and equality at the heart of liberal democracy? Even when liberty is thinned to the ideal of crafting one's own life and equality is reduced to equal opportunity or equal standing before the law—that is, even bracketing more substantive formulations of freedom and equality than those featured by classical political liberalism—can these values survive the evisceration of an educated public?

Frank Donoghue, in *The Last Professors*, has told much of the story we need to know here, though he has not drawn from this story all of its implications for an educated citizenry and hence for democracy.[8] The saturation of higher education by market rationality has converted higher education from a social and public good to a personal investment in individual futures, futures construed mainly in terms of earning capacity. According to Donoghue, the implications of this transformation are especially significant for the mission of public universities. A few dozen elite private institutions can and will continue to market prestige and alumni networks, but job training becomes the implicit mandate for all other higher-education institutions, a mandate that pushes both the instructional mission and the economics of public universities ever closer to those of the for-profit colleges. Just as students pay the University of Phoenix not for the cultural capital, citizenship capacities, or abstract value of a college education, but for the vocational training and future income it promises, the same is rapidly becoming true for students at public universities. Skyrocketing tuition abets this instrumental view of college among students and their families, reducing the value of the degree and hence the very project of higher education to its income-generating promise.

Thus, public universities are increasingly competing with for-profit and mainly online educational institutions such as Kaplan and the University of Phoenix, rather than with private universities and colleges for market share of various student populations.[9] More than overlapping admissions markets and student expectations, however, describe the growing kinship of the publics with the proprietaries: as tuition becomes a primary source of revenue for the publics, both kinds of institutions bank on high levels of student indebtedness to generate this revenue.[10] Both also feature job and professional-school placement rates at the front end of their recruitment strategies. And both eschew the liberal arts as their main attraction.

These kinds of transformations in the purpose and image of public universities suggest the disappearance of two dominant conceits in the United States about the value of higher education in the second half of the twentieth century. On the one hand, we are no longer governed by the idea that upward mobility and middle-class status require schooling in the liberal arts.[11] On the other hand, the idea of a well-educated public, one that has the knowledge and understanding to participate thoughtfully in public concerns and problems, has gone the way of public goods and provisions themselves. As it dispenses with the very idea of the public, neoliberal rationality recognizes and interpellates the subject only as human capital, making incoherent the idea of an engaged and educated citizen.

This transmogrification of the valuation and approach to higher education, combined with a severely constrained public purse, threatens to divorce what remains of public universities from undergraduate education in the liberal arts. Students are pressured by families and cultural norms into choosing business, engineering, and preprofessional majors over those in the arts, humanities, and interpretive social sciences. Meanwhile, universities search incessantly for ways to trim costs by compressing time to degree and making extensive use of summer and online courses taught by casual academic labor, moves that in turn exert pressure to trim breadth and general-education requirements and also discourage double majors—the latter is significant, because many public-university students currently finesse the "practicality" problem by combining a preprofessional major with one in the arts or humanities. Degree requirements and courses are also transformed as their stewardship by faculty is replaced by governance oriented to satisfying consumers and investors, including students, states, and corporations.[12] The growing demand for job training and exclusively marketable research marginalizes, when it does not eliminate, academic practices and undertakings at variance with market norms or understood to block market flows; these include tenure, academic freedom, faculty governance, nine-month appointments (and summer reprieves from teaching), research without inherently marketable purposes or outcomes (including basic research in the sciences), as well as courses and teaching oriented toward developing capacities of reflection and insight, the acquisition of multiple literacies, and obtaining a long, large view of human and nonhuman orders.[13]

As I have suggested, the most serious and sustained entailments of this transformation pertain neither to the corporatization and commercialization of university life nor to the shrinking size and falling status of the liberal arts professoriat. Certainly, those effects are lamentable. But the most dire entailments pertain to the effects on democratic citizenship of this conversion in the purpose, organization, and content of public higher education. After more than half a century of public higher education construed and funded as a medium for egalitarianism and social mobility and as a means of achieving a broadly educated democracy, as well as for providing depth and enrichment to individuality, public higher education, like much else in neoliberal orders, is increasingly structured to entrench, rather than redress class trajectories. As it devotes itself to enhancing the value of human capital, it now abjures the project of producing a public readied for participation in popular sovereignty.

Before pursuing this point further, it is (past) time to ask: Why do the liberal arts matter?[14] What was the origin and purpose of a liberal arts education? How, if at all, does this origin and purpose bear upon the present? The term "liberal arts" came into regular use in the fourteenth century and, as Raymond Williams argues, was "predominantly a class term," identifying "the skills and pursuits appropriate...to men of independent means and assured social position, as distinct from other skills and pursuits...appropriate to a lower class."[15] Even in classical antiquity, the liberal arts (rooted in *liberus*, the Latin word for individual freedom) denoted the education appropriate to free men, in contrast to that of slaves. A liberal arts education, in other words, was necessary for free men to know and engage the world sufficiently to exercise that freedom. It was the knowledge that enabled the use of freedom, but that in an important sense also made men free insofar as it lifted them from the immediate present to a longer temporal and larger spatial domain, one accessible only through knowledge. Thus did Martianus Capella define the seven liberal arts in the fifth century A.D.: grammar, dialectic, rhetoric, geometry, arithmetic, astronomy, and music. Later, history, theology, and art would be added, along with the natural sciences.[16]

This background makes clear that extending liberal arts education from the elite to the many was nothing short of a radical democratic event, one in which all became potentially eligible for the life of freedom long reserved for the few. The notion that all colleges and universities ought to offer a liberal arts degree and that such a degree is one to which all intellectually qualified citizens should have access heralded an order in which the masses would be educated for freedom. Regardless of the quantitative and qualitative limits on its realization, the radicalism of this event cannot be overstated: for the first time in human history, higher-educational policy and practice were oriented toward the many, tacitly destining them for intelligent engagement with the world, rather than economic servitude or mere survival. In this respect, far more than class mobility and equality of opportunity were advanced by a liberal arts education generalized across society. Rather, the ideal of democracy was being realized in a new way insofar as the demos was being prepared through education for a life of freedom, understood as both individual sovereignty (choosing and pursuing one's ends) and participation in collective self-rule.

Nowhere else and at no other time was this radically democratic idea more fully embraced and institutionalized than in the United States after World War II.[17] Most European nations continued to adhere to postsecondary entrance-examination systems that sent a select few on to academic study while the majority of postsecondary learners were channeled into training for specific vocations or professions. Certainly, higher education in France, Germany, and England also expanded in the postwar period, an expansion that facilitated class mobility to a historically unprecedented extent. But only in the United States did a postsecondary education contoured toward developing the person and the citizen, not merely the job holder, ubiquitously come to structure university curriculums, and only in the United States was such an education on offer to a wide swath of the population from the 1940s forward.

The prime carriers and executors of this value were the public higher educational systems comprising universities, colleges, and community colleges that expanded exponentially from the end of World War II through the end of the twentieth century. These were the institutions that accommodated massive numbers of war veterans, as well as other populations historically excluded from higher education: middle-class white women; African Americans; and working-class, lower middle-class, and new immigrant students.[18] This expansion and openness to new populations, of course, did not bring class stratification in higher education to an end. Selective private universities and colleges have always reproduced a socioeconomic elite, even as this mission was partially dissimulated in the recent decades by recruitment for modest racial diversity and promulgation of "need-blind admissions." Many states, too, built multitiered higher-education systems that divided roughly along class lines. In California, for example, better-off students tend to go straight to the University of California; the less advantaged are more likely to move through the community colleges and state colleges close to their homes.[19] Other states feature heavy investment in highly ranked research flagship campuses coupled with relative starvation of often rurally located stepsiblings: such are the state university systems of Michigan, Minnesota, and Wisconsin, among others. And community colleges largely remain institutions of vocational training for clerical, mechanical, and low-level health and social service workers, even as they can also be launching grounds for ambitious students, often from new immigrant families, aspiring to four-year universities.

While the remarkable postwar extension of liberal arts education to the many did not generate true educational equality let alone social equality, this extension importantly *articulated* equality as an ideal. It also articulated the value of an American public educated for the individual and collective capacity for self-governance. And while the fact of a college degree promised upward social and economic mobility for working-class or lower-middle-class students, the material of such degrees exceeded this narrow utility. College stood for expanded individual opportunity, but also for the acquisition of a vastly enlarged view of and encounter with the world—its diverse peoples, sciences, languages, literatures, and histories.[20] This ideal never ceased to be a classically liberal one, but it was a liberalism of profound egalitarian commitments, rich humanism, and a strong ethos of the public good. It expressed that part of liberal thought, found in a range of thinkers including Adam Smith, Alexis de Tocqueville, John Dewey, John Stuart Mill, and John Rawls, that regarded raw economic interest as too thin a reed and too crude a principle on which to build either an individual life or a democracy; cultivation of mind and character through education was one crucial counter to this thinness and crudeness.[21] Consider this justification, from the 1946 President's Commission on Higher Education, for immense federal investment in public higher education: "It is an investment in social welfare, better living standards, better health and less crime. It is an investment in a bulwark against garbled information, half-truths and untruths, against ignorance and intolerance. It is an investment in human talent, better human relationships, democracy and peace."[22]

We can no longer speak this way about the public university, and the university no longer speaks this way about itself. Instead, the market value of knowledge—its income-enhancing prospects for individuals and industry alike—is now understood as both its driving purpose and leading line of defense. Even when the humanities and interpretive social sciences are accounted as building the analytical thinkers needed by the professions or as building the mind and hence securing a more gratifying life for the individual, they align with the neoliberal notion of building human capital.[23] In neither defense are the liberal arts depicted as representing, theorizing, interpreting, creating, or protecting the world. They are not conceived as binding, developing, or renewing us as a people, alerting us to dangers, or providing frames, figures, theories, and allegories for altering our practices or collective trajectories. Above all, they are not conceived as providing the various capacities required for democratic citizenship. Rather, they are conceived as something for individuals to imbibe like chocolate, practice like yoga, or utilize like engineering. They are presumed to inhabit a land apart from the material world, the practical world, the world of power, profit, and achievement, although bits of the skills one learns in studying them may be broken off and honed as instruments for that world. This is a measure of how far neoliberalization has already gone. Even its critics cannot see the ways in which we have lost a recognition of ourselves as held together by literatures, images, religions, histories, myths, ideas, forms of reason, grammars, figures, and languages. Instead, we are presumed to be held together by technologies and capital flows. That presumption, of course, is at risk of becoming true, at which point humanity will have entered its darkest chapter ever. We would be the entities of human capital, and nothing else, of the contemporary economic theoretical imagination.

Did the principle of broadly educating the masses, generated in the aftermath of World War II, really improve democracy? Did it make U.S. citizens more thoughtful, less easily manipulated, more democratic in instinct, more public minded, more insistent on transparent governance, or more oriented toward justice than self-interest? Did it bring about better leadership or more political accountability? If such accomplishments seem dubious during the four long decades of the Cold War that would constitute the test period for this experiment in what Christopher Newfield has dubbed "high-quality mass higher education," it is important to remember that these same decades featured the civil rights movement, feminism, sustained challenges to inequality and to Cold War ideology, and an explosion of other justice-minded cultural, artistic, and civic practices.[24] Moreover, mass quality education held out the promise of citizens who were knowing enough about history, power, foreign affairs, language, affect, and meaning to give substance to the notion of choosing their own ends in life, as well as choosing and checking political representatives. To be "knowing enough," Socrates would remind us, above all entails humility before the vastness and complexity of the world, an appreciation of what one does not know.[25] Such humility and appreciation are precisely what is disappearing from popular political discourse in the United States; smugness in ignorance is notably more common.

The political significance of the provision of a liberal arts education to the many might be compressed this way: if, historically, a liberal arts education pertained to a leisured class that was also a ruling class, the extension of such an education to the general citizenry configures an ideal of this leisure and power as widely shared. Extending such an education to the masses draws a utopian vision in which freedom from toil is generalized and political rule is widely shared. Crucially, citizens educated in the liberal arts are being prepared for what Aristotle called "the good life," which he understood as cultivating the higher human faculties for thoughtful civic engagement and *eudamonia*, that special Greek term for happiness comprising rich fulfillment through the elaboration of human possibility.[26] The notion of the "good life" may sound arcane, effete, or even decadent. Thus, it is important to remember that for Aristotle, it signifies the capacity for human pursuits beyond toiling for survival. "Mere life" (mere existence) is the good life's opposite, and the difference between them is marked by the difference between freedom and necessity and even between freedom and enslavement.

The specific content of Aristotle's binary is contestable, especially in its conjoining of work and servitude, on the one hand, and of freedom with aristocratic leisure, on the other. Yet the point is sustainable beyond these challenges and can be made into a sharp critique of a neoliberal table of values. Human life wholly bound to the production of wealth, whether laboring to produce it or hovering over its accumulation, is small and unrealized. The same is true of human life that does not develop creative or intellectual capacities and does not seek to govern its own affairs. A liberal arts education, whatever its aporias and occlusions consequent to its class basis (and its markedly raced and gendered historical unfolding and content), is the most comprehensive affirmation of this truth contained in Western history. The proffering of this education to broad swaths of the population thus includes them in the projects of humanism and democratic governance so long reserved for the few.[27]

THE NEOLIBERALIZED ACADEMY

If the extension of a liberal arts education to the many carried an ideal of radically democratized knowledge, human perfectibility, freedom, and political rule, what is signified by the reversal of this move today? By the diminution of a liberal arts education in the two higher-education destinations of most working-class and middle-class students today, the proprietaries and the state universities? Certainly, depreciating liberal arts higher education for the masses retreats from the promise of upward socioeconomic mobility, of emancipation from being born to one's position in a class-stratified social order. But it retreats as well from the value of a citizenry educated for democracy, from the idea that education offers the prospect of intrinsically richer and more gratifying lives and from the idea that education fosters an enhanced capacity to participate in public life and contribute to the public good. Thus, the popular contemporary wisdom that a liberal arts education is outmoded is true only to the extent that social equality, liberty (understood as self-governance and sharing in the powers that govern us together), and worldly development of mind and character are outmoded and have been displaced by another set of metrics: income streams, profitability, technological innovation, and contribution to society construed narrowly as the development and promulgation of marketable goods or services.

It is easy enough to see this displacement of the value of developed, free, and equal citizens by the value of capital appreciation (human or otherwise) in today's halls of heroism: popular culture does not celebrate inventors of vaccines, advocates for peace, revolutionary leaders, or even astronauts opening new frontiers; it celebrates Hollywood or sports celebrities; creators of Apple, Facebook, Netflix, or eBay; and above all the very rich…some of whom are college or even high school drop-outs. "Who needs a college degree?" is the theme not only of Kanye West's debut CD, but also countless get-rich-quick blogs, and it was the headline of a 2010 *Businessweek* story about megarich CEOs.[28] Apart from glorifying uneducated and often vacuous celebrity, much in popular and maverick business culture suggests that higher education is irrelevant to success defined as fame, wealth, or even ingenuity and invention: billionaire Peter Theil's "fellowship competition," which pays college-age students $100,000 to drop out and pursue business ventures instead, makes this point explicit. At the same time, of course, university curriculums and culture have been demonized by the Right as saturated with Left agendas and political correctness, while the common rage of the common citizen has been glorified and exploited.[29]

Two other things are striking here. First, while throughout the twentieth century, college was the proven ticket to income enhancement, the skyrocketing costs of tuition, coupled with the decline of well-paying white-collar jobs in the United States, means that "the college wage premium," while still significant, no longer automatically fulfills this promise. Neither end of the vastly unequal wealth scale in the United States is governed by this premium: the wealth of the superrich is not tied to their college degrees, and many college graduates are unemployed or earning poorly. Indeed, the income of the average college graduate has not increased for a decade.[30] Direct appeal to this reality and to the imagined advantages of being trained for a particular job is why the proprietary schools are thriving, despite their sky-high attrition rates, their scant job-placement records, and the scandals plaguing their ruthless exploitation of student access to federal loan programs.[31] Second, the bottom line has become the only line in the current cultural valuation of college and a life beyond it. The debate about the "worth" of expensive college educations today turns almost entirely on the question of return on investment.[32]

These economic and cultural shifts, the new college ranking systems that endorse them, along with the dismal contemporary economics of higher education itself exert enormous pressures on colleges and universities and especially on liberal arts curriculums to abandon all aims and ends other than making students "shovel ready" when they graduate. Other values—of being a well-educated or worldly person, of being discerning in relation to information gluts or novel concentrations and circulations of power—cannot and do not defend themselves in terms of student desire or demand, economic necessity or benefit, or cost efficiencies within the university. Thus, while Christopher Newfield brilliantly deposes the myth that the sciences subsidize the humanities, demonstrating instead that the cost of scientific research vastly exceeds the extramural grant funding that the sciences bring in, this factual correction of a popular misconception does not reach to a larger problem: the viability of providing humanities instruction and research by many students, their families, businesses, the state, or the culture at large.[33]

Again, it is important to underscore differences here between public universities and the elite privates. While the numbers of students headed or herded into "practical" education may be everywhere on the increase, the elite privates continue to offer two unique commodities to their students that strongly mitigate these pressures: prestige and social networks that themselves yield socioeconomic access and status, hence increasing the value of human capital. This is why, amid the declining cultural and economic value of the *content* of a college education, competition for admission to the top privates grows ever more ferocious. Put another way, as the chasm grows between the elites and all other institutions of higher learning, the elites remain what they have always been: a gateway or guarantor of belonging to the American plutocracy, a status belied by the continued admissions advantage enjoyed by legatees and full-fee-paying students, no matter how many new immigrants and underrepresented minorities these institutions also admit.[34] Ironically, only the private elites can preserve liberal arts curriculums while performing this crude economic function; what is taught or learned (or not) at Princeton or Amherst is largely irrelevant to the prestige obtained and the networks accessed and reproduced. Certainly, there are faculty and administrators in these institutions calling for dramatic curricular and organizational overhauls, but the truth is that what students learn at these institutions is mostly irrelevant to their future in worlds of business, finance, and tech, which is where most of them are going.[35]

As the gap widens between the private elites and quality public universities, the "mission creep" or "mission disorientation" of the public universities grows.[36] Derailed from the project of providing inexpensive liberal arts education to the many, even the most distinguished of state universities are positioned unhappily between elite institutions granting prestige, on the one side, and community colleges and for-profits whose purpose has always been job training, on the other. If state universities are not select and pedigreed enough to rival the former, it is also the case that the ground on which they have distinguished themselves from the latter is washing away. More than merely sharing a mission, the increasingly privatized "publics" are also becoming structured more like their for-profit and community college kin as they search relentlessly for ways to cheapen undergraduate education through online instruction, casual academic labor, credit for coursework elsewhere, and treating students themselves as cash cows in the form of high tuition rates for MA programs and out-of-state undergraduates. Of course, the more that state universities move in this direction, the more they will drive away top-tier research faculty once drawn to working in high-quality public institutions, the more they will decline in rankings, and thus the more they price themselves out of a market in which they also are trapped.

State universities will survive these sea changes, but what will likely not survive is their core in undergraduate liberal arts education offered by prestigious faculty researchers. Written and oral skills can be developed in writing and speech classes taught by inexpensive lecturers, who can also offer courses in American politics, Latin American literature, and Chinese history. There is no reason for public universities to keep eminent or promising scholars on their payrolls in these fields; indeed, from a fully marketized perspective, there is no reason for the public universities to sustain these research fields at all.[37] As tuition levels continue to rise, fast-tracked degrees making extensive use of advanced-placement units, summer sessions, and online courses will increasingly appeal to families, administrators and governments alike. This, in turn, will exert pressure on breadth and general-education requirements already thinned in recent years by increased major requirements in the sciences and preprofessional programs and by lack of consensus on what a well-educated university graduate ought to know. While three decades ago the elimination of great books or Western civilization courses and foreign-language proficiency was ubiquitous in public universities, soon, all concern with educational breadth will likely give way to demands for the specialization and professionalization of undergraduates, on the one side, and efficient provision of technical training, on the other. Moreover, as increased use of casual academic labor, online instruction, and neoliberal governance erodes research-faculty control over curriculums, degrees, and major requirements, the last force within public universities potentially sustaining the ideal of the well-educated citizen, the liberal arts professoriat itself, will be dramatically diminished in both size and power to exert its vision.[38]

Even now, public-university faculty are poorly positioned, intellectually and organizationally, to fight these trends. For two decades, neoliberal rationality has steered faculty ever farther from forms of association, knowledge, and teaching that serve the public good, defined either as developing thoughtful citizens or as research oriented toward solving public problems. One irony of neoliberal entrepreneurialism and debt-financed investment is that it often draws producers and investors into niche industries and products that are unsustainable over time—derivatives, bubble markets, and so forth. Current norms and metrics for academic success are an example of this. Faculty gain recognition and reward according to standing in fields whose methods and topics are increasingly remote from the world *and* the undergraduate classroom. Graduate students are professionalized through protocols and admonitions orienting them toward developing their own toeholds in such fields This professionalization aims at making young scholars not into teachers and thinkers, but into human capitals who learn to attract investors by networking long before they "go on the market," who "workshop" their papers, "shop" their book manuscripts, game their Google Scholar counts and "impact factors," and above all, follow the money and the rankings. "Good investment" is the way departments speak of new hires, and "entrepreneurial" has become a favored term for describing exceptionally promising young researchers; it is deployed to capture both a researcher's capacity to parlay existing accomplishments into new ones and the more quotidian business of grant getting. These commonplaces in the sciences, social sciences, business, and law schools will soon dominate the entirety of university and scholarly activity.

Paradoxically, however, these forms of academic capital appreciation degrade, rather than augment the value of public research universities in the eyes of the public and the legislators who hold the purse strings. Vital to academic success, these norms and practices render faculty research activity less relevant to teaching or to public knowledge and the public good than was the case even a generation ago.[39] They promulgate standards, career pathways, and rungs of achievement that widen the breach between research valued and rewarded by the disciplines and research that is profound, useful, exciting, or relevant to making better worlds or better citizens. This is as true of economics and sociology as of linguistics, literature, and astronomy.[40]

The point is not to castigate a rising generation of scholars for participating in practices that index the degree to which all academic practices have been transformed by neoliberal economization. Rather, the point is that relentless configuration of liberal arts research by academic market norms paradoxically weakens the capacity of liberal arts scholars to defend the liberal arts at the moment of their endangerment.[41] It renders what scholars do increasingly illegible and irrelevant to those outside the profession and even outside individual disciplines, making it difficult to establish the value of this work to students or a public. The move to judge every academic endeavor by its uptake in nonacademic venues (commerce, state agencies, NGOs), as the British Research Excellence Framework (REF) does, is equally damaging. Of course, these metrics abjure humanistic inquiry, but they also cannot capture the value of basic scientific research from which technical applications derive, thus threatening to shut off the spring waters whose exploitation the REF aims to affirm.[42]

Along with intensifying the distance between academic research and undergraduate teaching, neoliberalization has dramatically depressed the status of undergraduate teaching within the academic profession as a whole and at public research universities, in particular. Since research is all that enhances scholarly value, all savvy young faculty learn to allocate most of their human capital portfolio to it. Teaching steals precious time from research, and too much care for undergraduate teaching also stigmatizes academics as lacking "market smarts."[43] Consequently, dedicated undergraduate teachers tend to be regarded by their peers as losers, anachronisms, or both. Tuition-driven institutions require such teachers, of course, and carry on publicly about recognizing and rewarding them. But these rewards amount mostly to local prizes and ceremonies. Tenure and promotion, let alone targeted recruitments and lucrative counteroffers, are never based on teaching excellence in research universities. Yet the devaluation of teaching among research faculty, like the trend toward research contoured by narrow professional norms and concerns, undercuts public universities' ability to protect or advance the liberal arts. Tuition and taxpaying parents rightly query why professors are not teaching more and better, and administrators are caught between answering to this public and cultivating or retaining premier research faculty, which depends on minimizing teaching duties. This predicament, along with cost-cutting imperatives, speeds the replacement of research faculty with casual academic labor in the undergraduate classroom, which further denigrates the value of teaching among the professoriat and raises more questions for taxpayers about what they are paying for at a public university.

Taken together, these forces of neoliberalized knowledge on faculty endeavor and priorities are disastrous for the future of liberal arts education. This future is imperiled by, on the one hand, academic market metrics that sever research from teaching or public purposes, and, on the other hand, nonacademic market metrics that value scholarly endeavor according to its commercial uptake or attractiveness to would-be investors. Only among the ever-growing, woefully paid casual academic labor force does teaching quality matter. Yet here, precisely because teaching is delinked from research, that quality is increasingly measured according to consumer satisfaction, that is, popularity with students, themselves increasingly oriented by return on investment, whether in the form of entertainment or the enhancement of human capital. Thus, as research faculty are pulled away from dedication to rich and challenging undergraduate education by research-market metrics, adjunct faculty are pulled away from it by entertainment-market metrics or by demands for knowledge with immediate applicability.

It is remarkable how quickly all strata in public universities—staff, faculty, administrators, students—have grown accustomed to the saturation of university life by neoliberal rationality, metrics, and principles of governance. Faculty are used to corporately funded research centers, professorships, programs and departments and have, with a few exceptions, largely accepted the erosion of their power to govern the university. Senior faculty enjoying privileges (often including marketized salaries that jump off university scales) at the top end of the privatized public universities are preoccupied with their publications, invitations, prizes, rankings, offers, and counteroffers. Younger faculty, raised on neoliberal careerism, are generally unaware that there could be alternative academic purposes and practices to those organized by a neoliberal table of values. The support staff who survive downsizing are immersed in endless rounds of training for new systems, new best practices, new techniques of assessment and management. Students are used to mall-style food courts, corporate sponsorship of student activities and athletics, privatized educational loans, and above all, education approached in terms of career bang for the buck and the replacement of intellectual curiosity with gaming every element of their education—course selection, test preparation, homework completion, and choice of major.[44] Also on the horizon are new "enterprise zones" encircling public universities, where businesses large and small will make direct use of university goods, including research, technology, consultants, and cheap student labor.[45] Not only does this vision pose a striking contrast with the classic university-town ambiance of cafés, bookshops, pubs, and thrift stores, it literalizes as it spatializes the domination of the university by the needs and purposes of capital and spatializes as well the merging of business, state, and academe.

This merger, of course, has been underway for decades, but accelerated in the years of rapid state disinvestment in higher education and the growing integration—in finance, parlance, and governance—of the business and public sectors. Thus, while corporations developed research and administrative "campuses," universities have become increasingly corporate in physical appearance, financial structure, evaluation metrics, management style, personnel, advertising, and promotion.[46] It is telling in this regard that the bloat in administrative staff accompanying slash-and-burn reductions in other campus venues pertains heavily to jobs in private fundraising, money management, and public relations. The Haas School of Business at Berkeley, for example, has three dozen full-time positions related to alumni relations and development, one for every three faculty members.[47] The UCLA business school, the Anderson School of Management, privatized in 2012. The school chose to forego $8 million a year in state funds in order to gain the flexibility to raise tuition, spurn salary caps, and spurn limitations on fundraising, partnerships, and admissions protocols, all of which compromised its competitiveness with Harvard, Yale, and Stanford.[48] Such developments, which could soon extend to professional schools in medicine, engineering, and law, combined with the withdrawal of public support from universities, intensify pressure on administrators and faculty to contour university endeavors in terms of attractiveness for business. It also accounts for why there is barely a whimper of protest against developments such as corporately sponsored research institutes and schools and even donor-sponsored and donor-organized programs of study and courses.[49]

———

Democracy in an era of enormously complex global constellations and powers requires a people who are educated, thoughtful, and democratic in sensibility.[50] This means a people modestly knowing about these constellations and powers; a people with capacities of discernment and judgment in relation to what it reads, watches, or hears about a range of developments in its world; and a people oriented toward common concerns and governing itself. Such knowledge, discernment, and orientation are what a university liberal arts education has long promised and what are now severely challenged by neoliberal rationality inside and outside universities. Contesting this challenge democratically would place us squarely within Rousseau's paradox: to support good institutions, the people must be antecedently what only good institutions can make them.[51] The survival of liberal arts education depends on broad recognition of its value for democracy. The survival of democracy depends upon a people educated for it, which entails resisting neoliberalization of their institutions and themselves.

Put the other way around, a liberal arts education available to the many is essential to any modern democracy we could value, but is not indigenous to it.[52] Democracy can defund, degrade, or abandon the education it requires, undermining its resources for sustaining or renewing itself, even for valuing or desiring itself. Indeed, one crucial effect of neoliberal rationality is to reduce the desire for democracy, along with its discursive intelligibility when it does appear. Hence, another variation on Rousseau's paradox: to preserve the kind of education that nourishes democratic culture and enables democratic rule, we require the knowledge that only a liberal arts education can provide. Thus, democracy hollowed out by neoliberal rationality cannot be counted on to renew liberal arts education for a democratic citizenry.

Losing Bare Democracy
and the Inversion of Freedom into Sacrifice

My critique of neoliberalization does not resolve into a call to rehabil-itate liberal democracy, nor, on the other hand, does it specify what kind of democracy might be crafted from neoliberal regimes to resist them. Rather, the purpose has been to chart how neoliberal rational-ity's ascendance imperils the ideal, imaginary, and political project of democracy. The primary focus has been on the grammar and terms of this rationality and on the mechanisms of its dissemination and inter-pelletive power. Of course, these are buttressed by concrete policies that dismantle social infrastructure, privatize public goods, deregu-late commerce, destroy social solidarities, and responsibilize subjects. However, even if many neoliberal economic policies were abandoned or augmented, this would not abate the undermining of democracy through the normative economization of political life and usurpation of *homo politicus* by *homo oeconomicus*. Strong bank regulation (even nationalization of the banks), public reinvestment in education, cam-paign finance reform, renewed commitment to equal opportunity, or even wealth redistribution, for example, could coexist with the econ-omization of political life, the remaking of education by business metrics, or the formulation of elections as marketplaces and political speech as market conduct. Thus, neoliberal economic policy could be paused or reversed while the deleterious effects of neoliberal reason on democracy continued apace unless replaced with another order of political and social reason. This is the meaning of a governing rationality and why NGOs, nonprofits, schools, neighborhood organizations, and even social movements that understand themselves as opposing neoliberal economic policies may nonetheless be organized by neoliberal rationality.

LOSING BARE DEMOCRACY

Still, why care about democracy in the first place? Isn't neoliberalism imperiling many less ambiguous goods, for example, all planetary life, or all local forms of sustenance and community? What about health care and affordable housing? What about sleep, the soul, the sacred, the intimate, the ineffable?[1] Moreover, hasn't actually existing democracy always been saturated with class domination and inequality, racial subordination and exclusions, institutionalized sexual difference, colonial and imperial premises and practices, unavowed religious privileges and erasures? Why worry about neoliberal damage to this troubled field of meanings, practices, and institutions?

Demos/kratia. The people rule. "Democracy" signifies the aspiration that the people, and not something else, order and regulate their common life through ruling themselves together.[2] Conversely, democracy negates the legitimacy of rule by a part of the people, rather than by the whole—for example, only by those with property, wealth, education, or expertise—or by any external principle, such as power, god(s), violence, truth, technology, or nationalism, even as the people may decide that one or more of these ought to guide, even determine, their shared existence. The term "democracy" contains nothing beyond the principle that the demos rules, although as the only political form permitting us all to share in the powers by which we are governed, it affords without guaranteeing the possibility that power will be wielded on behalf of the many, rather than the few, that all might be regarded as ends, rather than means, and that all may have a political voice. This is the bare promise of bare democracy.[3]

The term does not specify the arrangements, agreements, or institutions by which popular rule could or should be fulfilled. It does not say whether the people will delegate their authority or exercise it directly, whether they will be superordinate (sovereign) or subordinate (subject) to extant laws, whether they will actively assert their sovereignty in formulating and executing a common good or subscribe only to minimalist agreements for living in proximity with each other. Hence, on the one hand, Occupy participants shout "This is what democracy looks like!" when they seize private property (or privatized public space) for the commons, when they deliberate for hours in general assemblies, and when they refuse to produce accountable leaders, representatives, or even make demands. On the other hand, mayors, university administrators, and police invoke democratic law and principle when they evict or arrest the occupiers. There is a deep argument here about what democracy entails—not mere hypocrisy, dissimulation, or instrumentalization of the term. However, a long historical shadow and a contemporary struggle are also in play: Is democracy destined always to be captured and co-opted by the socially dominant? Will the demos always be contained, divided, or subdued in the name of its own political form?

More than leaving its contents and particulars unspecified, the bare concept of democracy (or the concept of bare democracy) features no continuous or consistent account of why the people ought to rule, only the negative one that we should not be ruled by others.[4] Even Rousseau, nearly singular in Western political thought for closely specifying why democracy alone secures (or recovers) the moral dignity of man, theorizes democracy as a way not to violate this dignity, rather than by delineating democracy's positive *political* value. Democracy alone is "the form of association…under which each individual, while uniting with the others, obeys no one but himself, and remains as free as before."[5]

Curiously, political theorists have been more forthcoming on the value of political participation as an intrinsic value. For Aristotle (no democrat, he), participating in the life of the polis is an expression of the "good life"; taking turns "ruling and being ruled" fulfills and perfects members of the species that is by nature political.[6] Tocqueville formulated local participation as a vital counterweight to the ethos of self-interest promulgated by a growing world of commerce and as a prophylactic against the vulnerability to political domination produced by this ethos. In Tocqueville's account, local political participation offsets private interest with orientation toward the common, it also reduces the alienation from government that citizens of large states otherwise experience, thereby nourishing a citizenry that would check natural tendencies toward concentrated governmental power.[7] As an antidote to what he characterizes as the inherently undemocratic nature of both states and constitutions, Sheldon Wolin highlights the value of citizens routinely "sharing and handling power" in local politics and also of an episodically active demos, one that asserts itself in occasional, rather than continuous ways.[8] Strikingly, none of these arguments praising participation make the case for the value of democracy as such.

Over the centuries, of course, there have been many accounts of democracy's superiority and advantages over other political forms. However, most of them have little or nothing to do with popular rule and instead attribute features to democracy that are not inherent to it: equality, liberty, rights or civil liberties, individuality, tolerance, equal opportunity, inclusiveness, openness, proceduralism, the rule of law, peaceful conflict resolution and change. None of these belong exclusively to democracy defined as rule of the people.[9] Each could be promulgated or secured by nondemocratic regimes. Moreover, any demos could affirm one or more of the following: extreme inequality;

invasive policing and surveillance; limited or nonsupervenient rights; nonuniversal rights; severe restrictions on speech, assembly and worship; conformism; intolerance; exclusions or persecutions of targeted peoples and practices; rule by experts or bureaucrats; war, colonialism, or a domestically militarized society. Many have done so.[10] It will not do to say that such phenomena are undemocratic, if the demos willed or sanctioned them.

From its emergence in the late eighteenth century through the present, European liberal democracy has always been saturated with capitalist powers and values. More generally, through its political and legal abstractions, it has secured the power and privileges of the socially dominant, consecrating not only private property and capital rights, but racialism and a subordinating and gender-normative sexual division of labor. Liberal democracy's imbrication with privileges, inequalities, and exclusions is masked through explicit formulations such as equality before the law and freedom based in rights and through a trove of tacit precepts such as moral autonomy and abstract personhood. Together, these precepts secure unequal and unfree social, cultural, and economic life as they disavow their intersection with entrenched divisions of labor and class stratifications and their mobilization of norms of personhood heavily inflected by race, gender, and culture.[11] Through their formal context and content neutrality, liberal democratic ideals of personhood, freedom, and equality appear universal while being saturated with norms of bourgeois white male heterosexual familialism.[12] This is but one reason why the historically excluded, long after political enfranchisement, have yet to achieve substantive equality and belonging.

Liberal democracy is rightly criticized for its disavowals of these imbrications and effects. However, the dissonances that such disavowals produce—for example, between paeans to freedom and equality, on the one hand, and lived realities of exploitation and poverty, on the other—have also been the material for a political imaginary exceeding liberal democratic precepts, one that aims to realize a democracy precluded by its liberal form. Thus, for the early Marx, bourgeois democracy contained an aspirational popular sovereignty and justice that it could not materialize within existing unfree and inegalitarian social conditions. Yet for Marx, it was precisely by abstracting from those very social conditions that bourgeois democracy could figure political liberty, equality, and universality in such a way as to "ideally negate" those conditions. Thus, the abstract formulations of liberty, equality, fraternity, and man that kept it from representing the truth of the lives it governed were also the abstractions enabling its emancipatory vision. From this angle, Marx implies, bourgeois or liberal democracy is not merely a duplicitous shroud for dominant social powers and their effects, but heralds the overcoming of structural inequalities, unfreedoms, and lack of collective power over existence. Thus, for Marx, bourgeois or constitutional democracy does more than "represent a great progress" over the naturalized stratification and exclusions of the *ancien régime*. It also signifies both the desire and the promise of popular sovereignty, freedom, equality, and community in excess of what can be realized in the context of bourgeois (capitalist) social relations.[13]

In addition to harboring an ideal in excess of itself, liberal democracy's divide between formal principles and concrete existence provides the scene of paradox, contradiction, and at times, even catachresis that social movements of every kind have exploited for more than three centuries.[14] Women, racial and religious minorities, slave descendants, new immigrants, queers, not to mention the poor and working classes, have seized on the universalism and abstraction of liberal democratic personhood to insist on belonging to the category of "man" (when they did not), to stretch liberal meanings of equality (to make them substantive, not only formal), and to press outward on freedom as well (to make it bear on controlling conditions of existence, not mere choice within existing conditions). Similarly, if the promise of popular sovereignty was constantly compromised in one way by that other, illegitimate sovereign ever-present in liberalism—the state—and in another way by what Marx called "social power" and what Foucault would call "biopower," the promise nevertheless forced episodic reckonings with the operation of wealth and other privileges in organizing common life. Never did the demos really rule in liberal democracies, nor could it in large nation-states. But the presumption that it *should* rule placed modest constraints on powerful would-be usurpers of its ghostly throne, helped to leash legislation aimed at benefiting the few, rather than the many, and episodically incited political action from below oriented toward the "common concerns of ordinary lives."[15]

This containment of antidemocratic forces and this promise of the fuller realization of democratic principles are what neoliberal political rationality jeopardizes with its elimination of the very idea of the demos, with its vanquishing of *homo politicus* by *homo oeconomicus*, with its hostility toward politics, with its economization of the terms of liberal democracy, and with its displacement of liberal democratic legal values and public deliberation with governance and new management. Despite routine claims by proponents that governance techniques are more democratic than those associated with hierarchical or state-centered forms, there is simply no place for the demos or its political activity (especially political contestation about broad principles organizing and directing the polity) within these techniques or more generally within a neoliberal table of values.[16] In addition, insofar as economization of the political and suffusion of public discourse with governance eliminate the categories of both the demos and sovereignty, the value—even the intelligibility—of popular sovereignty is rubbed out. Economization replaces a political lexicon with a market lexicon. Governance replaces a political lexicon with a management lexicon. The combination transforms the democratic promise of shared rule into the promise of enterprise and portfolio management at the individual and collective level. In place of citizens sharing and contesting power, the resulting order emphasizes, at best, consensus achieved through stakeholder consultation, focus groups, best practices, and teamwork. The unruliness of democracy is stifled by a form of governing that is soft and total.

The neoliberal economization of the political not only divests the terms of liberal democratic justice of their capacity to contest or to limit the reach of market values and distributions into every quarter of life. Economization inverts this capacity into its opposite as it makes justice terms consecrate and confirm market values and distributions. Again, this is not to suggest that the interval between economic and political life articulated by liberal democracy meant that this form of democracy was ever uncontaminated by capitalism. The point is simply that as long as it operated in a different lexical and semiotic register from capital, liberal democratic principles and expectations could be mobilized to limit capitalist productions of value and market distributions; they could be a platform for critiques of those values and distributions, and they could gestate more radical democratic aspirations. When this other register is lost, when market values become the only values, when liberal democracy is fully transformed into market democracy, what disappears is this capacity to limit, this platform of critique, and this source of radical democratic inspiration and aspiration.

———————

In the Euro-Atlantic world today, there would seem to be a fair amount of discontent, or at least unease, about the neoliberalization of everyday life. However, this quotidian unhappiness tends to focus on neoliberalism's generation of extreme inequalities, on its invasive or crass levels of commodification, or on its dismantling of public goods and commercialization of public life and public space. There is far less worry expressed about neoliberalism's threat to democracy, perhaps because the incursions, inversions, and transformations I have been describing are more subtle than the juxtapositions of billionaire bankers with slum dwellers, perhaps because of the shell form democracy already had prior to neoliberalization (its reduction to rights and elections), perhaps because of ubiquitous cynicism and alienation from political life. Above all, no doubt, neoliberal rationality has been extremely effective in identifying capitalism with democracy.

As I have suggested, democracy does not promise to save us from domination by either the direct imperatives or wily powers of capitalism. Democracy is an empty form that can be filled with a variety of bad content and instrumentalized by purposes ranging from nationalist xenophobia to racial colonialism, from heterosexist to capitalist hegemony; it can be mobilized within the same regimes to counter these purposes.[17] But if democracy stands for the idea that the people, rather than something else, will decide the fundamentals and coordinates of their common existence, economization of this principle is what can finally kill it.

The idea of the people ruling themselves together in a polity is important for many reasons, but not least because the alternative is to be ruled by others.[18] Yet by no means does this render democracy a pure good or suggest that it can or should be exhaustive and comprehensive in political life. Even a radical or direct democracy, or one not saturated with capital, racialism, and so forth, is capable of dark trajectories or simply of neglecting critical issues such as climate change, species extinction, or genocidal warfare beyond its borders. Thus, there are times when democracy may have to be intermixed with practices of nondemocratic stewardship or contained by moral absolutes. Moreover, democracy is not inherently self-sustaining; it often requires undemocratic or ademocratic sources of supplementation or reinforcement. Rousseau is openhanded about this, infamously proclaiming that we must sometimes be "forced to be free" and underscoring the problem, as well, in the importance he places on a founder or lawgiver external to a self-ruling demos.[19] The degeneration of democracy and its conditions is also no small problem; democracy has no intrinsic mechanisms for renewing itself. Thus, Chapter 5 concluded with the worry that the Supreme Court's neoliberalization of the constituent elements of democracy could extinguish the very imaginary that would resist this, and Chapter 6 concluded with the argument that democracy could not be counted on to save the higher education on which it depends. In sum, democracy is neither a panacea nor a complete form of political life. Without it, however, we lose the language and frame by which we are accountable to the present and entitled to make our own future, the language and frame with which we might contest the forces otherwise claiming that future.

SACRIFICE

I have been arguing that neoliberal rationality's economization of the political, its jettisoning of the very idea of the social, and its displacement of politics by governance diminish significant venues for active citizenship and the meaning of citizenship itself. However, as this rationality eliminates the last classical republican traces of citizenship formulated as engagement with the public interest, it retains and transforms the idea of citizen sacrifice. In fact, as I will suggest below, neoliberalism may require sacrifice as a supplement, something outside of its terms, yet essential to its operation.[20]

While, in the transition from liberal to neoliberal democracy, citizen virtue is reworked as responsibilized entrepreneurialism and self-investment, it is also reworked in the austerity era as the "shared sacrifice" routinely solicited by heads of state and heads of businesses.[21] Such sacrifice may entail sudden job losses, furloughs, or cuts in pay, benefits, and pensions, or it may involve suffering the more sustained effects of stagflation, currency deflation, credit crunches, liquidity crises, foreclosure crises, and more.[22] "Shared sacrifice" may refer to the effects of curtailed state investment in education, infrastructure, public transportation, public parks, or public services, or it may simply be a way of introducing job "sharing," that is, reduced hours and pay. Regardless, as active citizenship is slimmed to tending oneself as responsibilized human capital, sacrificial citizenship expands to include anything related to the requirements and imperatives of the economy.[23]

This slimming of active citizenship and the expansion of citizen sacrifice are facilitated through the neoliberal supplanting of democratic political values and discourse with governance, the consensus model of conduct integrating everyone and everything into a given project with given ends. As governance replaces law with benchmarking, structurally conflicting interests with "stakeholders," political or normative challenges with a focus on the technical and the practical (best practices), it also replaces class consciousness with team consciousness. Thus, neoliberal governance converts the classically modern image of the nation comprising diverse concerns, issues, interests, points of power, and points of view into the nation on the model of Wal-Mart, where managers are "team leaders," workers are "junior associates," and consumers are "guests"—each integrated into the smooth functioning of the whole and bound to its ends.

In this context, outsourcing, downsizing, salary and benefits reductions, along with slashed public services all present themselves as business decisions, not political ones.[24] This also means that when economic "reality" requires it, even the most thoroughly responsibilized individuals may be legitimately cast off from the ship. Human capital for itself bears the responsibility of enhancing and securing its future; it is expected to self-invest wisely and is condemned for dependency. However, human capital for the firm or the nation is bound to the project of the whole and is valued according to macroeconomic vicissitudes and exigencies. This means that neither its responsibility nor its fealty guarantees its survival. It also means that the solidarity and sacrifice that workers once directed toward unions in the form of union dues, stay-aways, or strikes are now redirected toward capital and the state in the form of accepting layoffs, furloughs, and reduced hours and benefits. It means tolerating the substitution of undocumented or prison labor for one's own or losing business to firms with access to such labor.[25] It means willingness to suffer regressive taxation and bankrupt state coffers on the rationale that corporate and mineral-extraction taxes discourage investment, chase away businesses, or stymie growth. It means accepting encomiums to spend, borrow, or save according to the changing needs of the economy, rather than the needs of oneself, one's family, community, or planet. And where austerity measures are most severe, as all of Southern Europe has recently learned, it means accepting persistent high rates of joblessness combined with life-threatening cuts in social protections and services.

The notion that loyal citizens must "share sacrifice" in accepting austerities, the encomium one hears today from Right to Left, relocates this classic gesture of patriotism from a political-military register to an economic one, a relocation that itself indexes the neoliberal economization of the political. Yet a depoliticized economy and economized polity does not terminate the economy as a *political end*; rather, as we have seen, competitive positioning, credit rating, and growth become *the* national ends, and citizenship entails reconciliation to those ends. Virtuous citizenship undertakes this reconciliation; bad citizenship (greedy public employees, lazy consumers of benefits, or intransigent labor unions) does not. Thus, while neoliberalism formally promises to liberate the citizen from the state, from politics, and even from concern with the social, practically, it integrates both state and citizenship into serving the economy and morally fuses hyperbolic self-reliance with readiness to be sacrificed.

The "shared sacrifice" discourse of neoliberalism's austerity epoch differs sharply from that accompanying the "trickle-down" economics of the 1980s. The Reagan-Thatcher era promised that wealth generated by the giants would benefit the small; today's sacrificial citizen receives no such promise. Economic ends are delinked from the general welfare of the population but, in addition, as citizens are integrated into these ends via governance, they may be sacrificed to its needs, vicissitudes, and contingencies in a nation, just as they are in a firm. Thus, a political rationality born in reaction to National Socialism (recall that the theories of F. A. Hayek and the Ordo School of neoliberalism were retorts to that formation) paradoxically comes to mirror select aspects of it. In place of the social-contractarian promise—that the political aggregate (or an authorized precipitate of it) will secure the individual against life-threatening danger from without and within—individual *homo oeconomicae* may now be legitimately sacrificed to macroeconomic imperatives. Instead of being secured or protected, the responsibilized citizen tolerates insecurity, deprivation, and extreme exposure to maintain the competitive positioning, growth, or credit rating of the nation as firm.

Shared sacrifice is also different from "shared pain," "lowered expectations," or "trimming the fat"—other signatures of earlier decades in American political-economic life. Of course, where ostensibly bloated public sectors or indulgent subjects or nations are targeted for cuts or restructuring, a blaming discourse still circulates, and measures are taken to punish or discipline lazy or freeloading peoples, regions, or practices. However, when we are called to share sacrifice, we are neither being punished nor simply suffering a necessity. Something else is afoot.

So why *is* shared sacrifice the lingua franca of business and governments today, circulating across firms large and small and accompanying the fiscal restructuring or bailouts in the EU, states, municipalities, or certain economic or public sectors?[26] What work is this call doing and upon what tropes is it drawing? Sacrifice is a historically and culturally ubiquitous, yet disunified and shape-shifting practice.[27] It has supremely religious, as well as utterly prosaic usages—there are ritual sacrifices of animals and other treasures to god(s), parental sacrifices of time, sleep, and money for children, and strategic sacrifices in games—of a pawn in chess or to advance a runner in baseball.[28] Which orbit of meaning harbors the call for shared sacrifice in neoliberal austerity politics?

Moishe Halbertal, in a meditation largely focused on the Hebrew Bible and contemporary just-war theory, argues for distinguishing between religious sacrifice and moral-political sacrifice. He formulates the distinction as turning on the difference between "sacrificing to" something (usually collectively) and "sacrificing for" something (usually individually).[29] Thus, we sacrifice *to* the sacred, but *for* the nation, *to* the gods, but *for* war. Halbertal's distinction, useful, albeit obviously unstable,[30] could also be cast as that between sacrifice in the idioms of ancient and modern, religious and secular, theological and political, communal and personal.

Here is how we might further develop Halbertal's distinction: religious sacrifice is generally (but not always) communal, ritualistic, and oriented toward restoring order or harmony. While such sacrifice generally entails killing a designated victim, and while it is the killing itself that is crucial in the eyes of some theorists,[31] others have argued that its importance lies in making an offering of life to the wellspring of life, to the supreme power from which life emanates and on which all life depends. The life of an animal or a child is offered up to the sacred origin of life as a way of restoring or feeding that source. Sacrifice is a communal ritual that renarrates the community's origin and expresses its conscious dependence on the sacred, but is distinct from other expressions of devotion or servitude in that we feed the life-giving powers of the sacred with life. Thus, Henri Hubert and Marcel Mauss argue that sacrifice acts to establish a relationship between the sacred and the profane: "the profane enters into a relationship with the divine…because it sees in it the very source of life."[32]

In soft contrast with religious sacrifice, moral-political (or, perhaps, secular) sacrifice also involves giving up life (or an aspect of it), but importantly, what is given up is one's own. Invoked today in relationship to families, communities, nations, and coworkers, this kind of sacrifice is always self-sacrifice, which, Halbertal implies without quite saying, modern moral life requires as a counter to a world otherwise organized exclusively by self-interest.[33] Like religious sacrifice, this kind may entail death, especially in war, and it may also be an expression of dependence and devotion, especially in patriotism and familialism. But it is a sacrifice of oneself, rather than another, and is above all a sacrifice *for* rather than *to* something or someone. We give up something we care about for an outcome and in so doing have not departed the modern world of the self and its interests, but rather confirm that world through naming the act a sacrifice. The idea of "taking one for the team," an idiomatic expression that has spread from sports to politics, love, and work, captures something of the difference. The expression neither assumes a natural community nor implicates the sacred; rather, it iterates an individual choice of membership or belonging and a willingness to override personal desires or glory for a larger entity or longer purpose.

For our purposes, what is important is that both religious and moral-political sacrifice are premised upon a noneconomistic and nonmarketized form of exchange.[34] Both involve and articulate belonging to an order larger than oneself. Both entail a destruction or deprivation of life in the name of sustaining or regenerating that order. These features remind us of the respects in which the logic of sacrifice is external to neoliberal reason, working as a supplement to it. The supplement is required in part because a world of capitals does not fully cohere or self-regulate, in part because there is slippage in neoliberal rationality between normative capital enhancement and normative economic growth, and in part because individual or federated nation-states remain the basis of political steering and legitimation in a global economic order.

As we are enjoined to sacrifice to the economy as the supreme power and to sacrifice for "recovery" or balanced budgets, neoliberal austerity politics draws on both the religious and secular, political meanings of the term. We appear to be in the orbit of the second, secular meaning insofar as "sharing" is called for, rather than assumed, the call itself is issued in a moral-political idiom, and the call implies overcoming self-interest for the good of the team. Yet the devastation of human well-being entailed in slashed jobs, pay, benefits, and services brings no immediate returns to those who sacrifice or are sacrificed. Rather, the putative aim is restoration of economic and state fiscal "health," a return from the brink of bankruptcy, currency collapse, debt default, or credit downgrade. Moreover, the addressee of sacrifice is not the nation, not the demos, but the spectacularly imbricated state and economy on which all life depends, but which also command destruction and deprivation. In the 2008 subprime mortgage crisis, for example, 700 billion taxpayer dollars and over five million homeowners were fed to banks "too big to fail."[35] Thus we are returned to the religious valence of sacrifice. In shared sacrifice for economic restoration, we sacrifice "to," rather than "for," and make an offering to a supreme power on which we are radically dependent, but that owes us nothing. We are called to offer life to propitiate and regenerate its life-giving capacities… but without any guarantee that the benefits of this sacrifice will redound to us.

As already suggested, the status of sacrifice as a supplement to neoliberal reason means that it carries the potential for breaking open or betraying the limitations of that logic. Exploring that political potential is beyond the scope of this book, but I will note two features of religious sacrifice that might open it.

Substitution and Displacement. Hubert and Mauss argue that substitution is an essential element of sacrifice: the victim takes the place of the sacrificer, "the sacrificer remains protected: the gods take the victim instead of him," and "the victim redeems him."[36] René Girard, drawing on the work of Samuel Leinhardt and Victor Turner, develops and transforms this point by emphasizing what the victim does for the community: sacrifice, Girard writes, is a "deliberate act of collective substitution performed at the expense of the victim and absorbing all the internal tensions, feuds, and rivalries pent up within the community."[37] Girard here lays groundwork for his renowned notion of "scapegoating": "the victim is a substitute for all the members of the community, offered up by the members themselves. The sacrifice serves to protect the entire community from its own violence; it prompts the entire community to choose victims outside itself. The elements of dissension scattered through the community are drawn to the person of the sacrificial victim and eliminated, at least temporarily, by its sacrifice."[38]

So, who or what might be the object of substitution in neoliberal citizen sacrifice? What "internal tensions, feuds, and rivalries" is sacrifice absorbing from the community? What are the "elements of dissension scattered throughout the community" temporarily eliminated or displaced by the call to sacrifice? Might interpellation by the call to sacrifice repress political dissension or uprising? Alternatively, perhaps "shared sacrifice" inverts while sustaining the general logic that Girard outlines: instead of preserving the community through sacrifice of a victim outside of it, the whole community is called to sacrifice in order to save particular elements within it. Thus, for example, rage appropriately directed at investment banks is redirected into a call for shared sacrifice undertaken by their victims. This would seem to be exactly the logic that Occupy was seeking to expose and reverse in its attempt to hold the banks, rather than the people, responsible for creating an unsustainable debt-based economy.

Restoration. Religious sacrifice often aims not only to nourish or propitiate the gods, but to rebalance the forces of life and common existence. Girard insists that "the purpose of sacrifice is to restore harmony to the community, to reinforce the social fabric."[39] What is the disharmony or torn social fabric at stake in the call to sacrifice in contemporary neoliberal regimes? Is it only fiscal and economic? Does it concern only debt, spending, or even improperly regulated financial institutions? Perhaps there is also at stake a crisis in values, a crisis in the identity or promise of the polity, even a crisis of democracy. Refusal of the encomium to sacrifice might productively reveal these other crises and in so doing, challenge their neoliberalized form.

Citizenship in its thinnest mode is mere membership. Anything slightly more robust inevitably links with patriotism, love of *patria*, whether the object of attachment is city, country, team, firm, or cosmos.[40] Patriotism itself may be expressed in many ways, from radical criticism to slavish devotion, engaged activity to passive obedience. In all cases, however, its consummate sign is the willingness to risk life, which is why soldiers in battle remain its enduring icon and why Socrates rendered acceptance of his death sentence as ultimate proof of his loyalty to Athens and compared himself to a soldier when doing so.[41] Today, as economic metrics have saturated the state and the national purpose, the neoliberal citizen need not stoically risk death on the battlefield, only bear up uncomplainingly in the face of unemployment, underemployment, or employment unto death. The properly interpellated neoliberal citizen makes no claims for protection against capitalism's suddenly burst bubbles, job-shedding recessions, credit crunches, and housing market collapses, its appetites for outsourcing or the discovery of pleasure and profit in betting against itself or betting on catastrophe. This citizen also accepts neoliberalism's intensification of inequalities as basic to capitalism's health—comprising the subpoverty wages of the many and the bloated compensation of bankers, CEOs, and even managers of public institutions and comprising as well reduced access of the poor and middle class to formerly public goods, now privatized. This citizen releases state, law, and economy from responsibility for and responsiveness to its own condition and predicaments and is ready when called to sacrifice to the cause of economic growth, competitive positioning and fiscal constraints.

Thus, again, does a political rationality originally born in opposition to fascism turn out to mirror certain aspects of it, albeit through powers that are faceless and invisible-handed and absent an authoritarian state. This is not to say that neoliberalism is fascism or that we live in fascist times. It is only to note convergences between elements of twentieth-century fascism and inadvertent effects of neoliberal rationality today. These convergences appear in the valorization of a national economic project and sacrifice for a greater good into which all are integrated, but from which most must not expect personal benefit.[42] They appear as well in the growing devaluation of politics, publics, intellectuals, educated citizenship, and all collective purposes apart from economy and security.

This is the order of things challenged by the protests of recent years against austerity measures and privatization. In place of the image of the nation (or of Europe) on the model of the firm, these protests often struggle to revive the image of the nation as *res publica*, a public thing, and of the people as a living political body. Ironically, these protests emerge in part from the broken solidarities of neoliberalism. The "99 percent" that Occupy claimed to represent, for example, was not founded on associations of workers, students, consumers, welfare clients, or debtors. Rather, Occupy in fall 2011 was a public coalescing and uprising of solidarities dismantled and citizenries fragmented and dispersed by neoliberal rationality. This eruption, like those in Southern Europe in 2012 or Turkey, Brazil, and Bulgaria in spring 2013, repossessed private space as public space, occupied what is owned, and above all, rejected the figure of citizenship reduced to sacrificial human capital and neoliberal capitalism as a life-sustaining sacred power. It sought to reclaim the *political* voice hushed by those figures. But a voice on behalf of what future?

DESPAIR: IS ANOTHER WORLD POSSIBLE?

The Euro-Atlantic Left today is often depicted, from within and without, as beset by a predicament without precedent: we know what is wrong with this world, but cannot articulate a road out or a viable global alternative. Lacking a vision to replace those that foundered on the shoals of repression and corruption in the twentieth century, we are reduced to reform and resistance—the latter being a favored term today in part because it permits action as reaction, rather than as crafting an alternative. While the Left opposes an order animated by profit instead of the thriving of the earth and its inhabitants, it is not clear today how such thriving could be obtained and organized. Capitalist globalization, which Marx imagined would yield a class that would universalize itself by inverting its denigration into shared power and freedom, has yielded instead paralyzing conundrums: What alternative planetary economic and political order(s) could foster freedom, equality, community, and earthly sustainability and also avoid domination by massive administrative apparatuses, complex markets, and the historically powerful peoples and parts of the globe? What alternative global economic system and political arrangements would honor regional historical, cultural, and religious differences? Within such arrangements, what or who would make and enforce decisions about production, distribution, consumption, and resource utilization, about population thresholds, species coexistence, and earthly finitude? How to use the local knowledges and achieve the local control essential to human thriving and ecological stewardship in the context of any worldwide economic system? How to prevent rogue subversions without military repression or prevent corruption and graft without surveillance and policing? Whither the nation-state or international law?

Where thinkers and actors have even been willing to pose and consider such questions, answers have been thin. However, the Left is not alone in faltering before the task of crafting, in ideas or institutions, a realizable alternative future trajectory. Rather, the Left's predicament refracts a ubiquitous, if unavowed, exhaustion and despair in Western civilization. At the triumphal "end of history" in the West, most have ceased to believe in the human capacity to craft and sustain a world that is humane, free, sustainable, and, above all, modestly under human control. This loss of conviction about the human capacity to craft and steer its existence or even to secure its future is the most profound and devastating sense in which modernity is "over." Neoliberalism's perverse theology of markets rests on this land of scorched belief in the modern. Ceding all power to craft the future to markets, it insists that markets "know best," even if, in the age of financialization, markets do not and must not know at all, and the hidden hand has gone permanently missing.[43]

Neoliberal rationality did not germinate this civilizational despair. However, its figuration of the human, its reality principle, and its worldview—"there *is* no alternative"—consecrates, deepens, and naturalizes without acknowledging this despair.[44] In letting markets decide our present and future, neoliberalism wholly abandons the project of individual or collective mastery of existence.[45] The neoliberal solution to problems is always more markets, more complete markets, more perfect markets, more financialization, new technologies, new ways to monetize. Anything but collaborative and contestatory human decision making, control over the conditions of existence, planning for the future; anything but deliberate constructions of existence through democratic discussion, law, policy. Anything but the human knowledge, deliberation, judgment, and action classically associated with *homo politicus*.

The task of the Left today is compounded by this generalized collapse of faith in the powers of knowledge, reason, and will for the deliberate making and tending of our common existence. Insistence that "another world is possible" runs opposite to this tide of general despair, this abandoned belief in human capacities to gestate and guide a decent and sustainable order, this capitulation to being playthings of powers that escaped from the bottle in which humans germinated them. The Left alone persists in a belief (or in a polemic, absent a belief) that all could live well, live free, and live together—a dream whose abandonment is expressed in the ascendency of neoliberal reason and is why this form of reason could so easily take hold. The perpetual treadmill of a capitalist economy that cannot cease without collapsing is now the treadmill on which every being and activity is placed, and the horizons of all other meanings and purposes shrink accordingly. This is the civilizational turning point that neoliberal rationality marks, its postpostmodernism and deep antihumanism, its surrender to a felt and lived condition of human impotence, unknowingness, failure, and irresponsibility.

Thus, the Left's difficulties are compounded by the seduction of such surrender to the overwhelmingly large, fast, complex, contingently imbricated, and seemingly unharnessable powers organizing the world today. Tasked with the already difficult project of puncturing common neoliberal sense and with developing a viable and compelling alternative to capitalist globalization, the Left must also counter this civilizational despair. Our work on all three fronts is incalculably difficult, bears no immediate reward, and carries no guarantee of success. Yet what, apart from this work, could afford the slightest hope for a just, sustainable, and habitable future?

Notes

CHAPTER ONE: UNDOING DEMOCRACY

1. Rousseau's appreciation of the difficulty of constructing democratic subjects from the material of modernity is told in the transition from his "Discourse on Inequality" to *The Social Contract*. In *On Liberty*, Mill is straightforward about the fact that we all want liberty, individuality, and tolerance for ourselves, but are less inclined to grant it to others. John Stuart Mill, *On Liberty and Other Writings*, ed. Stefan Collini (Cambridge: Cambridge University Press, 1989), pp. 11 and 16.

2. Giorgio Agamben, *Homo Sacer* (Stanford: Stanford University Press, 1998), p. 176.

3. Jacques Rancière, *Dissensus: On Politics and Aesthetics* (New York: Continuum, 2010), p. 70.

4. Etienne Balibar, *Equaliberty: Political Essays*, trans. James Ingram (Durham: Duke University Press, 2014), p. 207. Alas, Balibar's extraordinary text emerged in English just as *Undoing the Demos* was going to press. It deserves fuller treatment than I have given it here.

5. Jamie Peck, *Constructions of Neoliberal Reason* (New York: Oxford University Press, 2010); John Clarke, "Living With/in and Without Neo-Liberalism," *Focaal—European Journal of Anthropology* 51.1 (2008), pp. 135–47; Franco Barchiesi, *Precarious Liberation: Workers, the State and Contested Social Citizenship in Post-Apartheid South Africa* (Albany: State University of New York Press, 2011).

6. There is now a fine set of intellectual histories of neoliberalism, including Peck, *Constructions of Neoliberal Reason*; Daniel Stedman Jones, *Masters of the Universe: Hayek, Friedman, and the Birth of Neoliberal Politics* (Princeton: Princeton University Press, 2012); Pierre Dardot and Christian Laval, *The New Way of the World* (New York: Verso, 2014); Philip Mirowski, *Never Let a Serious Crisis Go to Waste* (New York: Verso, 2013); and Angus Burgin, *The Great Persuasion: Reinventing Free Markets since the Depression* (Cambridge, MA: Harvard University Press, 2012). Each of these works contributes to an appreciation of neoliberalism as emerging from several streams of dissident thought in the postwar period, eventually taking shape as a governing rationality that drew on and diverged from these waters. Each also contributes something distinctive to theorizing the novel powers and categories of neoliberal political regimes and subjectivities. Together, these studies implicitly contest a more orthodox Marxist view, exemplified by David Harvey in *A Brief History of Neoliberalism* (New York: Oxford University Press, 2005), that neoliberalism was a reformatting of capitalism in response to the falling rate of profit in the 1970s. For work that extends the more idea-centered analysis to examine the rise and spread of austerity politics, see Mark Blyth, *Austerity: The History of a Dangerous Idea* (New York: Oxford University Press, 2013). For a study of the ways that neoliberal think tanks continue to shape neoliberal policy and rationality, see P. W. Zuidhof, *Imagining Markets: The Performative Politics of Neoliberalism* (forthcoming with Zone). For the claim that neoliberalism has been made to signify so many different things that it is largely useless, see Taylor C. Boas and Jordan Gans-Morse, "Neoliberalism: From New Liberal Philosophy to Anti-Liberal Slogan," *Studies in Comparative International Development* 44.2 (2009), pp. 137–61.

7. For developed analyses of the significance of this transition, see, among others, Michel Feher, *Rated Agency: Investee Politics in a Speculative Age* (forthcoming with Zone); and Gerald F. Davis, *Managed by the Markets: How Finance Reshaped America* (New York: Oxford University Press, 2009); Davis, "After the Corporations," *Politics and Society* 41.2 (2013), and Davis, "Finance Capitalism 2.0: How BlackRock Became the new J. P. Morgan," Labor and Employment Relations Association Conference, January 7, 2012,

University of Michigan, available at http://webuser.bus.umich.edu/gfdavis/
Presentations/Davis%20LERA%20tak%201-7-12.pdf.

8. Michel Foucault, *The Birth of Biopolitics: Lectures at the Collège de France,
1978–79*, ed. Michel Senellart, trans. Graham Burchell (New York: Picador,
2004).

9. Koray Çalışkan and Michel Callon, "Economization, Part 1: Shifting
Attention from the Economy Towards Processes of Economization," *Economy
and Society* 38.3 (2009), pp. 369–98; Timothy Mitchell, *Rule of Experts: Egypt,
Techno-Politics, Modernity* (Berkeley: University of California Press, 2002);
Mitchell, *Carbon Democracy: Political Power in the Age of Oil* (London: Verso,
2011).

10. See Ariel Kaminer, "Lists that Rank Colleges' Value Are on the Rise,"
New York Times, October 27, 2013, p. A1.

11. While the rating system is clearly oriented to would-be investors in
higher education, Deputy Under Secretary of Education Jamienne Studley cast
it as a consumer service: "it's like rating a blender," she said to a gathering
of college presidents. Michael D. Shear, "Colleges Rattled as Obama Presses
Rating System," *New York* Times, May 25, 2014, http://www.nytimes.com/
2014/05/26/us/colleges-rattled-as-obama-presses-rating-system.html. Studley
has also compared choosing a college to making decisions about restaurants,
hotels, or cars, where "we use expert and peer reviews to determine which
establishments other consumers like best and how much each costs, compar-
ing them across a range of options." Doug Lederman, "Key Addition to U.S.
Higher Ed Team," *Inside Higher Ed*, September 22, 2013, http://www.inside-
highered.com/news/2013/09/22/jamienne-studley-named-key-education-
department-post#sthash.PQdCSwd5.dpbs. See also Kelly Field, "Obama Plan to
Tie Student Aid to College Ratings Draws Mixed Reviews," *Chronicle of Higher
Education*, August 22, 2013, http://chronicle.com/article/Obama-Proposes-
Tying-Federal/141229; Tamar Lewin, "Obama's Plan Aims to Lower Cost of
College," *New York Times*, August 22, 2013, http://www.nytimes.
com/2013/08/22/education/obamas-plan-aims-to-lower-cost-of-college.html.

12. "Remarks by the President in the State of the Union Address," February

12, 2013, White House Office of the Press Secretary, available at http://www.whitehouse.gov/the-press-office/2013/02/12/remarks-president-state-union-address, p. 1.

13. *Ibid.*, pp. 1–9. The one exception to this was gun control, which may also explain why Obama gave up on it so quickly in 2013.

14. *Ibid.*, p. 2.

15. *Ibid.*, p. 4.

16. *Ibid.*, p. 5.

17. *Ibid.*, p. 6.

18. *Ibid.*, p. 6.

19. *Ibid.*, p. 7.

20. *Ibid.*, p. 8.

21. *Ibid.*, pp. 8–9.

22. See Thomas Piketty, *Capital in the Twenty-First Century*, trans. Arthur Goldhammer (Cambridge, MA: Belknap Press of Harvard University Press, 2014) and "Dynamics of Inequality," an interview with Piketty, *New Left Review* 85 (January–February 2014). Many are arguing with Piketty's policy prescriptions, few with his
fundamental claim that capital accumulation without growth is at the bottom of intensifying inequality.

23. There are many other examples of the neoliberalization of social justice concerns by the Obama administration. Consider, for example, Obama's pet initiative, My Brother's Keeper, which aims to improve the chances of education and employment for at-risk boys and men of color by recruiting public and private "investors" in this population. The president summarized the project this way: "We've got a huge number of kids out there who have as much talent, and more talent, than I had, but nobody is investing in them." Tanzina Vega, "Administration Lays Out Ways Groups Can Support Program for Minority Men" *New York Times*, May 30, 2014, http://www.nytimes.com/2014/05/31/us/politics/white-house-releases-report-on-helping-minority-men-and-boys.html.

24. Joseph E. Stiglitz *The Price of Inequality: How Today's Divided Society Endangers Our Future* (New York: Norton, 2012); Joseph E. Stiglitz, *Freefall:*

America, Free Markets, and the Sinking of the World Economy (New York: Norton, 2010); Robert Reich, *Aftershock: The Next Economy and America's Future* (New York: Vintage, 2010) and Reich in *Inequality for All*, DVD, directed by Jacob Kornbluth, 72 Productions, 2013; Paul Krugman, "Hunger Games, U.S.A." *New York Times*, July 15, 2013, p. A15, http://www.nytimes.com/2013/07/15/opinion/krugman-hunger-games-usa.html; Krugman, *End This Depression Now!* (New York: Norton, 2012); Krugman, *The Return of Depression Economics and the Crisis of 2008* (New York: Norton, 2009); and Krugman, *The Great Unraveling: Losing Our Way in the New Century* (New York: Norton, 2003); James Ferguson, *Global Shadows: Africa in the Neoliberal World Order* (Durham: Duke University Press, 2006); Branko Milanović, *The Haves and the Have-Nots: A Brief and Idiosyncratic History of Global Inequality* (New York: Basic Books, 2010); Amartya Sen, *Development as Freedom* (New York: Random House, 1999); Joseph Stiglitz, Amartya Sen, and Jean-Paul Fitoussi, "Report by the Commission on the Measurement of Economic Performance and Social Progress," September 14, 2009, available at http://www.stiglitz-sen-fitoussi.fr/documents/rapport_anglais.pdf.

25. See Debra Satz, *Why Some Things Should Not Be for Sale: The Moral Limits of Markets* (New York: Oxford University Press, 2010); Michael Sandel, *What Money Can't Buy: The Moral Limits of Markets* (New York: Farrar, Strauss and Giroux, 2012); and also my review of these books in *Political Theory* 42.3 (2014).

26. Sheldon S. Wolin, *Democracy Incorporated: Managed Democracy and the Specter of Inverted Totalitarianism* (Princeton: Princeton University Press, 2008).

27. Jacob S. Hacker and Paul Pierson, *Winner-Take-All Politics: How Washington Made the Rich Richer—and Turned Its Back on the Middle Class* (New York: Simon and Schuster, 2011). In November 2013, National Public Radio aired an excellent story on the subtle mechanisms of corporate domination in state policy, tracking how neoliberal economization of government generates a new vulnerability of legislators to corporate interests. One interviewee explained how lobbyists now write legislation and organize its passage. He

offered the example of Citigroup's authorship of a bill to roll back a piece of financial regulation imposed after the 2008 finance-capital meltdown. "To me," says Lee Drutman of the Sunlight Foundation, a government watchdog group, "it is just another tick-tock on a story that's been developing for a long time—that Congress has basically outsourced its policy expertise to the private sector." As outrageous as this story seems, Drutman says, it's now unfortunately business as usual on Capitol Hill. "People on the Hill don't stay as long. You don't get as good people on the Hill. *The expertise on policymaking more and more has moved to the private sector*, and it's moved to represent those organizations and companies who can afford to pay for it, which generally isn't you and me. It's big banks and Big Oil and big companies." Drutman worked as a banking policy staffer in 2009 and 2010, handling financial-overhaul issues, and what he saw around the Capitol was that congressional staff members were stretched incredibly thin. Lobbyists know this, says Drutman, so what they offer lawmakers is an all-in-one package—they'll help a lawmaker round up cosponsors for the bill, even write talking points, as well as the bill's specific language. Ailsa Chang, "When Lobbyists Literally Write the Bill," National Public Radio, November 11, 2013, available at http://www.npr.org/blogs/itsallpolitics/2013/11/11/243973620/when-lobbyists-literally-write-the-bill.

28. Gérard Duménil and Dominique Lévy, *The Crisis of Neoliberalism* (Cambridge, MA: Harvard University Press, 2011); Michael Hudson, *Finance Capitalism and Its Discontents* (Dresden: Islet Verlag, 2012); Yves Smith, *E-CONned: How Unrestrained Self Interest Undermined Democracy and Corrupted Capitalism* (New York: Palgrave MacMillan, 2010); Matt Taibbi, *Griftopia: A Story of Bankers, Politicians, and the Most Audacious Power Grab in American History* (New York: Random House, 2010); Philip Mirowski, *Never Let a Serious Crisis Go to Waste: How Neoliberalism Survived the Financial Meltdown* (New York: Verso, 2013).

29. My early efforts at developing Foucault's account of neoliberalism as political rationality appear in "Neoliberalism and the End of Liberal Democracy," *Theory and Event* 7.1 (2003), reprinted in *Edgework: Critical*

Essays on Knowledge and Politics (Princeton: Princeton University Press, 2005) and "American Nightmare: Neoconservatism, Neoliberalism, and De-Democratization," *Political Theory* 34.6 (2006), pp. 690–714. This book revises some of those early formulations, which were fairly uncritical of Foucault, in some cases misinterpreted him, took no account of finance capital or financialization, and limited neoliberal corrosions of democracy to demotion or displacement, rather than the substantive conversion of liberal democratic principles to economic meanings.

30. Çalışkan and Callon, "Economization."

31. See, for example, Bruce Feiler, "Programming Families: How Kids Are Like Software, and What the Government Could Learn From It," in *The Secrets of Happy Families* (New York: William Morrow, 2013), also available at New Tech City, http://www.wnyc.org/story/programming-families-how-kids-like-software-what-the-government-could-learn. Feiler applies the language, metrics, and techniques of business to family life. These include family decisions arranged in the fashion of a stakeholder meeting, branding one's family, and creating a family mission statement. *The Week* describes it as "acknowledging that things can go wrong and introducing a system to address those things works the same in business and at home." See http://theweek.com/article/index/252829/the-secrets-of-happy-families. Similarly, TED Talks describes Feiler as introducing "family practices which encourage flexibility, bottom-up idea flow, constant feedback and accountability." See http://www.ted.com/talks/bruce_feiler_agile_programming_for_your_family.html. Thanks to Chantal Thomas for alerting me to Feiler's work. For another example, see physician and author Reed Tuckson's advice to patients to "become CEO of your own health." His website opens: "How do we work together to improve our quality of life? We start by assembling all available assets; engaging in best health behaviors and sharing innovations in both prevention and medical care delivery." "Meet Dr. Reed Tuckson," http://www.tucksonhealthconnections.com.

32. See also Stella Fayman, "7 Ways Finding Investors for Your Startup Is Just Like Dating," *Forbes*, August 19, 2013, http://www.forbes.com/sites/stellafayman/2013/08/19/7-ways-finding-investors-for-your-startup-is-just-

like-dating, and Jessica Bosari, "Is Dating a Good Investment?," *Forbes*, January 3, 2013, http://www.forbes.com/sites/moneywisewomen/2013/01/03/is-dating-a-good-investment.

33. A dating coach told a *New York Times* reporter, "On Match.com, you might not meet as many people in a month, but you will get to choose those people. Online dating has better return on investment." See Pagan Kennedy, "Who Made Speed Dating?," *New York Times*, September 29, 2013, p. MM17. http://www.nytimes.com/2013/09/29/magazine/who-made-speed-dating.html. Another dating website also construes dating as an investment: "In today's fast-paced world, high-achieving professionals seek experts to assist in a myriad of personal and professional goals. However, when it comes to finding love, many busy, successful singles continue to take a haphazard, needle-in-a-haystack approach when seeking a romantic partner.... If you're truly serious about finding that lasting relationship, be strategic and retain a service that has the experience, reputation and the time to invest in your personal future!! ...We have found that by offering The Premier Match 360™, which is derived from the corporate reviewing process, our clients can maximize their potential for successful dates and achieve the long-term relationship they desire." Premiere Match, http://www.premiermatchmaking.com/About.php. Yet another urges "outsourcing your love life": "Time is of essence, and if you are like most single rich men, you've wasted a lot of it on an attempt to date beautiful women. If you've spent your share of time screaming over music in bars and clubs to make conversation with women that are young enough to be your daughter, you won't want to waste anymore. If you have no problem attracting women, but have an issue with attracting the right ones, and transitioning into serious relationships, you should join our upscale matchmaking agency. It is frustrating to have a lot of failed attempts at finding love. The guess work, games, and hassle that accompany the dating process can be very trying—not to mention expensive. You can save so much time and energy by outsourcing your love life to experienced professionals, like those at Model Quality Introductions, the most trusted male-owned executive matchmaking agency in the nation," http://www.modelqualityintroductions.com/why-use-

an-upscale-dating-service. In the same vein, speed dating is promoted as a way to maximize productivity: "Speed dating is a fun and efficient way to meet more singles in one night.... Rather than going out to a bar or going on a blind date, you know that everyone is single, they are successful, and you don't have to spend more than five minutes with them." The Ivy Connection, "Why Speed Dating," http://www.theivyconnection.com/contents/whyspeeddating.

34. Carl Schmitt, *The Crisis of Parliamentary Democracy*, trans. Ellen Kennedy (Cambridge, MA: MIT Press, 1988), pp. 24–26. Hannah Arendt, *The Human Condition* (Chicago: University of Chicago Press, 1958), pp. 79–100; Claude Lefort, *Democracy and Political Theory*, trans. David Macey (Minneapolis: University of Minnesota Press, 1988), pp. 2–4 and 10–12.

35. Foucault, *The Birth of Biopolitics*, p. 148.

36. Michel Feher, the thinker who has most extensively theorized the implications for the subject and subjectivity of the shift from productive to finance capital, appears to argue that the shift is thoroughgoing and complete. I am suggesting that both modalities are present today, that human capital on the entrepreneurial model is not dead and may cohabit in the same person with human capital on the investment model. See Feher, *Rated Agency;* and Michel Feher, "Self-Appreciation; or, the Aspirations of Human Capital," *Public Culture* 21.1 (2009).

37. See chapter 4 in the excellent work by Murray Milgate and Shannon C. Stimson, *After Adam Smith: A Century of Transformation in Politics and Political Economy* (Princeton: Princeton University Press 2009).

38. Feher, "Self-Appreciation," pp. 21–41.

39. Foucault, *The Birth of Biopolitics*, pp. 118–19.

40. Consider the story of a young assistant professor at University of Victoria in Canada who gamed Academia.edu to acquire for his work the highest "impact" ranking out of five million users of the academic website: http://blog.academia.edu/post/53204075764/kindling-impact. What makes the beginning scholar's achievement especially poignant is his unblanched pride about this ranking on his own website, http://people.geog.uvic.ca/Springer. There is also the fact that he appears to identify with Occupy and the anarchist revival and

that his scholarship critically engages neoliberalism, violence, governmentality, and biopolitics.

41. Michel Feher, "On Credit, Self-esteem, and Sharing: an Introduction to the Neoliberal Condition" lecture, Cornell University, November 2013; and Feher, *Rated Agency*.

42. Florian Gathmann and Veit Medick, "German Chancellor on the Offensive: Merkel Blasts Greece over Retirement Age, Vacation," *Der Spiegel* Online International, May 18, 2011, http://www.spiegel.de/international/europe/german-chancellor-on-the-offensive-merkel-blasts-greece-over-retirement-age-vacation-a-763294.html.

43. Foucault, *The Birth of Biopolitics*, pp. 131 and 246.

44. Responsibilization combined with austerity capitalism requires us to self-invest in externally specified ways, yet our thriving is never guaranteed by this self-investment or responsible conduct insofar as we are appended to a larger order whose purposes do not include the promise to secure us.

45. Hannah Arendt, *The Human Condition* (Chicago: University of Chicago Press, 1958); Aristotle, *The Politics*, trans. Ernest Barker (Oxford: Clarendon, 1946); Karl Marx, "On the Realm of Necessity and the Realm of Freedom," from *Capital, Volume Three*, in *The Marx-Engels Reader*, ed. Robert C. Tucker (New York: Norton, 1978). When I have presented parts of this book to academic audiences, my use of Aristotle's "mere life," has so often been confused with Agamben's "bare life" that it seems important to explain why Agamben's thesis does not bear on my point. In *Homo Sacer*, Agamben uses the term "bare life" to depict a particular positioning of human beings in relation to sovereignty and law. Aristotle uses "mere life" to signify the limited existence of those bound to producing and reproducing human existence; he contrasts this with the lives of citizens who can realize humanness through political and intellectual life, both of which are distinctly human in part because they are free(d) from necessity defined as the basic sustenance and reproduction of life. Of course, with these formulations, Aristotle ontologized an unfree order, one based on slavery, gender, and class domination, and divided humanity between those condemned to mere life and those free to pursue the good life. Arendt

was infamously uncritical of Aristotle's ontology. Marx, however, seized upon Aristotle's distinction as a premise for liberation: all humans should be emancipated from mere life for the good life.

46. Marx, "On the Realm of Necessity and the Realm of Freedom," p. 441.

47. Mill, *On Liberty and Other Writings*, pp. 59–64.

CHAPTER TWO: FOUCAULT'S BIRTH OF BIOPOLITICS LECTURES

1. Stuart Hall, "The Neo-Liberal Revolution," *Soundings*, no. 48 (Summer 2011), pp. 9–28; Jamie Peck, *Constructions of Neoliberal Reason* (New York: Oxford University Press, 2010), pp. 8 and 30.

2. Peck, *Constructions of Neoliberal Reason*, p. 4.

3. Michel Foucault, *The Birth of Biopolitics: Lectures at the Collège de France, 1978–79*, ed. Michel Senellart, trans. Graham Burchell (New York: Picador, 2004), p. 2.

4. *Ibid.*, p. 149.

5. *Ibid.*, p. 313.

6. For speculations on why Foucault took the turn he did in his 1978–79 course, see, for example: Michael Behrent, "Liberalism without Humanism: Foucault and the Free Market Creed," *Modern Intellectual History* 6 (2009), pp. 539–68; Terry Flew, "Michel Foucault's *The Birth of Biopolitics* and Contemporary Neo-liberalism Debates," *Thesis Eleven* 108.1 (2012), pp. 44–65; Francesco Guala, "Critical Notice," *Economics and Philosophy* 22 (2006), pp. 429–39.

7. On this point, see Guala, "Critical Notice," p. 437.

8. Michel Foucault, "Nietzsche, Genealogy, History," in Paul Rabinow (ed.), *The Foucault Reader* (Pantheon, 1984), pp. 83 and 86.

9. Note Mike Gane's way of explaining this in "Foucault on Governmentality and Liberalism"—Foucault is questioning his earlier thesis that knowledge shifts have been dependent on developments of disciplinary and regulatory practices, that is, that they have been promulgated from below: thus, he begins working from "theories to practices in the 78–9 lectures" and also suggests that the eighteenth-century theorists (Adam Smith, Adam Ferguson) reflect

new economic governmentalities—see all this on p. 361, Gane, "Foucault on Governmentality and Liberalism," *Theory, Culture and Society* 25.7–8 (2008), pp. 353–63.

10. Keith Tribe, "The Political Economy of Modernity: Foucault's Collège de France Lectures of 1978 and 1979," *Economy and Society* 38.4 (2009), pp. 682–83, 684, 694. See also Gane, "Foucault on Governmentality and Liberalism."

11. Foucault, *The Birth of Biopolitics*, pp. 13, 63–64, 82. On "not being governed so much," see also Michel Foucault, "What is Critique?," in *The Politics of Truth*, ed. Sylvère Lotringer, trans. Lysa Hochroth and Catherine Porter (Los Angeles: Semiotext(e), 1997), p. 29.

12. Behrent, "Liberalism without Humanism"; Guala, "Critical Notice"; Tribe, "The Political Economy of Modernity"; Flew, "Michel Foucault's *The Birth of Biopolitics* and Contemporary Neo-liberalism Debates"; Gane, "Foucault on Governmentality and Liberalism"; Jacques Donzelot, "Michel Foucault and Liberal Intelligence," *Economy and Society* 37.1 (2008); Jason Read, "A Genealogy of Homo-Economicus: Neoliberalism and the Production of Subjectivity," *Foucault Studies*, 6 (2009). See also "Les néolibéralismes de Michel Foucault," ed. Frédéric Gros, Daniele Lorenzini, Ariane Revel, and Arianna Sforzini, special issue, *Raisons Politiques*, no. 52 (2013–14).

13. Behrent, "Liberalism without Humanism." Behrent's thesis that Foucault was deeply attracted to the neoliberal ideal of individual freedom misunderstands much about Foucault, both in the neoliberalism lectures and in his other work. Recall these remarks on freedom by Foucault: "The man described for us, whom we are invited to free, is already in himself the effect of a subjection much more profound than himself." Michel Foucault, *Discipline and Punish: The Birth of the Prison*, trans. Alan Sheridan (New York: Vintage, 1977), p. 30; and "The political, ethical, social, philosophical problem of our days is not to liberate the individual from the State and its institutions, but to liberate ourselves from the State and the type of individualization linked to it." Foucault, "The Subject and Power," in Hubert L. Dreyfus and Paul Rabinow (eds.), *Michel Foucault: Beyond Structuralism and Hermeneutics* (Chicago: University of Chicago Press, 1982), p. 216.

14. Foucault, *The Birth of Biopolitics*, pp. 294–95.

15. *Ibid.*

16. *Ibid.*, lecture 11, especially pp. 271–73. Foucault introduces the problem this way: "Is *homo oeconomicus* an atom of freedom in the face of all the conditions, undertakings, legislation and prohibitions of a possible government, or was he not already a certain type of subject who precisely enabled an art of government to be determined according to the principle of economy, both in the sense of political economy and in the sense of the restriction, self-limitation and fragility of government? Obviously the way in which I have formulated this question gives the answer straightaway ... *homo oeconomicus* as the partner, the vis-à-vis, and the basic element of the new governmental reason formulated in the eighteenth century." *Ibid.*, p. 271.

17. *Ibid.*, p. 6

18. *Ibid.*, p. 8.

19. *Ibid.*, p. 9.

20. *Ibid.*, pp. 12–15.

21. *Ibid.*, p. 28.

22. *Ibid.*, p. 29.

23. *Ibid.*, p. 37.

24. *Ibid.*, pp. 63–64.

25. *Ibid.*, pp. 69–70. Foucault is careful not to separate crises of liberalism from crises of capitalism, noting that the problems of the 1930s exemplify their intertwining. However, he then says: "But crises of liberalism are not just the pure and simple or direct project of these crises of capitalism in the political sphere. You can find crises of liberalism linked to crises of the capitalist economy. But you can also find them with a chronological gap with regard to these crises, and ... the way ... these crises manifest, are handled ... is not directly deducible from the crises of capitalism" (p. 70).

26. *Ibid.*, p. 104.

27. *Ibid.*, p. 242.

28. I attempted to think through certain aspects of the relation of American neoconservatism and neoliberalism in "American Nightmare: Neoliberalism,

Neoconservatism, and De-Democratization," *Political Theory* 34.6 (2006), pp. 690–714.

29. Foucault, *The Birth of Biopolitics*, p. 243.

30. *Ibid.*, pp. 117–18.

31. Tim Mitchell notes that the term "political economy" originally referred to an economical manner of governing. This suggests not that the economy becomes the model for government, but rather that governments can be economical, efficient, lean, qua governments. The difference is vast. See Timothy Mitchell, *Rule of Experts: Egypt, Techno-Politics, Modernity* (Berkeley: University of California Press, 2002).

32. Foucault, *The Birth of Biopolitics*, pp. 241–43.

33. *Ibid.*, p. 130.

34. *Ibid.*

35. *Ibid.*, p. 131.

36. *Ibid.*

37. *Ibid.*, p. 145.

38. *Ibid.*, p. 120.

39. *Ibid.*, pp. 120 and 145. In "Critical Notice," Guala says this claim is overstated.

40. *Ibid.*, p. 131.

41. *Ibid.*, p. 163.

42. *Ibid.*, p. 121.

43. *Ibid.*, p. 121 (italics added).

44. *Ibid.*, p. 144 (italics added).

45. *Ibid.*, p. 144.

46. *Ibid.*, p. 116.

47. *Ibid.*, p. 118.

48. *Ibid.*, pp. 223–25.

49. *Ibid.*, p. 175.

50. *Ibid.*, p. 241.

51. *Ibid.*, pp. 147 and 149.

52. See Michel Feher, "Self-Appreciation, or the Aspirations of Human

Capital," *Public Culture* 21.1 (2009), pp. 21–41; and *Rated Agency: Investee Politics in a Speculative Age* (forthcoming with Zone).

53. Foucault, *The Birth of Biopolitics*, p. 149.

54. *Ibid.*, p. 148.

55. *Ibid.*

56. *Ibid.*, pp. 121 and 163.

57. *Ibid.*, pp. 145–46 and 148–49.

58. *Ibid.*, p. 173.

59. *Ibid.*, p. 172.

60. *Ibid.*, pp. 243 and 268–69.

61. *Ibid.*, p. 47.

62. *Ibid.*, p. 84.

63. Jürgen Habermas, *Legitimation Crisis*, trans. Thomas McCarthy (Boston: Beacon Press, 1975); Nicos Poulantzas, *Political Power and Social Classes*, trans. Timothy O'Hagan (London: Verso, 1975); James O'Connor, *The Fiscal Crisis of the State* (New York: St. Martin's Press, 1973); Ralph Miliband, *The State in Capitalist Society* (New York: Basic Books, 1969); Claus Offe, "Structural Problems of the Capitalist State: Class Rule and the Political System," in Klaus von Beyme (ed.), *German Political Studies*, vol. 1 (Beverly Hills: Sage, 1974).

64. Foucault, *The Birth of Biopolitics*, p. 160.

65. *Ibid.*, p. 85.

66. *Ibid.*, p. 84.

67. *Ibid.*, p. 85.

68. See Zach Carter, "Scaling Back Our Bloated Financial Sector," Huffington Post, May 26, 2010, http://www.huffingtonpost.com/zach-carter/scaling-back-our-bloated_b_590930.html and Pat Garofalo, "The Financial Sector Now makes Up a Bigger Share of the Economy Than Before the Recession," Think Progress, December 14, 2011, http://thinkprogress.org/economy/2011/12/14/389487/financial-sector-gdp-recession.

69. Chapter 5's discussion of the Bremer Orders in post-Saddam Iraq offers an example of this imbrication.

70. While the account of Foucault's 1978–79 Collège de France lectures offered in this and subsequent chapters focuses not on biopolitics, but on neo-liberalism as a political rationality, there is now an expansive literature that reads these lectures in light of the former. See, for example, Nikolas Rose, *The Politics of Life Itself: Biomedicine, Power, and Subjectivity in the Twenty-First Century* (Princeton: Princeton University Press, 2006); Thomas Lemke, *Bio-politics: An Advanced Introduction* (New York: New York University Press, 2011); Roberto Esposito, *Bios: Biopolitics and Philosophy*, trans. Timothy Campbell (Minneapolis: University of Minnesota Press, 2008); Pheng Cheah, "Power Over Life / Power of Life: What Is a Non-organizational Politics?," in Alain Brossat, Yuan-Horng Chu, Rada Ivekovic, and Joyce C. H. Liu (eds.), *Biopolitics, Ethics and Subjectivation* (Paris: Éditions l'Harmattan, 2011); Melinda Cooper, *Life as Surplus: Biotechnology and Capitalism in the Neoliberal Era* (Seattle: University of Washington Press, 2011); Miguel Vatter, *The Republic of the Living: Biopolitics and the Critique of Civil Society* (New York: Fordham University Press, 2014) and Vanessa Lemm and Miguel Vatter, *The Government of Life: Foucault, Biopolitics and Neoliberalism* (New York: Fordham University Press, 2014).

71. Of course, this is hardly Foucault's first critique of Marx; each of his earlier genealogical works develops an element of his push away from Marx's historiography, materialism, dialectics, ideology, and primacy of capital and economic life.

72. Foucault, *The Birth of Biopolitics*, pp. 91–92 and 164–65.

73. See, for example, *Ibid.*, pp. 105 and 164–65.

74. Michel Foucault, "Two Lectures" in *Power/Knowledge: Selected Interviews and Other Writings*, ed. Colin Gordon (New York: Vintage, 1980), pp. 93–94.

CHAPTER THREE: REVISING FOUCAULT

1. Michael Sandel, *What Money Can't Buy: The Moral Limits of Markets* (New York: Farrar, Strauss and Giroux, 2012); Sandel, "How Markets Crowd Out Morals," *Boston Review* 37.3 (2012), p. 13, http://www.bostonreview.net/forum-sandel-markets-morals. See also responses from Richard Sennett, Matt Welch, Deborah Sachs, et al. in the same issue.

2. Albert O. Hirschman, *The Passions and the Interests: Political Arguments for Capitalism Before Its Triumph* (Princeton: Princeton University Press, 1977); Christian Laval, *L'homme économique: Essai sur les racines du néolibéralisme* (Paris: Gallimard, 2007); Marcel Mauss, *The Gift: The Form and Reason for Exchange in Archaic Societies*, trans. W. D. Halls (New York: Routledge: 1990); Samuel Bradford Tabas, "After Nature: *Homo Oeconomicus* and the Aesopic Fable," Ph.D. diss., Department of Comparative Literature, New York University, September 2009.

3. Samuel Bowles and Herbert Gintis, "The Revenge of *Homo oeconomicus*: Contested Exchange and the Revival of Political Economy," unpublished paper, 1992; William Dixon and David Wilson, *A History of* Homo Economicus*: The Nature of the Moral in Economic Theory* (New York: Routledge, 2012); Laval, *L'homme économique*.

4. Marshall Sahlins, *Stone-Age Economics* (Chicago: Aldine Publishing, 1972); Karl Polanyi, *The Great Transformation* (Boston: Beacon, 2001); Alain Caille, "Anti-Utilitarianism, Economics and the Gift Paradigm, " *Revue du MAUSS* (Mouvement anti-utilitariste dans les sciences sociales), www.revuedumauss.com.fr/media/ACstake.pdf; Mauss, *The Gift*.

5. Max Weber, "Politics as a Vocation," in *From Max Weber: Essays in Sociology*, ed. and trans. H. H. Gerth and C. Wright Mills (New York: Routledge, 1948); Pierre Thuillier, *La grande implosion* (Paris: Fayard, 1995); Ario Klamer, "Late Modernism and the Loss of Character in Economics," in Stephen Cullenberg, Jack Armariglio, and David F. Ruccio (eds.), *Postmodernism, Economics, and Knowledge* (London: Routledge, 2001); Marshall Sahlins, "On the Culture of Material Value and the Cosmography of Riches," *HAU: Journal of Ethnographic Theory* 3.2 (2013), pp. 161–95; Laval, *L'homme économique*; Caille, "Anti-Utilitarianism, Economics and the Gift Paradigm."

6. Michel Foucault, *The Birth of Biopolitics: Lectures at the Collège de France, 1978–79*, ed. Michel Senellart, trans. Graham Burchell (New York: Picador, 2004), pp. 225–26.

7. *Ibid.*, p. 225.

8. *Ibid.*, p. 226.

9. See the journal *Cultural Economy*, where a great deal of this theorizing is taking place.

10. Timothy Mitchell, *Rule of Experts: Egypt, Techno-Politics, Modernity* (Berkeley: University of California Press, 2002), pp. 3–7. See also Mitchell's *Carbon Democracy* (London: Verso, 2011), pp. 123–26 for another variation on this argument.

11. *Ibid.*, p. 81.

12. Koray Çalışkan and Michel Callon. "Economization, Part 1: Shifting Attention from the Economy Towards Processes of Economization," *Economy and Society* 38.3 (August 2009), pp. 369–98. See p. 370 for a definition of the term. See also Michel Callon, "The Embeddedness of Economic Markets in Economics," in Michel Callon (ed.), *The Laws of the Markets* (Oxford: Blackwell, 1998), pp. 1–57, where Callon first uses the term.

13. Karl Marx, *The German Ideology*, in *The Marx-Engels Reader*, ed. Robert C. Tucker (New York: Norton, 1978).

14. David Ricardo, *The Works and Correspondence of David Ricardo* (London: Cambridge University Press, 1973).

15. Thomas Malthus, *An Essay on the Principle of Population,* ed. Geoffrey Gilbert. (New York: Oxford University Press, 1993).

16. John Maynard Keynes, *The General Theory of Employment, Interest and Money* (Kissimmee: Signalman, 1936).

17. Gary Becker, *Human Capital: A Theoretical and Empirical Analysis, with Special Reference to Education* (Chicago: University of Chicago Press, 1964).

18. Foucault, *The Birth of Biopolitics*, p. 278.

19. *Ibid.*, p. 276.

20. For responsibilization, see Pat O'Malley, s.v. "Responsibilization," in *The SAGE Dictionary of Policing*, ed. Alison Wakefield and Jenny Fleming (London: SAGE Publications Ltd., 2009), pp. 277–79; See also John Clarke, "Living With/in and Without Neo-Liberalism," *Focaal–European Journal of Anthropology* 51 (2008), pp. 135–47; and Ronen Shamir, "The Age of Responsi-bilization: On Market-Embedded Morality," *Economy and Society* 37.1 (2008), pp. 1–19.

21. Adam Smith, *The Wealth of Nations* (Chicago: University of Chicago Press, 1976), p. 477

22. Thus the persistent effort to fathom why working and middle-class voters can often be mobilized "against their interests" operates within an anachronistic paradigm of liberalism; such voters are behaving like good neo-liberal subjects. See Thomas Frank, *What's the Matter With Kansas?: How Conservatives Won the Heart of America* (New York: Holt, 2004).

23. Foucault, *The Birth of Biopolitics*, pp. 274 and 282.

24. *Homo juridicus*, Foucault says, differs from *homo oeconomicus* insofar as the latter has no sovereign and cannot be subject to sovereignty. Thus, the coexistence of sovereign and economic governance, of *homo oeconomicus* and *homo juridicus*, constitutes a fundamental problematic of liberalism, in Foucault's view. Foucault, *The Birth of Biopolitics*, pp. 292–93.

25. *Ibid.*, p. 282.

26. *Ibid.*, pp. 282–97.

27. *Ibid.*, p. 274.

28. Aristotle, *The Politics*, trans. Ernest Barker (Oxford: Clarendon, 1946) 1.7.9.

29. *Ibid.*, 1.2.13

30. *Ibid.*, 1.2.14

31. *Ibid.*, 1.8.15

32. *Ibid.*, 1.9.1

33. *Ibid.*, 1.9. Marx will articulate this distinction as being between use value and exchange value, even though, again, the same process or object might harbor both. See Karl Marx, "Capital," in *The Marx-Engels Reader*, volume 1, part 1, chapter 1.

34. *Ibid.*, 1.9.7

35. *Ibid.*, 1.10.4

36. *Ibid.*, 1.9.12–13

37. *Ibid.*, 1.9.15–17

38. *Ibid.*, 1.9,15–18

39. *Ibid.*, 1.9.14

40. Laval, *L'homme économique*; Hirschman, *The Passions and the Interests.*

41. C. B. MacPherson, *The Political Theory of Possessive Individualism: Hobbes to Locke* (Oxford: Oxford University Press, 1962), p. 3.

42. Smith, *The Wealth of Nations.*

43. Marx, *The German Ideology.*

44. In chapter 2 of the *Wealth of Nations*, Smith writes: "whether this propensity [to truck and barter] be one of those original principles in human nature of which no further account can be given; or whether, as seems more probable, it be the necessary consequence of the faculties of reason and speech, it belongs not to our present subject to inquire." (Note how this modifies the Aristotelian move—resting the putatively distinctive human qualities, reason and speech, at the base of our economic rather than our political nature.)

45. In this passage from *Theory of Moral Sentiments*, Smith's depiction of what we care about actually casts quite a wide net: "The administration of the great system of the universe...the care of the universal happiness of all rational and sensible beings, is the business of God and not of man. To man is allotted a much humbler department, but one much more suitable to the weakness of his powers, and to the narrowness of his comprehension: the care of his own happiness, of *that of his family, his friends, his country*...But though we are...endowed with a very strong desire of those ends, it has been entrusted to the slow and uncertain determinations of our reason to find out the proper means of bringing them about. Nature has directed us to the greater part of these by original and immediate instincts. Hunger, thirst, the passion which unites the two sexes, and the dread of pain, prompt us to apply those means for their own sakes, and without any consideration of their tendency to those beneficent ends which the great Director of nature intended to produce by them." Adam Smith, *Theory of Moral Sentiments* (Indianapolis: Liberty Classics, 1976), p. 378. Useful considerations of Smith's account of human nature include Samuel Fleischacker, *On Adam Smith's Wealth of Nations: A Philosophical Companion* (Princeton: Princeton Univ. Press, 2004) and Manfred J. Holler, "Adam Smith's Model of Man and Some of its Consequences," *Homo Oeconomicus* 23.3 (2006), pp. 467–88.

46. John Locke, *Two Treatises of Government*, in *Political Writings*, ed. David Wooston (New York: Penguin, 1993).

47. Foucault says that interest is what drives us into the social contract for Locke. But this reading eclipses the place of the laws of nature in the *Second Treatise*—both our desire to have them enacted and our frustration with trying to enact them ourselves. Lockean laws of nature are principles of natural justice, not simply principles of self-interest. Locke, *Two Treatises*, chapter 2, sections 6–13, pp. 270–74. "The State of Nature has a Law of Nature to govern it, which obliges every one . . . that being all equal and independent, no one ought to harm another in his Life, Health, Liberty or Possessions . . . . Every one as he is bound to preserve himself . . . ought he, as much as he can, to preserve the rest of Mankind" (p. 271).

48. Jean Jacques Rousseau, *The Social Contract*, trans. Maurice Cranston (New York, NY: Penguin, 1968).

49. Georg Wilhelm Friedrich Hegel, *The Philosophy of Right*, trans. T. M. Knox. (Oxford: Oxford University Press, 1952).

50. Karl Marx, "On The Jewish Question," in *The Marx-Engels Reader*.

51. Karl Marx, *The Eighteenth Brumaire of Louis Bonaparte*, in *The Marx-Engels Reader*.

52. Karl Marx, *Economic and Philosophic Manuscripts of 1844*" and Marx, "On The Jewish Question," in *The Marx-Engels Reader*.

53. Jeremy Bentham, "An Introduction to the Principles of Morals and Legislation," in *A Bentham Reader*, ed. Mary Peter Mack (New York: Pegasus, 1969).

54. "What then is the rightful limit to the sovereignty of the individual over himself? Where does the authority of society begin?" John Stuart Mill, "On Liberty," in *On Liberty and Other Writings*, ed. Stefan Collini (Cambridge: Cambridge University Press, 1989), p. 75.

55. John Stuart Mill, "On the Definition of Political Economy and on the Method of Investigation Proper to It," in *The Collected Works of John Stuart Mill*, vol. 4, *Essays on Economics and Society, Part II*, ed. John M. Robson (Toronto: University of Toronto Press, 1967), p. 321.

56. *Ibid.*, p. 322.

57. *Ibid.*

58. Sigmund Freud, *Civilization and Its Discontents*, trans. James Strachey (New York: Norton, 2010), p. 84.

59. Here would be the historical sketch compressed to a paragraph: At the dawn of what we have come to call "the West," the citizen was an overtly political being, participating in rule of the common through which he is also realized, perfected, and freed. During the long centuries of feudalism, this strenuous notion of citizenship faded as the authority of the church and monarchies came to the fore. From this dark night, the revolutions of modernity were born. Coterminous with (and partly inciting) these political revolutions was the emergence of a mode of production that bore heavily on political life—shaping its institutions, driving its contents, conditioning it languages—but that still did not fuse with it, let alone fully commandeer its terms or organize its principles. At this point, a figure of the citizen emerged who, on the one hand, formally shared in political sovereignty and, on the other hand, was relentlessly concerned with the citizen's own interests and well-being, finding its freedom in the pursuit of its own ends. Animated by desire, armed with rights, this figure ceded concern with shared political rule to its representatives and chased after its own satisfactions. This is the subject split between "citizen" and "bourgeois" that dogged liberal democratic theory for two centuries, that Marx makes the basis of his critique of the liberal state, and that the neoliberal form of *homo oeconomicus* will finally leave behind.

60. See Melinda Cooper's *Family Values: Between Neoliberalism and the New Social Conservatism* (New York: Zone, 2017).

61. See Jean Elshtain, *Public Man / Private Woman: Women in Social and Political Thought* (Princeton: Princeton University Press, 1993); Wendy Brown, *Manhood and Politics: A Feminist Reading in Political Theory* (Totowa, NJ: Rowman and Littlefield, 1988); Kathy Ferguson, *The Man Question: Visions of Subjectivity in Feminist Theory* (Berkeley: University of California Press: 1993); Linda Zerilli, *Signifying Woman: Culture and Chaos in Rousseau, Burke, and Mill* (Ithaca: Cornell University Press, 1994). Plato in *The Republic* could be

considered an interesting exception, except that Plato dispatches *homo politicus* as he establishes the rule of the republic by philosophy.

62. Joan Scott, *Only Paradoxes to Offer: French Feminists and the Rights of Man* (Cambridge, MA: Harvard University Press, 1997).

63. Milton Friedman, *Capitalism and Freedom* (Chicago: University of Chicago Press, 1962), p. 12.

64. *Ibid.,* p. 33.

65. Gary S. Becker, *A Treatise on the Family,* enlarged edition (Cambridge, MA: Harvard University Press, 1991), p. 78.

66. See Paula England, "Separative and Soluble Selves: Dichotomous Thinking in Economics," and Deirdre McCloskey, "The Demoralization of Economics: Can We Recover from Bentham and Return to Smith?" both in Martha Albertson Fineman and Terence Dougherty (eds.), *Feminism Confronts Homo Oeconomicus: Gender, Law, and Society* (Ithaca: Cornell University Press, 2005). See also Annette Baier, "What Do Women Want with a Moral Theory?," in Roger Crisp and Michael Slote (eds.), *Virtue Ethics* (Oxford: Oxford University Press, 1997), Carol M. Rose, "Property as Storytelling: Perspectives from Game Theory, Narrative Theory, Feminist Theory," *Yale Journal of Law and the Humanities* 2.1 (1990), pp. 37–57; Julie Nelson, "Feminism and Economics," *Journal of Economic Perspectives* 9.2 (Spring 1995), pp. 131–48, and Nelson, *Beyond Economic Man: Feminist Theory and Economics,* ed. Marianne A. Ferber and Julie Nelson (Chicago: University of Chicago Press, 1993).

67. McCloskey, "The Demoralization of Economics," pp. 28–29. Hobbes well understood the fundamental noncoherence of families made of wholly self-regarding humans, which is why he, unlike Thatcher and many modern economists, did not formulate families as a priori.

68. In addition to McCloskey, see Dixon and Wilson, *A History of Homo Oeconomicus* and Albert O. Hirschman, "Against Parsimony: Three Easy Ways of Complicating Some Categories of Economic Discourse, *Bulletin of the American Academy of Arts and Sciences* 37.8 (1984), pp. 11–28.

69. McCloskey, "The Demoralization of Economics," p. 30.

70. See England, "Separative and Soluble Selves" and McCloskey, "The

Demoralization of Economics." Joan Tronto's work on care spans two decades. The volume setting out the general parameters of the argument is *Moral Boundaries: A Political Argument for an Ethic of Care* (New York: Routledge, 1993).

71. See, for example, this argument by Becker: "The responsibility of married women for childcare and other housework has major implications for earnings and occupational differences between men and women, even aside from the effect on the labor force participation of married women. I submit that this is an important reason why the earnings of married women typically are considerably below those of married men, and why substantial occupational segregation persists." Becker, *A Treatise on the Family*, p. 78.

72. Some have argued that gender stratification is reduced by neoliberalism, insofar as it involves a shift from an economy based on private property economy to an economy based on human capital. Elizabeth Mayes, for example, thinks the decreasing importance of private property is positive for women, for Engels-like reasons: if women's subordination has been linked historically to their status as private property, women are now freed to be individuals rather than property. See Elizabeth Mayes, "Private Property, the Private Subject, and Women: Can Women Truly Be Owners of Capital?" in Fineman and Dougherty (eds.), *Feminism Confronts Homo Oeconomicus*.

73. See Sam Dillon, "Harvard Chief Defends His Talk on Women," *New York Times*, January 18, 2005, http://www.nytimes.com/2005/01/18/national/18harvard.html.

74. I live in a progressive city in 2014. Women constitute 90 percent of those providing support—driving, organizing, provisioning—for my son's high school sports team and music ensemble. Almost all of the women providing this support are college educated and work in the professions.

75. Abstractly free and autarkic, human capital is distinguished from other kinds by virtue of its subordination to its employer, its nondissolubility, and its enhancement by itself or another.

76. A definition s.v. "Human Capital" from Investopedia.com: "A measure of the economic value of an employee's skill set. This measure builds on the

basic production input of labor measure where all labor is thought to be equal. The concept of human capital recognizes that not all labor is equal and that the quality of employees can be improved by investing in them. The education, experience and abilities of an employee have an economic value for employers and for the economy as a whole." Investopedia, "Human Capital," http://www. investopedia.com/terms/h/humancapital.asp.

77. Clarke, "Living With/in and Without Neo-Liberalism," pp. 135–47.

78. Foucault, *The Birth of Biopolitics*, pp. 270–71.

CHAPTER FOUR: POLITICAL RATIONALITY AND GOVERNANCE

1. Mitchell Dean, *Critical and Effective Histories: Foucault's Methods and Historical Sociology* (New York: Routledge, 1994), p. 181.

2. *Ibid.*, p. 187.

3. William Callison, "A Genealogy of Political Rationality: Capitalist Governance and Power beyond Weber and Foucault," dissertation prospectus, University of California, Berkeley, 2013, p. 15.

4. Pierre Dardot and Christian Laval, *The New Way of the World: On Neo-liberal Society* (London: Verso, 2013), p. 3.

5. Michel Foucault, *The Birth of Biopolitics: Lectures at the Collège de France, 1978–79*, ed. Michel Senellart, trans. Graham Burchell (New York: Picador, 2004), pp. 83–91; Daniel Stedman Jones, *Masters of the Universe: Hayek, Friedman, and the Birth of Neoliberal Politics* (Princeton: Princeton University Press, 2013), chapters 3, 6, 7.

6. Max Weber, *Economy and Society: An Outline of Interpretive Sociology*, ed. Guenther Roth and Klaus Wittich, 2 vols. (New York: Bedminister Press, 1968), vol. 1 p. 24.

7. *Ibid.*, p. 26.

8. *Ibid.*

9. See, for example, *Ibid.*, vol. 2, pp. 809–15.

10. Max Weber, *The Protestant Ethic and the Spirit of Capitalism*, trans. Talcott Parsons (New York: Routledge, 1992), pp. 181—82. Weber, *The Vocation Lectures*, ed. David Owen and Tracy B. Strong (Indianapolis: Hackett, 2004).

11. Herbert Marcuse, *One-Dimensional Man: Studies in the Ideology of Advanced Industrial Society* (Boston: Beacon Press, 1964), pp. xvi and 1.

12. *Ibid.* see especially chapters 6–8.

13. Foucault, *The Birth of Biopolitics*, p. 94. Foucault defines liberalism as a governing rationality, rather than an ideology, recognizing the function of each while making an important distinction between them.

14. Foucault, *The Birth of Biopolitics*, pp. 269–70.

15. Here is a tiny sampling of this literature: Jan Kooiman (ed.), *Modern Governance* (London: Sage, 1993); Jon Pierre, *Debating Governance* (Oxford: Oxford University Press, 2000); R. A. W. Rhodes, *Understanding Governance: Policy Networks, Governance, Reflexivity and Accountability* (Buckingham: Open University Press, 1997) and Rhodes, "The New Governance: Governing without Government," *Political Studies* 44.4 (1996), pp. 652–67; Gerry Stoker, "Governance as Theory: Five Propositions," *International Social Science Journal* 50.155 (1998), pp. 187–95; Aseem Prakash and Jeffrey A. Hart (eds.), *Globalization and Governance* (London: Routledge, 1999); James Rosenau and Ernst-Otto Czempiel (eds.), *Governance without Government: Order and Change in World Politics* (Cambridge: Cambridge University Press, 1992); Simon Hix, "The Study of the European Union II: The 'New Governance' Agenda and its Rivals," *Journal of European Public Policy* 5.1 (1998), pp. 38–65; Markus Jachtenfuchs, "The Governance Approach to European Integration," *Journal of Common Market Studies* 39.2 (2001), pp. 245–64; and Gary Marks, Fritz W. Scharpf, Philippe Schmitter, and Wolfgang Streeck, *Governance in the European Union* (London: Sage, 1996).

16. Rhodes, *Understanding Governance*, p. 47.

17. *Ibid.*, especially chapter 3.

18. Philippe Ryfman "Governance and Policies in Nongovernmental Organizations" in Michel Feher (ed.), *Nongovernmental Politics* (New York: Zone, 2007), p. 289.

19. Rhodes, *Understanding Governance*, pp. 48–49.

20. Grammarist.com, s.v. "Governance vs. Government," http://grammarist.com/usage/governance.

21. Thomas Lemke, "An Indigestible Meal?: Foucault, Governmentality and State Theory," *Distinktion: Scandinavian Journal of Social Theory* 8.2(2007), pp. 43–64.

22. United Nations Economic and Social Commission for Asia and the Pacific, "What is Good Governance?," http://www.unescap.org/sites/default/files/good-governance.pdf.

23. *Ibid.*

24. William Walters, "Some Critical Notes on 'Governance,'" *Studies in Political Economy* 73 (Spring–Summer 2004), pp. 29–30 and 32.

25. Elizabeth Meehan, "From Government to Governance, Civic Participation and 'New Politics': The Context of Potential Opportunities for the Better Representation of Women," Center for Advancement of Women in Politics, School of Politics and International Studies, Queen's University, Belfast, Occasional Paper no. 5 (October 2003), p. 3.

26. *Ibid.*, p. 2.

27. Lester M. Salamon, "The New Governance and the Tools of Public Action: An Introduction," *Fordham Urban Law Journal* 28.5 (2000), p. 1624.

28. *Ibid.*, p. 1633.

29. *Ibid.*, p. 1636.

30. *Ibid.*, p. 1634.

31. *Ibid.*, p. 1636.

32. Meehan, "From Government to Governance," p. 3.

33. Niccolò Machiavelli, *Discourses on the First Decade of Titus Livius*, in *Machiavelli: The Chief Works and Others*, trans. Allan Gilbert (Durham: Duke University Press, 1965), book 1, chapter 4, pp. 202–204.

34. Meehan, "From Government to Governance," p. 7.

35. United Nations Economic and Social Commission for Asia and the Pacific, "What is Good Governance?"

36. Walters, "Some Critical Notes on 'Governance,'" p. 34.

37. Michel Foucault, "Omnes et Singulatim: Toward a Critique of Political Reason," in *Power*, ed. James D. Faubion, trans. Robert Hurley, vol. 3 of *The Essential Works of Foucault* (New York: New Press, 2000).

38. Walters, "Some Critical Notes on 'Governance,'" p. 36.

39. *Ibid.*, p. 43.

40. Joe Soss, Richard C. Fording, and Sanford F. Schram, "The Color of Devolution: Race, Federalism, and the Politics of Social Control," *American Journal of Political Science* 52.3 (2008), p. 1.

41. Ronen Shamir, "The Age of Responsibilization: On Market-Embedded Morality," *Economy and Society* 37.1 (February 2008), p. 1.

42. *Ibid.*, p. 4.

43. Recently, my university used this language to discuss the handling of political demonstrations and occupations as it attempts to fold all segments of the university into consensus about policing them. Here is an example from a university-wide invitation from then president Mark Yudof to a forum on this subject: "On behalf of the UC Office of the President, you are invited to attend an Open Forum entitled 'How Would You Respond to the Next Occupy?' The UC General Counsel and the Dean of the UC Berkeley School of Law invite students and faculty to share their opinions and experiences on: Best Practices for pre-event planning, such as event observers and pre-event coordination; Best Practices during events, including such as mutual aid and the role of campus administrators and faculty; Best post-event practices, including such issues as civilian review; Educating police, students, faculty administrators regarding policies and Best Practices." "Invitation to UCOP Town Hall, 1/31, 4 PM: How Would you Respond to the Next Occupy?" From "Claire Holmes, Associate Vice Chancellor- Public Affairs (campus-wide)," 1/27/2012. This best-practices-saturated invitation was issued by the vice chancellor for public affairs and communications, a fact that is noteworthy because of the neoliberal governance aim to generate consensus or "buy-in." Thus, the university's legal counsel, the president's right-hand man, and the lead public relations administrator invite all "stakeholders"—police, protestors, staff, administrators, students, and faculty—to develop best practices for policing demonstrations that are protesting the privatization of the public university. If this were not irony enough, the prompt for the invitation was an episode at the Berkeley campus in which police beat, clubbed, dragged, and charged with felony trespass a small group of peaceful

protestors assembled in an outdoor university space, a reaction so violent and out of proportion that it provoked solidarity round the world and nearly brought down the UC Berkeley chancellor, Robert Birgeneau. The formally apolitical nature of the best practices that the forum aimed to develop brackets the politics of such events, police responses to them, and the disparate power and positions of the various actors. Instead, it attempts to knit all stakeholders into consensus about how demonstrations ought to be planned, observed, conducted, monitored by administrators and faculty, and policed.

44. Philip Mirowski, *Never Let a Serious Crisis Go to Waste: How Neoliberalism Survived the Financial Meltdown* (London: Verso, 2013), p. 112.

45. "H.R.3172—BEST Practices Act," Congress.gov, http://beta.congress.gov/bill/113th-congress/house-bill/3172.

46. Selected Independent Funeral Homes. "The Best Practices Competition," http://www.selectedfuneralhomes.org/Best-Practices-Competition-437.

47. Julia Elyachar, "Best Practices: Research, Finance, and NGOs in Cairo," *American Ethnologist* 33.3 (August 2006), pp. 413–26.

48. Robert C. Camp, *Benchmarking: The Search for Industry Best Practices that Lead to Superior Performance* (Milwaukee: Quality Press, 1989), pp. 6–7; Juhani Kulmala, "Approaches to Benchmarking," a white paper for the Finnish Employers' Management Development Institute, pp. 2–3, available at http://www15.uta.fi/yksikot/entrenet/hankerekisteri/hanke5_benchmarking.htm.

49. Benchmarking, Robert Camp argues, has two parts: practices and metrics. "Practices are defined as the methods that are used; metrics are the quantified effect of installing the practices." Camp, *Benchmarking*, p. 4. Camp is very clear that the investigation of practices should come first and that the metrics quantifying their effect should come later (*ibid.*, pp. 4–5). However, it is noteworthy that leading with the metrics in order to produce the practices has become an important governance tool. The British REF (Research Excellence Framework) is but one example; almost all the efforts at assessing teaching and educational outcomes in U.S. K–12 education has the purpose of altering pedagogical and curricular practices.

50. *Ibid.*, p. xii.

51. *Ibid.*, p. xi.

52. *Ibid.*, p. 3.

53. Patricia Keehley and Neil N. Abercrombie, *Benchmarking in the Public and Nonprofit Sectors: Best Practices for Achieving Performance Breakthroughs* (San Francisco: Jossey-Bass, 2008), p. 24.

54. *Ibid.*, pp. 21–22.

55. Kulmala, "Approaches to Benchmarking," p. 12.

56. Investopedia, s.v. "Best Practices," www.investopedia.com/terms/b/best_practices.asp.

57. Best-Practice.com, "The Best Practice Network—Definition of a Best Practice," www.best-practice.com/definition-of-best-practice.

58. The Bremer Orders, including the preamble and purpose, are available at http://www.iraqcoalition.org/regulations.

59. William Engdahl, "Iraq and Washington's 'Seeds of Democracy,'" *Current Concerns* no. 5 (2005), http://www.currentconcerns.ch/archive/2005/05/20050507.php.

60. Bremer Orders, http://www.iraqcoalition.org/regulations.

61. Engdahl, "Iraq and Washington's 'Seeds of Democracy.'"

62. The full text of Coalitional Provisional Authority Order Number 81, "Patent, Industrial Design, Undisclosed Information, Integrated Circuits and Plant Variety Law," is available at http://www.bibliotecapleyades.net/ciencia/ciencia_geneticfood18a.htm.

63. See *The World According to Monsanto*, a documentary film directed by Marie-Monique Robin, France, Image et Compagnie, 2008.

64. Jeremy Smith, "Order 81: Re-engineering Iraqi Agriculture," *Global Research*, August 27, 2005, available at http://www.globalresearch.ca/order-81-re-engineering-iraqi-agriculture/870.

65. *Ibid.*; Engdahl, "Iraq and Washington's 'Seeds of Democracy.'"

66. Engdahl, "Iraq and Washington's 'Seeds of Democracy,'" p. 3.

67. Smith, "Order 81: Re-engineering Iraqi Agriculture," p. 2.

68. Engdahl, "Iraq and Washington's 'Seeds of Democracy'"; Smith, "Order 81: Re-engineering Iraqi Agriculture"; Nancy Scola, "Why Iraqi Farmers Might

Prefer Death to Paul Bremer's Order 81," Alternet, September 19, 2007, http://www.alternet.org/story/62273/why_iraqi_farmers_might_prefer_death_to_paul_bremer%27s_order_81.

69. Smith, "Order 81: Re-engineering Iraqi Agriculture," *ibid.*; Engdahl, "Iraq and Washington's 'Seeds of Democracy,'" pp. 3–4.

70. Engdahl, "Iraq and Washington's 'Seeds of Democracy,'" p. 4.

71. Scola, "Why Iraqi Farmers Might Prefer Death to Paul Bremer's Order 81." See also Vandana Shiva, *Biopiracy: The Plunder of Nature and Knowledge* (Boston: South End Press, 1999).

72. Scola, "Why Iraqi Farmers Might Prefer Death to Paul Bremer's Order 81," p. 2.

73. *Ibid.*, p. 5.

74. Coalitional Provisional Authority Order Number 81.

75. Nancy Scola, "Why Iraqi Farmers Might Prefer Death to Paul Bremer's Order 81," p. 1.

76. "Victorious capitalism, since it rests on mechanical foundations, needs [the support of Protestant asceticism] no longer." Weber, *The Protestant Ethic and the Spirit of Capitalism*, pp. 181–82.

77. This created problems for the process of ratifying the constitution because of an initial proposal to exclude from the process all political parties that opposed the occupation.

78. If states also face challenges and tasks other than this goal, such as mollifying the people or securing the nation from danger, that, too, can be dealt with by executive fiat: hence Order 2, which abolished the Iraqi Army.

79. The erasure of the distinction between the form and the content of government and business by neoliberal governance is important. However, so are its effects in conjoining business and research. Since neoliberal governance is legitimated by its effectiveness in promulgating efficient means to ends, rather than, say, by its upholding of the principles of justice or of provisioning for its members, it has a distinctive relationship to knowledge. Good governance promotes economic growth, a good investment climate, and a high credit rating and requires the knowledge necessary to do this. Bad governance does

not. Thus, the contouring of all knowledge to economic usefulness (evident in steadily accelerating moves to support academic research with high "impact factors" and to starve or eliminate research that does not have commercial impact) and of all government to economic health are two faces of the same phenomenon. Best practices express the convergence. Again, agribusiness financing of Texas A&M University research, and Texas A&M development of demonstration plots for genetically modified seed in India, and USAID staff joining with World Wide Wheat Company sales and distribution representatives in Iraq— all of these are just the surface empirics. They represent a much deeper reconfiguration in and by neoliberal governance of what were formerly important moats and intervals, however modest, however routinely breached, between the domains and undertakings of business, scholarship, and government.

CHAPTER FIVE: LAW AND LEGAL REASON

1. Michel Foucault, *The Birth of Biopolitics: Lectures at the Collège de France, 1978–79*, ed. Michel Senellart. Trans. Graham Burchell (New York: Picador, 2004), p. 163; Terry Flew, "Michel Foucault's *The Birth of Biopolitics* and Contemporary Neo-liberalism Debates," *Thesis Eleven* 108.1 (2012), p. 60.

2. Jack Jackson notes that this is not an even or consistent process. Obamacare, he argues, was a significant challenge to neoliberalization. Jack Jackson, "Not Yet an End: Neoliberalism and the Jurisprudence of Obamacare," unpublished paper presented at the 2013 Annual Meeting of the American Political Science Association. Certainly, Jackson has a point, but the neoliberal form of Obamacare as a national health plan can be lost on no one. There is also a question of whether it will survive.

3. Citizens United v. Federal Election Commission, 130 S. Ct. 876, 558 U.S. 310, 175 L. Ed. 2d 753 (2010).

4. AT&T Mobility LLC v. Concepcion, 130 S. Ct. 3322, 176 L. Ed. 2d 1218 (2010).

5. Brian Fitzpatrick, quoted in Adam Liptak, "Supreme Court Allows Contracts That Prohibit Class-Action Arbitration," *New York Times*, April 28, 2011, p. B3, www.nytimes.com/2011/04/28/business/28bizcourt.html. See for

example, David Segal, "A Rising Tide Against Class-Action Suits," *New York Times*, May 5, 2012, http://www.nytimes.com/2012/05/06/your-money/class-actions-face-hurdle-in-2011-supreme-court-ruling.html. See also the Public Citizen report on the effects of the decision, Public Citizen & National Association of Consumer Advocates, "Justice Denied. One Year Later: The Harms to Consumers from the Supreme Court's Concepcion Decision Are Plainly Evident,"availableathttp://www.citizen.org/documents/concepcion-anniversary-justice-denied-report.pdf.

6. State ex rel. Ozanne v. Fitzgerald, 798 N.W.2d 436, 2011 W.I. 43, 334 Wis. 2d 70 (2011).

7. The Associated Press, "Wisconsin: Governor Wins a Round in Fight Over Union Bargaining Rights," *New York Times*, January 18, 2013, p. A12, http://www.nytimes.com/2013/01/19/us/wisconsin-governor-wins-a-round-in-fight-over-union-bargaining-rights.html; Reuters, "Wisconsin: Union Curbs Are Upheld," *New York Times*, September 11, 2013, p. A21, http://www.nytimes.com/2013/09/12/us/wisconsin-union-curbs-are-upheld.html.

8. Wal-Mart Stores, Inc. v. Dukes, 131 S. Ct. 2541, 564 U.S., 180 L. Ed. 2d 374 (2011).

9. "[I]t isn't that I set out on economic policies; it's that I set out really to change the approach, and changing the economics is the means of changing that approach. If you change the approach you really are after the heart and soul of the nation. Economics are the method; the object is to change the heart and soul." Quoted in Ronald Butt, "Mrs. Thatcher: The First Two Years," *Sunday Times*, May 3, 1981, http://www.margaretthatcher.org/document/104475.

10. See, for example, Timothy K. Kuhner, "*Citizens United* as Neoliberal Jurisprudence: The Resurgence of Economic Theory," *Virginia Journal of Social Policy and the Law*, 18:3 (2011).

11. *Ibid.*, pp. 460 and 468.

12. *Ibid.*, pp. 448 and 460.

13. Kuhner writes, "January 21, 2010, stands as the day that the Roberts Court solidified its commitment to defining democracy on the basis of a controversial form of economic theory." And, "Two things stand out in the majority

opinion: first, it espouses a dogmatic free market form of economic theory; and second, it is printed on the pages of a judicial opinion that authoritatively defines the terms of the First Amendment. This combination of capitalist ideology and case law makes up what I call *neoliberal jurisprudence*, the use of neoclassical economic theory as judicial reasoning." *Ibid.*, pp. 396 and 397.

14. Citizens United v. FEC, 558 U.S. (2010), p. 314.

15. *Ibid.*, p. 327, citing WRTL, 551 U.S. at 469, citing New York Times Co. v. Sullivan, 376 U.S. 254, 269070 (1964).

16. *Ibid.*, p. 329, citing Federal Election Commission v. Wisconsin Right to Life, Inc.

17. *Ibid.*, p. 334.

18. *Ibid.*, p. 335.

19. *Ibid.*, pp. 312 and 339.

20. Following one lengthy account of all the record keeping, accounting, and reporting that PACs must do "just to speak," Kennedy concludes that "given the onerous restrictions, a corporation may not be able to establish a PAC in time to make its views known" in an election. Such a "ban on speech," he continues, injures not only the would-be speaker, but the public, insofar as it "necessarily reduces the quantity of expression by restricting the number of issues discussed, the depth of their exploration, and the size of the audience reached." *Ibid.*, p. 339, quoting Buckley v. Valeo.

21. No one has offered a better set of discussions about the problematic of the marketplace metaphor in interpreting and adjudicating twentieth-century First Amendment cases than Steven Shiffrin. In a series of articles and books, as well as in his casebook, Shiffrin decisively cuts asserted connections between an imagined marketplace of ideas and truth, fairness, dissent, deliberation, or even genuine choice. See, for example, *The First Amendment, Democracy, and Romance* (Princeton: Princeton University Press, 1990) where he argues: "A . . . commitment to sponsoring dissent does not require a belief that what emerges in the 'market' is usually right or that the 'market' is the best test of truth. Quite the contrary, the commitment to sponsor dissent assumes that societal pressures to conform are strong and that incentives to keep quiet are

often great. If the marketplace metaphor encourages the view than an invisible hand or voluntaristic arrangements have guided us patiently, but slowly, to Burkean harmony, the commitment to sponsoring dissent encourages us to believe that the cozy arrangements of the status quo have settled on something less than the true or the just. If the marketplace metaphor encourages the view that conventions, habits, and traditions have emerged as our best sense of the truth from the rigorous testing ground of the marketplace of ideas, the commitment to sponsoring dissent encourages the view that conventions, habits, and traditions are compromises open to challenge. If the marketplace metaphor counsels us that the market's version of truth is more worthy of trust than any that the government might dictate, a commitment to sponsoring dissent counsels us to be suspicious of both. If the marketplace metaphor encourages a sloppy form of relativism (whatever has emerged in the marketplace is right for now), the commitment to sponsoring dissent emphasizes that truth is not decided in public opinion polls." Cited in Steven Shiffrin and Jesse Choper, *First Amendment: Cases, Comments, Questions*, 3rd ed. (Saint Paul, MN: West Academic Publishing, 2001), pp. 15–16. See also, Steven Shiffrin, *The First Amendment and Economic Regulation: Away From a General Theory of the First Amendment, Northwestern University Law Review* 78.5 (1983).

22. Citizens United v. FEC, 558 U.S. (2010), p. 339.

23. *Ibid.*, p. 364.

24. *Ibid.*, pp. 349–50.

25. *Ibid.*, p. 356.

26. *Ibid.*, p. 354.

27. *Ibid.*, p. 364.

28. *Ibid.*, pp. 339–40, 349–50, 353, 356.

29. *Ibid.*, 339.

30. *Ibid.*, p. 353.

31. *Ibid.*, p. 356.

32. *Ibid.*, pp. 356, 354, 355

33. *Ibid.*, 354.

34. *Ibid.*, pp. 313 and 369.

35. *Ibid.*, p. 313.

36. *Ibid.*

37. *Ibid.*, pp. 339–40.

38. *Ibid.*, p. 354, citing Austin, 494 US 660.

39. *Ibid.*, p. 354.

40. *Ibid.*, 340.

41. *Ibid.*, pp. 340–41.

42. *Ibid.*, p. 336.

43. *Ibid.*, pp. 469–71.

44. *Ibid.*, p. 472.

45. *Ibid.*, p. 441.

46. *Ibid.*, p. 446.

47. *Ibid.*, p. 446.

48. *Ibid.*, p. 364.

49. *Ibid.*, p. 359.

50. *Ibid.* There is plenty of evidence that neoliberalization has brought with it tremendous growth in this kind of overt corruption in liberal democracies, accompanied by decreased penalties for it. See Perry Anderson's brilliant and chilling "The Italian Disaster" in *The London Review of Books* 36.10–22 (May 2014), pp. 3–16, available at http://www.lrb.co.uk/v36/n10/perry-anderson/the-italian-disaster.

51. Niccolò Machiavelli, *The Prince* (Cambridge: Cambridge University Press, 1988), Jean-Jacques Rousseau, *The Social Contract and Other Late Political Writings* (Cambridge: Cambridge University Press, 1997).

52. See Eric Lipton and Ben Protess, "Banks' Lobbyists Help in Drafting Bills on Finance," *New York Times*, May 24, 2013, p. A1, http://dealbook.nytimes.com/2013/05/23/banks-lobbyists-help-in-drafting-financial-bills; "Wall St. Lobbyists and Financial Regulation," *New York Times*, October 28, 2013, at http://www.nytimes.com/interactive/2013/10/29/business/dealbook/29lobbyists-documents.html; and Ailsa Chang, "When Lobbyists Literally Write the Bill," National Public Radio, November 11, 2013, http://www.npr.org/blogs/itsallpolitics/2013/11/11/243973620/when-lobbyists-literally-write-the-bill.

53. Citizens United v. FEC, 558 U.S. (2010), p. 355.

54. McConnell, 540 U.S., at 297 (opinion of Kennedy, J.), cited in *ibid.*, p. 359.

55. *Ibid.*, p. 360.

56. United States v. Automobile Workers, 352 U.S. 593, 597, dissenting opinion of Douglas, J. joined by Warren, C. J. and Black, J., cited in Citizens United, p. 344.

57. *Ibid.*

CHAPTER SIX: EDUCATING HUMAN CAPITAL

1. See Frank Donoghue, *The Last Professors: The Corporate University and the Fate of the Humanities* (New York: Fordham University Press, 2008); Christopher Newfield, *Unmaking the Public University: The Forty-Year Assault on the Middle Class* (Cambridge, MA: Harvard University Press, 2008); The journal *Reclamations*; "The Humanities and the Crisis of The Public University," ed. Colleeen Lye, Christopher Newfield, and James Vernon, *Representations* 116.1 (2011); Henry A. Giroux, "Neoliberalism, Corporate Culture, and the Promise of Higher Education: The University as a Democratic Public Sphere," *Harvard Educational Review* 72.4 (2002), pp. 186–94; Bill Readings, *The University in Ruins* (Cambridge, MA: Harvard University Press, 1997); Jane Kelsey, "Privatizing the Universities," *Journal of Law and Society* 25.1 (1998), pp. 51–70; Matthew Fitzsimons, "Managerialism and the University," *New Zealand Journal of Tertiary Education Policy* 1.1 (2004), pp. 1–3; Suzanne Mettler, *Degrees of Inequality: How Higher Education Politics Sabotaged the American Dream* (New York: Basic Books, 2014); Roger Brown and Helen Carasso, *Everything for Sale?: The Marketisation of UK Higher Education* (London: Routledge, 2013); Andrew McGettigan, *The Great University Gamble: Money, Markets and the Future of Higher Education* (London: Pluto, 2013); Jordan Weissman, "The 38 States That Have Slashed Higher Education Spending," *Atlantic*, January 23, 2013, http://www.theatlantic.com/business/archive/2013/01/the-38-states-that-have-slashed-higher-education-spending/267427/ .

2. For an outline of President Obama's proposal, see "FACT SHEET on the

President's Plan to Make College More Affordable: A Better Bargain for the Middle Class," http://www.whitehouse.gov/the-press-office/2013/08/22/fact-sheet-president-s-plan-make-college-more-affordable-better-bargain-.

3. In making this point, Rousseau says, "In truth, laws are always useful to those with possessions and harmful to those who have nothing; from which it follows that the social state is advantageous to men only when all possess something and none has too much." Rousseau does not intend "that degrees of power and wealth should be absolutely the same for all." However, "where wealth is concerned . . . no citizen shall be rich enough to buy another and none so poor as to be forced to sell himself." Jean-Jacques Rousseau, *The Social Contract*, ed. and trans. Maurice Cranston (New York: Penguin, 1968), pp. 68n and 96.

4. After decades of shrinking income and wealth inequality in the postwar period, inequality has risen steadily since the early 1980s. The vast preponderance of economic growth since that time has benefitted the richest Americans: in the most recent decade, 65 percent of all income growth went to the top 1 percent of the population, while the median income of nonelderly households fell, and the share of Americans living in poverty rose. See Jacob S. Hacker and Paul Pierson, *Winner-Take-All Politics* (New York: Simon and Schuster, 2011), pp. 21, 24, 28. See also Joseph E. Stiglitz, *The Price of Inequality: How Today's Divided Society Endangers Our Future* (New York: Norton, 2013); Robert Reich, *Aftershock: The Next Economy and America's Future* (New York: Vintage, 2011); and Reich, *Inequality for All*, dir. Jacob Kornbluth, 72 Productions, 2013, the documentary in which Robert Reich explains growing inequality in a neoliberal economy without ever saying the word "neoliberalism." But income and wealth disparities are only a fraction of the story. At the same time, housing and health care costs skyrocketed, welfare provisions eroded, and access to equal opportunity embodied in public institutions—affordable high-quality education, for example—shrunk dramatically. Middle-class and working-class Americans became supersaturated in debt, employer-sponsored pensions shrank or vanished, union-secured jobs and benefits moved offshore. On the other side, an unprecedented plutocracy, comprising both the well off and the

superrich, emerged to dominate politics in new ways through the organization and manipulation of finance capital. None of this is news, but what is too rarely considered is the effect of such extreme and growing inequality on the principles and practices of democracy.

5. Alexis de Tocqueville, *Democracy in America*, ed. and trans. Harvey C. Mansfield and Delba Winthrop (Chicago: University of Chicago Press, 2000), pp. 662–64.

6. This point has been made by many others, among the most thoughtful of whom is Newfield in *Unmaking the Public University*. Traces of this ideal and practice persist in the structure of public secondary school curriculums and university baccalaureate requirements, where all students are expected to learn subjects—from higher mathematics, to great literature, to ancient histories— that they are unlikely to "use" in their jobs. It is a matter of little time before such expectations are queried and found spurious, irrelevant to the project of training human capital and allocating it efficiently. The high school in my markedly progressive city is not alone in contemplating the reintroduction of a vocational education track; the track would replace upper-level letters and sciences with "technology" courses, becoming the twenty-first-century version of what were formerly called "shop courses."

7. See, for example, Mark Taylor, "Academic Bankruptcy," *New York Times*, August 14, 2010, p. wk10, http://www.nytimes.com/2010/08/15/opinion/ 15taylor.html. In 2009, an op-ed piece by Taylor titled "End the University as We Know It" argued for that outcome, since, he claimed, "each academic becomes the trustee not of a branch of the sciences, but of limited knowledge that all too often is irrelevant for genuinely important problems." *New York Times*, April 27, 2009, p. a23, http://www.nytimes.com/2009/04/27/opinion/ 27taylor.html.

8. Donoghue, *The Last Professors*.

9. This competition is made palpable by hard sells on the part of public and for-profit universities to military veterans and other federally funded students.

10. See presentations made by Robert Meister, former president of The Council of UC Faculty Associations, on the University of California's use of

tuition as collateral for construction bonds. "They Pledged Your Tuition Index," http://cucfa.org/news/tuition_bonds.php.

11. See John Guillory, *Cultural Capital: The Problem of Literary Canon Formation* (Chicago: University of Chicago Press, 1993).

12. Stefan Collini, "Impact on Humanities: Researchers Must Take a Stand Now or Be Judged and Rewarded as Salesmen," *Times Literary Supplement*, November 13, 2009, http://firgoa.usc.es/drupal/node/44651; and Colleen Flaherty, "New Threat to Shared Governance," *Inside Higher Ed*, September 9, 2013, http://www.insidehighered.com/news/2013/09/09/wisconsin-faculty-object-idea-shared-governance-should-change.

13. In December 2013, the regents of the University of Kansas waged a direct assault on academic freedom, allowing the "CEO" of a state university to "suspend, dismiss or terminate from employment any faculty or staff member who makes improper use of social media." "Improper use" includes speech that "interferes with the regular operation of the university, or otherwise adversely affects the university's ability to efficiently provide services," or "is contrary to the best interests of the University." The justification of such radical curtailment of academic freedom was to protect transactions and relations between the university and state legislators. See William K. Black, "The Kansas Regents (Casually) End Academic Freedom," *New Economic Perspectives*, December 19, 2013, http://neweconomicperspectives.org/2013/12/kansas-regents-casually-end-academic-freedom.html; and Julene Miller, "Summary and Staff Recommendation," December 18–19, 2013, http://worldonline.media.clients.ellingtoncms.com/news/documents/2013/12/18/discussion_agenda_socialmediapolicy.pdf.

14. A number of scholars have addressed this issue in recent years, though each makes a somewhat different argument from the one presented here. See, for example, Martha Nussbaum, *Not for Profit: Why Democracy Needs the Humanities* (Princeton: Princeton University Press, 2010); Jonathan R. Cole, *The Great American University: Its Rise to Preeminence, Its Indispensable National Role, Why It Must Be Protected* (New York: Public Affairs Press, 2009); Sheila Slaughter and Gary Rhoades, *Academic Capitalism and the New Economy:*

Markets, State, and Higher Education (Baltimore: Johns Hopkins University Press, 2004); Derek Bok, *Universities in the Marketplace: The Commercialization of Higher Education* (Princeton: Princeton University Press, 2003); Newfield, *Unmaking the Public University,* chapter 3; and Geoffrey Harpham, "From Eternity to Here: Shrinkage in American Thinking about Higher Education," *Representations,* 116.1 (2011), pp. 42–61.

15. Raymond Williams, *Keywords: A Vocabulary of Culture and Society,* rev. ed. (New York: Oxford University Press, 1985), p. 179.

16. *Ibid.*

17. See Harpham, "From Eternity to Here."

18. To grasp the increase in provisioning a liberal arts education over the course of the second half of the twentieth century, consider just the University of California system. In 1940, there were only two campuses (Berkeley and Los Angeles), together enrolling fewer than twenty thousand students. By 1960, there were six campuses (Santa Barbara, Davis, Riverside, and San Francisco had been added) enrolling more than fifty thousand students. By 1980, with the addition of the Santa Cruz, Irvine, and San Diego campuses and expansion of the others, enrollment was one hundred and forty thousand. Today, ten campuses enroll more than two hundred and twenty thousand students. University of California History Digital Archives, "A Brief Historical Tour," http://sunsite.berkeley.edu/uchistory/general_history/overview/tour2.html; and University of California Office of the President, "Statistical Summary and Data on UC Students, Faculty and Staff," http://legacy-its.ucop.edu/uwnews/stat.

19. The Transfer Center at Santa Barbara City College estimated in February 2008 that the average annual income of parents of freshmen entering the California State University system is $40,000 and the average annual income of parents of freshmen entering the UC system is $80,000; Santa Barbara City College Transfer Center, "UC and CSU Comparison Chart," http://www.sbcc.edu/transfercenter/files/UC_CSU_Comparison_Chart.pdf; and The California State University, "Analytic Studies," http://www.calstate.edu/as. The University of California Annual Accountability Report indicates

that over the past decade, there has been increased enrollment by students from lower-income families (under $50,000) and upper-income families (more than $149,000), while there has been more than a 10 percent drop in enrollees from middle-income families ($50,000 to $149,000), with the greatest proportion of that drop coming from students of families earning between $100,000 and $150,000. "Income Profile," University of California Accountability Report, 2013, http://accountability.universityofcalifornia.edu/index/3.5.2.

20. Chris Newfield describes this ideal as pertaining to "the numerical majority of the population whose contact with college was interwoven with the mainstream and politically powerful ideal that this majority was to have interesting work, economic security, and the ability to lead satisfying and insightful lives in which personal and collective social development advanced side by side." Newfield, *Unmaking the Public University*, p. 3.

21. Consider Adam Smith's concern with cultivating what he termed "the moral sentiments," Tocqueville's notion of "self-interest, properly understood" as the antidote to a capitalist ethic run amok, and John Stuart Mill's insistence that individual liberty requires cultivation by education and mores if it is not to reduce to individual debauchery and civil ruin.

22. Quoted in Ansel Adams and Nancy Newhall, *Fiat Lux: The University of California* (New York: McGraw-Hill 1967), p. 192.

23. See, for example, Verlyn Klinkenborg, "The Decline and Fall of the English Major," op-ed, *New York Times*, June 23, 2013, http://www.nytimes.com/2013/06/23/opinion/sunday/the-decline-and-fall-of-the-english-major.html; and David Brooks, "The Humanist Vocation," op-ed *New York Times*, June 21, 2013, http://www.nytimes.com/2013/06/21/opinion/brooks-the-humanist-vocation.html.

24. Newfield, *Unmaking the Public University*, pp. 191, 193, 273.

25. See Plato, *Crito*, in *Euthyphro, Apology, Crito*, trans. F. J. Church (New York, 1956).

26. See Aristotle, *Politics*, trans. E. Barker (Oxford: Oxford University Press, 1946), book 1.

27. Unsurprisingly, including those who were previously excluded from a liberal arts education soon generated tremendous new pressures on both the style and the content of that education, pressures that eventuated in women's studies, ethnic studies, and a welter of disciplinary and pedagogical critiques.

28. Rebecca Reisner, "Who Needs a Higher Education," *Businessweek*, June 1, 2009, http://images.businessweek.com/ss/09/05/0522_no_college_ceos/ index.htm; Denise-Marie Balona, "Who Needs College?: Many Students Skip Higher Education for Jobs, Military," *Orlando Sentinel*, June 30, 2010, http:// articles.orlandosentinel.com/2010-06-30/news/os-students-skip-college-062810-20100630_1_college-trade-school-skipping; Jacob Lund Fisker, "Who Needs a College Degree Anyway," *Early Retirement Extreme* (blog), May 19, 2014, earlyretirementextreme.com/who-needs-a-college-degree-anywa.html; Dale J. Stevens, "Do You Really Have to Go to College?" *New York Times*, March 7, 2013, http://thechoice.blogs.nytimes.com/2013/03/07/do-you-really-have-to-go-to-college; Sarah Kavanagh, Katherine Schulten, and Daniel E. Slotnik, "When College May Not Be Worth the Cost: Examining Student Loan Debt," *New York Times*, May 15, 2012, http://learning.blogs.nytimes.com/2012/05/15/ when-college-may-not-be-worth-the-cost-examining-student-loan-debt; William Cohan, "Degrees of Influence," *New York Times*, March 16, 2011, http://opinionator.blogs.nytimes.com/2011/03/16/degrees-of-influence.

29. Consider Rick Santorum's comments that universities are "undermining the very principles of our country every single day by indoctrinating kids with left-wing ideology." Felicia Sonmez, "Santorum: Obama Is 'a Snob' Because He Wants 'Everybody in America to Go to College,'" *Washington Post*, February 5, 2012, http://www.washingtonpost.com/blogs/post-politics/post/ santorum-obama-is-a-snob-because-he-wants-everybody-in-america-to-go-to-college/2012/02/25/gIQATJffaR_blog.html; Peter Wood, "Rick Santorum Is Right," *Chronicle of Higher Education*, February 29, 2012, http://chronicle.com/ blogs/innovations/rick-santorum-is-right/31769.

30. See Hacker and Pierson, *Winner-Take-All Politics*, for details on increases of income among the highest earners. And it may be generous to say that

college graduates have seen wage stagnation: real wages have decreased in several of the past years. One report found "the average starting salary for a graduate in 2009 was $48,633, according to the National Association of Colleges and Employers, a decrease of 1.2 percent from 2008. From 2000 to 2007, real starting pay for those with bachelor's degrees fell 3.2 percent among men and 1.7 percent among women. In contrast, between 1995 and 2000, real starting pay for college-educated men and women increased 20.9 percent and 11.7 percent, respectively." Kathleen Murray, "Why Your Best Paycheck May Be Behind You," *CBS Money Watch*, January 7, 2010, http://www.cbsnews.com/news/why-your-best-paycheck-may-be-behind-you.

31. Recent attention to this issue has been paid by the national media and Congress. See, for example, Tamar Lewin, "Flurry of Data as Rules Near for Commercial Colleges," *New York Times*, February 4, 2011, http://www.nytimes.com/2011/02/04/education/04colleges.html; Lewin, "U.S. Revises Report on Commercial Colleges," *New York Times*, December 8, 2010, http://www.nytimes.com/2010/12/09/education/09gao.html; Mary Beth Marklein, "For-Profit Colleges Under Fire Over Value, Accreditation," *USA Today*, September 29, 2010, http://usatoday30.usatoday.com/news/education/2010-09-29-1Aforprofit29_CV_N.htm; Marklein, "More Lawsuits Target For-Profit Colleges," *USA Today*, September 27, 2010, http://usatoday30.usatoday.com/news/education/2010-09-27-1Aforprofit27_ST_N.htm; Tiffany Stanley, "On For-Profit Colleges, Congress Gets Schooled—Again," *New Republic*, October 12, 2010, http://www.newrepublic.com/blog/jonathan-cohn/78333/profit-colleges-congress-gets-schooled-again.

32. In 2013, the *Chronicle of Higher Education* listed Mark Schneider as one of the most influential people in the field that year. His accomplishment? "He pushed colleges to prove the return on students' investments," the *Chronicle* reports. Schneider formed an organization that provides reports on graduates' salaries by institution and major for five different states. He had hoped it would be utilized not only by students, but by policy makers—and, indeed, lawmakers and policy makers in Tennessee and Florida are now doing just that. See Goldie Blumenstyk, "The 2013 Influence List," *Chronicle of Higher Education*,

December 9, 2013, http://chronicle.com/article/The-Chronicle-List-This/143485/#article-scroll-section-5.

33. Newfield, *Unmaking the Public University*, chapter 13; Tamar Lewin, "As Interest Fades in the Humanities, Colleges Worry," *New York Times*, October 31, 2013, p. A1, http://www.nytimes.com/2013/10/31/education/as-interest-fades-in-the-humanities-colleges-worry.html.

34. Both George Washington University and Wesleyan have ended need-blind admissions, while MIT, Cornell, and the University of Virginia have curtailed promises to replace loans, which can burden students for years, with grants for low-income or middle-class families. See Marcella Bombardieri, "College Aid Offers Fail to Grow with Economy," *Boston Globe*, August 5, 2013, http://www.bostonglobe.com/metro/2013/08/24/even-economy-improves-colleges-lower-ambition-their-financial-aid-programs/A5Ly5bs77uBtke5HqrwMXL/story.html; Kevin Kiley, "Need Too Much," *Inside Higher Ed*, June 1, 2012, http://www.insidehighered.com/news/2012/06/01/wesleyan-shifts-away-need-blind-policy-citing-financial-and-ethical-concerns; Beckie Supiano, "George Washington U. Now Admits It Considers Financial Need in Admissions," *Chronicle of Higher Education*, October 22, 2013, http://chronicle.com/article/George-Washington-U-Now/142527.

35. Taylor, "End the University as We Know It."

36. James J. Duderstadt and Farris W. Womack, *The Future of the Public University in America: Beyond the Crossroads* (Baltimore: Johns Hopkins University Press, 2003), cited in Donoghue, *The Last Professors*, p. 131.

37. The question of whether the public universities remain a viable place for research in science, technology, and business depends heavily on what degree of subsidy they continue to provide for this research. The current struggle over who covers the overhead for large projects—grantees or hosts—is part of the shifting political economy of such research. States long willing to provide this subsidy themselves because of its benefit to state economies can no longer afford to do so and/or no longer see the benefit in doing so. But corporate grants will go wherever the research environment is cheapest, so

as public universities attempt to recoup larger portions of research overhead from grantees, they may end up driving the research elsewhere.

38. F. King Alexander, "Private Institutions and Public Dollars: An Analysis of the Effects of Federal Direct Student Aid on Public and Private Institutions of Higher Education," *Journal of Education Finance* 23.3 (1998), pp. 390–416, quoted in David Hursh and Andrew Wall, "Re-politicizing Higher Education and Research Within Neoliberal Globalization," *Policy Futures in Education* 9.5 (2011).

39. It would seem that many faculty have departed from the values of the priesthood for those of the market, rendering the notion that "you don't go into academia for the money" a quaint shibboleth of a tweedy past, one spurned by market-smart young professionals who just happen to study Chaucer or South Asian politics.

40. The tendency of neoliberalism to generate products with zero use value and for which there is often no clientele apart from those in the industry is brilliantly portrayed in the "Xtra Normal" cartoon videos satirizing academe through the figures of eager undergraduates yearning to go to graduate school. While each cartoon indicts the specific absurdities, fetishes, and dead ends of a particular discipline, together, they portray contemporary academic orders of recognition and reward that drive liberal arts scholarship in increasingly trivial or meaningless directions. For the cartoons, see YouTube, http://www.youtube.com/watch?v=obTNwPJvOI8.

41. "The University of District of Columbia, which was desperate to cut costs, is eliminating 17 low-enrolled academic programs—including physics, history and economics—but is keeping for now an NCAA Division II athletics program that cost $3 million more last year than it generated in revenue." Valerie Strauss, "UDC Drops Physics, History but Keeps Money-Losing Sports Program. Really," *Washington Post*, November 20, 2013, http://www.washington post.com/blogs/answer-sheet/wp/2013/11/20/udc-drops-psychics-history-but-keeps-money-losing-sports-program-really; Nick Anderson, "UDC Trustees Keep Athletics for Now, but Cut 17 Academic Programs," *Washington Post*, November 19, 2013, http://www.washingtonpost.com/local/education/udc-trustees-to-debate-cuts-to-athletics-academics/2013/11/19/a31a858a-5129-11e3-

9e2c-e1d01116fd98_story.html. Similar cuts are happening at Minnesota State University, Moorhead; see "MSUM Considers Cuts in Tenured Faculty, Program Closures to Fix Projected $5 Million Deficit," *Inforum*, http://www.inforum.com/event/article/id/419024 (subscription required).

42. Stefan Collini has offered unmatched commentaries on the British metrics. See Stefan Collini, "Impact on Humanities," *Times Literary Supplement* 5563, November 13, 2009; Collini, "Sold Out," *London Review of Books* 35, no. 20 (October 2013); and Collini, *What Are Universities For?* (New York: Penguin, 2012). See also Joan Scott, "On Assessment" (forthcoming).

43. Graduate teaching is excepted from this insofar as training successful Ph.D. students may enhance faculty capital in the profession.

44. Consider one prosaic example, drawn from a page on the U.C. Berkeley registrar's website. There, a software package called ScheduleBuilder, recently purchased from Ninja Scheduling, helps students choose and schedule classes for upcoming terms. Self-described as a "planning tool," ScheduleBuilder offers students no information about course content apart from catalog descriptions, but does link directly to four things: past grade distributions of courses, past exams of courses, informal student opinions about courses, and ways to build a class schedule around sleeping late and other personal preferences. In short, the university registrar's website now provides officially what fraternities used to do informally. Unsurprisingly, ScheduleBuilder was incubated, built, and licensed to Berkeley by recent Berkeley graduates who originally had "grown" the project during their college years. The ScheduleBuilder is at https://schedulebuilder.berkeley.edu. For the Berkeley student newspaper account of the design and implementation, see Geena Cova, "Schedule-Building Program to Launch in Fall," *Daily Californian*, January 19, 2012, http://www.dailycal.org/2012/01/19/schedule-building-program-to-launch-in-fall. Ninja Scheduling is but one example of the hundreds of transformations in higher education wrought by consumer values, such as minimal expenditure and the fungibility of all goods, driving the enterprise. Ninja Scheduling supplants course choices derived from faculty advising aimed at developing well-educated and well-rounded graduates with choices derived

from a platform reliant on other consumers for advice, valorizing easy A grades and endorsing a party schedule.

45. See Joe Matthews, "Finally, a New Idea in the Governor's Race," *PropZero: Changing the State of California Politics* (blog), NBC Bay Area, http://www.nbcbayarea.com/blogs/prop-zero/OneNewIdea-92069984.html.

46. Durham University in the United Kingdom is headed not by a chancellor or a president, but a CEO.

47. Many—perhaps most—of the articles in the mainstream press reporting this move focused on the presumed savings to the public purse, with rare mention of larger issues pertaining to the public good. See, for example, Matthew Garrahan, "UCLA Business School to End Public Funding," *Financial Times*, September 6, 2010, http://www.ft.com/cms/s/0/d5745294-b9d9-11df-8804-00144feabdc0.html#axzz31QiqGMj6; Larry Gordon, "UCLA's Anderson School Aims to Fund Itself," *Los Angeles Times*, September 9, 2010, http://articles.latimes.com/2010/sep/09/local/la-me-uc-bizschool-20100909; "UCLA Business School Wants to Wean Off State Funds," *San Diego Union-Tribune*, September 8, 2010, http://www.utsandiego.com/news/2010/sep/8/?page=4&.

48. Jon Wiener, "UCLA Business School to Go Private: A Blow to the Public University," *Nation*, June 8, 2012, http://www.thenation.com/blog/168305/ucla-business-school-go-private-blow-public-university.

49. Examples of this kind of sponsorship that receive a great deal of attention include the British Petroleum–sponsored Energy Biosciences Institute at U.C. Berkeley, where the big question is not whether corporate money may underwrite scientific research—it can and does—but what degree of control over the hiring and promotion of university scholars BP might have at the Institute. Recently, J. P. Morgan made a direct bid for such control in the graduate program it will sponsor at the University of Delaware. *Inside Higher Ed* reported, "JPMorgan Chase plans to give $17 million to start a doctoral program at the University of Delaware. . . . As part of the plan, JPMorgan will renovate a building to house the program, put up money to pay program faculty and pay a full ride for students seeking a degree, according to an internal

university plan. In addition, JPMorgan employees may sit on dissertation committees and advise the university on which faculty members should teach in the program, according to the planning document and a top university official." Ry Rivard, "A JP Morgan PhD?" *Inside Higher Ed*, October 7, 2013, http:// www.insidehighered.com/news/2013/10/07/proposed-phd-funded-jpmorgan-chase-raises-questions-u-delaware.

Less well known are stories such as the outright reach for control over curriculum exercised by the BB&T Charitable Foundation when it donated $500,000 to Guilford College, a small liberal arts school with Quaker roots located in North Carolina. The BB&T Foundation is linked to the BB&T banking powerhouse built by John Allison, a devotee of Ayn Rand. The half-million-dollar grant to Guilford committed the college to the following: offering a course called "The Moral Foundations of Capitalism" once a year for the next ten years; including as required reading in that course *Atlas Shrugged* in its entirety; several designated "Ethics of Capitalism Scholars" who will be sustained by the BT&T grant and will also be required to read *Atlas Shrugged*; and provision by the college of a copy of *Atlas Shrugged* to every junior majoring in business or economics. As Guilford College faculty member Richie Zweigenhaft queried, "What are our students likely to conclude about Guilford's endorsement of *Atlas Shrugged* as the only book now required in our entire curriculum?" Richie Zweigenhaft, "Is This Curriculum For Sale?" *Academe: Magazine of the AAUP*, July–August 2010, p. 38. Also striking is the willingness of Guilford administrators and faculty to sell its curriculum for a mere half million dollars.

The ultraconservative and megarich Koch brothers recently donated $1.5 million to the Florida State University, Tallahassee, Department of Economics to hire new faculty who will "promote free enterprise." The funding agreement specifies that an advisory board appointed by the Kochs will review potential candidates, eliminating those it deems not to meet its ideological threshold, and will also recommend withdrawing the funds if it determines that the hires are not meeting the objectives of the foundation. Administrators at the FSU have defended the arrangement. See Kris Hundley, "Billionaire's Role in

Hiring decisions at Florida State University Raises Questions," *Tampa Bay Times*, May 9, 2011, http://www.tampabay.com/news/business/billionaires-role-in-hiring-decisions-at-florida-state-university-raises/1168680.

50. See Dana Villa, *Socratic Citizenship* (Princeton: Princeton University Press, 2001).

51. "For a . . . people to understand wise principles of politics and follow basic rules of state craft, the effect would have to become the cause; the social spirit which must be the product of social institutions would have to preside over the setting up of those institutions; men would have to have already become before the advent of law that which they become as a result of law." Rousseau, *The Social Contract*, pp. 86–87.

52. John Dewey understood this. See John Dewey, *Democracy and Education* (Carbondale: Southern Illinois University Press, 2008). Tocqueville and Mill dealt with it by trying to cultivate an aristocratic strain within democracies. See Tocqueville, *Democracy in* America; and John Stuart Mill, "On Liberty," in *On Liberty and Other Writings*, ed. Stefan Collini (Cambridge: Cambridge University Press, 1989).

EPILOGUE: LOSING BARE DEMOCRACY

1. See Jonathan Crary, *24/7: Late Capitalism and the Ends of Sleep* (New York: Verso, 2013); Philip Mirowski, *Never Let a Serious Crisis Go to Waste: How Neoliberalism Survived the Financial Meltdown* (New York: Verso, 2013); Lauren Berlant, *Cruel Optimism* (Durham: Duke University Press, 2011); Elizabeth Povinelli, *Economies of Abandonment: Social Belonging and Endurance in Late Liberalism* (Durham: Duke University Press, 2011); Noam Chomksy, *Profit over People*: *Neoliberalism and Global Order* (New York: Seven Stories, 2011); William Connolly, *The Fragility of Things* (Durham: Duke University Press, 2013); Bonnie Honig, "The Politics of Public Things: Neoliberalism and the Routine of Privatization," *No Foundations: An Interdisciplinary Journal of Law and Justice* 10 (2013); and Lisa Duggan, *The Twilight of Equality* (Boston: Beacon Press, 2004).

2. Sheldon Wolin, "Norm and Form: The Constitutionalizing of Democracy," in J. Peter Euben, John R. Wallach, and Josiah Ober (eds.), *Athenian*

Political Thought and the Reconstruction of American Democracy (Ithaca: Cornell University Press, 1994).

3. Within the enormous literature on democracy's meanings, Bonnie Honig provides especially thoughtful reflections on its internal paradoxes in *Democracy and the Foreigner* (Princeton: Princeton University Press, 2001) and *Emergency Politics: Paradox, Law, Democracy* (Princeton: Princeton University Press, 2009).

4. I have discussed the problem of "democracy's lack" at greater length in a short commentary by that name in *Public Culture* 10.2 (1998), pp. 425–29 and in chapter 6 of Wendy Brown, *Politics Out of History* (Princeton: Princeton University Press, 2001).

5. Jean Jacques Rousseau, *On the Social Contract*, ed. and trans. Maurice Cranston (New York: Penguin, 1968), p. 60.

6. Aristotle, *The Politics*, trans. Ernest Barker (Oxford: Clarendon, 1946); Aristotle, *The Nicomachean Ethics*, trans. J. A. K. Thomson (New York: Penguin, 2003).

7. Alexis de Tocqueville, *Democracy in America*, ed. and trans. Harvey C. Mansfield and Delba Winthrop (Chicago: University of Chicago Press, 2000), pp. 56–90, 231–34, pp. 489–92, 496–500.

8. Sheldon Wolin, "Fugitive Democracy," *Constellations* 1.1 (1994), pp. 14, 17, 19, 22, 23.

9. Within the subfield of political theory known as democratic theory (which, for all its internal subdivisions and arguments, operates within the orbit of liberalism in the classic sense) John E. Roemer is especially alert to this point. See "Does Democracy Engender Justice?," in Ian Shapiro and Casiano Hacker-Cordon (eds.), *Democracy's Value* (Cambridge: Cambridge University Press, 1999). Roemer's acknowledgment is rare. Even when democracy is expressly detached from liberalism, it is presumed to host certain values. Sheldon Wolin, for example, asserts that the values of liberty and equality belong exclusively to democracy and have done so since antiquity. See "Fugitive Democracy," p. 21.

10. Another way of specifying democracy would involve distinguishing "true" or "genuine" from false, corrupt or disqualified versions. There are

Lockean, Rousseauist, Marxist, and Rawlsian efforts in this direction. Each involves stipulating either the precise set of powers that the people must share or the precise means by which they will share or transfer them. But this is part of the ongoing political argument about what democracy means and what it involves, not a way of determining its essence.

11. See Karl Marx, "On the Jewish Question," in *The Marx-Engels Reader*, ed. Robert C. Tucker (New York: Norton, 1978); and Wendy Brown, "Rights and Losses," chapter 5 of *States of Injury* (Princeton: Princeton University Press, 1995).

12. See Carole Pateman, *The Sexual Contract* (Stanford: Stanford University Press, 1988); Joan W. Scott, *Only Paradoxes to Offer: French Feminists and the Rights of Man* (Cambridge, MA: Harvard University Press, 1997); and Wendy Brown, "Liberalism's Family Values," chapter 6 of *States of Injury*.

13. Marx, "On the Jewish Question," pp. 34, 35, 46. In this essay, Marx does not use the terms "capital" or "capitalism," and only occasionally refers to "democracy" or "bourgeois democracy." So I am doing some filling in here, but I do not believe I have distorted Marx's meaning.

14. Joan W. Scott's *Only Paradoxes to Offer: French Feminists and the Rights of Man* (Cambridge: Harvard University Press, 1997) remains one of the best historical and theoretical accounts of how these constraints of liberalism may be mobilized for progressive purposes.

15. Wolin offers as examples of these concerns "low-income housing, worker ownership of factories, better schools, better health care, safer water, controls over toxic waste disposals." Wolin, "Fugitive Democracy," p. 24.

16. Sometimes this insistence reaches new heights of tautological reasoning. Consider this from Pierre-Yves Gomez and Harry Korine, two management specialists writing about democracy and governance: "One can discern a process of transformation in corporate governance that accompanies economic development over time. We show that this process can be understood as the *democratization* of corporate governance. Our reflection is based upon the observation that, in modern liberal society, the governance of human beings tends, over time, to democratize: the more the entrepreneurial force becomes concentrated in ever larger corporations, the greater the need for social frag-

mentation to maintain the legitimacy of governance—so as to ensure that corporations are governed according to the liberal spirit." *Entrepreneurs and Democracy: A Political Theory of Corporate Governance* (Cambridge: Cambridge University Press, 2008), pp. 8–9. In this remarkable book, the authors argue that what they call the "democratization of corporate governance" and the growth of economic performance depend upon a natural fragmentation of power that they regard as indigenous to entrepreneurial and democratic societies.

17. See Wendy Brown, "We Are All Democrats Now..." in Giorgio Agamben, et al., *Democracy in What State?* (New York: Columbia University Press, 2011).

18. I do not think the value of democracy is properly extended to every venue or activity of life. I think it fits poorly with decision making in most classrooms, in hospitals, in emergency response teams, or other places where expertise or other bases of authority are more relevant than self-rule.

19. Rousseau, *Social Contract*, pp. 64 and 84–88.

20. A crucial and complex term in *Of Grammatology*, the "supplement" may be crudely defined as something that is formally outside of a primary term or binary, but that supports or sustains it. Pressure on or exposure of the supplement can thus help to denaturalize or delegitimate the ontological status of the original term, or reveal its internal incompleteness or incoherence. That is why there is political possibility in the supplement. See "'...*That Dangerous Supplement*...'" in Jacques Derrida, *Of Grammatology*, trans. Gayatri Spivak, corrected ed. (Baltimore: Johns Hopkins University Press, 1997), pp. 141–64.

21. "Shared sacrifice" is used everywhere by politicians and managers imposing austerity measures, downsizing, engaged in layoffs, greening operations, and more. Democratic House leader Nancy Pelosi famously uttered these words when voting for the Reid deficit reduction bill in 2011: "It is clear we must enter an era of austerity; to reduce the deficit through shared sacrifice." In an interview with George Stephanopoulos on *ABC This Week*, President Obama insisted that everyone must sacrifice (and "have skin in the game") to balance the budget and reform government priorities. "Obama tells

Stephanopoulos Everyone Must Sacrifice," http://www.youtube.com/watch?v= 6GJX8bXduLM. However, the term is frequently flipped by Left activists to argue for "chopping from the top," especially outsized salaries, pensions and bonuses, severance agreements, golden parachutes, and other perks for politicians and executives. See for example: Lorenzo Totaro and Chiara Vasarri, "Monti's Austerity Debut Risks Italian Wrath" *Bloomberg News*, December 5, 2011, http://www.bloomberg.com/news/2011-12-04/monti-s-debut-austerity-package-risks-rousing-italian-wrath-euro-credit.html; Salvatore Babones, "What is Austerity, and Why Should We Care?," Inequality.org, May 21, 2012, http://inequality.org/austerity-care; Sasha Abramsky, "No Age of Austerity for the Rich," *Guardian*, July 2, 2010, https://www.commondreams.org/view/ 2010/07/02-5; AntiConformist911, "President Obama and the Myth of "Shared Sacrifice,'" *Daily Kos*, March 22, 2009 http://www.dailykos.com/story/2009/ 03/22/711737/-President-Obama-and-the-myth-of-shared-sacrifice#. Or see this account from the United Airlines employee union: "UAL Union Coalition Demands Shared Rewards," March 27, 2007, http://www.alpa.org/portals/ alpa/pressroom/pressreleases/2007/2007-3-27_UALUnionCoalition.htm.

22. Consider Barry Eichengreen's use of the term, sacrifice, in a *Guardian* commentary on the Greek response to restructuring amidst its debt crisis: "Greek Debt Crisis: Lessons in Hindsight," *Guardian*, June 14, 2013, http:// www.theguardian.com/business/2013/jun/14/greek-debt-crisis-lessons.

23. Individuals need not consciously "believe" in sacrifice for a sacrificial logic to be at work in citizenship remade by neoliberal rationality. Rather, the very notion of "shared sacrifice" interpellates and binds us *as* a citizenry—this is how the "sharing" works across extreme and obscene differences in how the sacrifice is experienced.

24. In this *New York Times* story about the city of Chicago's likely restructuring of public worker pension funds, the article itself frames every choice as an economic, not political one. Rick Lyman, "Chicago Pursues Deal to Change Pension Funding," *New York Times*, December 4, 2013, p. A1, http:// www.nytimes.com/2013/12/05/us/chicago-pursues-deal-to-change-pension-funding.html.

25. See, for example, Diane Cardwell, "Private Businesses Fight Federal Prisons for Contracts," *New York Times*, March 15, 2012, p. B1, http://www.nytimes.com/2012/03/15/business/private-businesses-fight-federal-prisons-for-contracts.html. The ironies of these substitutions are sometimes spectacular. See Ian Urbina, "Using Jailed Migrants as a Pool of Cheap Labor," *New York Times*, May 25, 2014, http://www.nytimes.com/2014/05/25/us/using-jailed-migrants-as-a-pool-of-cheap-labor.html.

26. Here is an example of the way that shared sacrifice is deployed in cutbacks to the U.S. court system: "31 Court Facilities to be Downsized in First Year of Cost-Cutting Project," United States Courts, October 15, 2013, http://news.uscourts.gov/31-court-facilities-be-downsized-first-year-cost-cutting-project.

27. One could no longer proclaim a scholarly intention, as did Henri Hubert and Marcel Mauss in their remarkable 1898 essay, "to define *the* nature and social function of sacrifice." Hubert and Mauss, *Sacrifice: Its Nature and Function*, trans. W. D. Halls (Chicago: University of Chicago Press, 1964), p. 1. In the intervening century, rich reflections on sacrifice from psychoanalysis, anthropology, philosophy, and political theories of theology have revealed the infinite depth and complexity of sacrificial rituals, as well as great variation across epochs, cultures, and practices.

28. Here, we are approaching the threshold of capitalism's theological dimensions, which a number of scholars have explored in recent years. See for example, Giorgio Agamben, *Homo Sacer: Sovereign Power and Bare Life*. trans. Daniel Heller-Roazen (Stanford: Stanford University Press, 1998); Walter Benjamin, "Capitalism as Religion," trans. Chad Kautzer, in Eduardo Mendieta (ed.), *The Frankfurt School on Religion: Key Writings by the Major Thinkers* (New York: Routledge, 2005); Wendy Brown, "Sovereignty and the Return of the Repressed," in David Campbell and Morton Schoolman (eds.), *The New Pluralism: William Connolly and the Contemporary Global Condition* (Durham: Duke University Press, 2008); Brown, *Walled States, Waning Sovereignty* (New York: Zone, 2010); Brown, "Is Marx (Capital) Secular?," in "Capitalist Force Fields: Sovereignty, Power and Law," special issue, *Qui Parle: Critical Humanities and Social Sciences* 23.1 (2014); Phillip Goodchild, *Capitalism and Religion* (New

York: Routledge, 2002); and Goodchild, *Theology of Money* (Durham: Duke University Press, 2009); Robert Meister, *After Evil: A Politics of Human Rights* (New York: Columbia University Press, 2010); William Connolly, *Why I Am Not a Secularist* (Minnesota: University of Minnesota Press, 1999), and Connolly, *Capitalism and Christianity, American Style* (Durham: Duke University Press, 2008).

29. Moishe Halbertal, *On Sacrifice* (Princeton: Princeton University Press, 2012), pp. 2 and 4.

30. Among other things, Halbertal's distinction is confounded by sacrifice in holy war, which, arguably, most wars are, including those fought by secular states. But the distinction is leaky in other ways as well.

31. Many anthropologists and other theorists of sacrifice insist that destruction of the victim is key to sacrifice. See, for example, Hubert and Mauss, *Sacrifice*, pp. 97–98; and René Girard, "Violence and the Sacred," in Jeffrey Carter (ed.), *Understanding Religious Sacrifice: A Reader* (London: Continuum, 2003), p. 242. "The victim is sacred only because he is to be killed," writes Girard.

32. Hubert and Mauss, *Sacrifice*, p. 98.

33. Halbertal, *On Sacrifice*, pp. 63–67.

34. This is not true of strategic sacrifice in a game, such as chess, where one calculates the gains expected from the move.

35. According to many analysts, the "too big to fail" problem is far worse than it was in 2008. "The six largest banks in the nation now have 67% of all the assets in the U.S. financial system, according to bank research firm SNL Financial. That amounts to $9.6 trillion, up 37% from five years ago." Stephen Gandel, "By Every Measure, the Big Banks are Bigger," *CNN Money*, September 13, 2013, http://finance.fortune.cnn.com/2013/09/13/too-big-to-fail-banks.

36. Hubert and Mauss, *Sacrifice*, pp. 98–99.

37. Girard, "Violence and the Sacred," p. 247.

38. *Ibid.*, p. 247.

39. *Ibid.*, p. 248.

40. See Nicholas Xenos, "Buying Patriotism," *Pioneer*, November 12, 2012, http://pioneerwired.x10.mx.

41. *The Apology*, in Plato, *The Last Days of Socrates*, trans. Hugh Tredennick (Harmondsworth, UK: Penguin, 1954), 28c, p. 60.

42. See Asaf Kedar. "National Socialism before Nazism: Friedrich Naumann and Theodor Fritsch, 1890–1914," Ph.D. diss., Department of Political Science, University of California, Berkeley, May 2009. Sheldon Wolin articulates the resonance with fascism in a different way by coining, "inverted totalitarianism." See Wolin, *Democracy Incorporated: Managed Democracy and the Specter of Inverted Totalitarianism* (Princeton: Princeton University Press, 2008).

43. Foucault, reading Hayek, says that what is distinctive about liberal (economic) governmentality is that the state cannot and should not *touch* the economy, because it cannot *know* the economy. See Michel Foucault, *The Birth of Biopolitics: Lectures at the Collège de France, 1978–79*, ed. Michel Senellart, trans. Graham Burchell (New York: Picador, 2004), p. 283. Similarly, *homo oeconomicus* is a creature led by interest and calculation, not knowledge: he, too, does not know because he cannot know. "So we have a system in which *homo oeconomicus* owes the positive nature of his calculation precisely to everything which eludes his calculation" (*ibid.*, p. 278). The premise is that man and state are inherently and necessarily ignorant about the economy, a field of logics that is rational, yet "naturally opaque" because of its nontotalizable quality (*ibid.*, pp. 279–83). But if man and state do not know, does the market know? Theories of supply, demand, and pricing notwithstanding, the assumption persists that the market acts, rather than knows; economics can explain and even predict that action, but it cannot bring it into being. However, financialization changes even this correlation between knowledge and action—its explanatory or predictive quality and its relation to calculation. It evaporates predictability. Financialization changes markets from predictable reactions to supply, demand, and price into markets where speculation is the driving dynamic— from interest to gambling, from stability to instability, from following the crowd to shorting it. But this also means that *homo oeconomicus* can no longer act on the basis of calculation; rather, he acts on the basis of speculation. And it is very easy to crash.

44. Margaret Thatcher, "Speech to Australian Institute of Directors Lunch," September 15, 1976, Margaret Thatcher Foundation, http://www.margaretthatcher.org/document/103099.

45. While its critique is supremely important, contemporary prescriptive posthumanism expresses this historical conjuncture and colludes with it.

Index

Foucault's normative stakes in, 55–56; liberalism and, 52, 54–59, 61–70; limitations of, 53, 56–57, 73–78; Marx and, 55, 58, 65, 74, 77.

Brazil: auterity protests in, 220.

Bremer Order 81, 142–150; as drafted by Monsanto, 149; as neoliberal jurisprudence, 148–50; best practices and, 147–48; effect on traditional agriculture, 145, 147–48; US corporate profits and, 146–50. *See also* Bremer Orders; Monsanto; Iraq.

Bremer Orders, 142–43. *See also* Bremer Order 81.

Bremer, Paul, 142, 149–50. *See also* Bremer Order 81; Iraq.

British Petroleum, 271 n. 49.

Brown, Gordon, 49.

Buckley v Valeo, 154, 163, 167–68, 256 n. 20.

Bulgaria: austerity protests in, 220.

Bush, George H. W., 49.

Bush, George W., 49, 142–50. *See also* Bremer Orders; Bremer Order 81; Iraq.

CALIFORNIA STATE UNIVERSITY, 264 n. 19.

Çalışkan, Koray, 30, 82, 102. *See also* econimization.

Callison, William, 116.

Callon, Michel, 30, 82, 102, 240 n. 12. *See also* econimization.

Camp, Robert, 251 n. 49.

Capella, Martianus, 184.

Capital, 40, 76. *See also* human capital; finance capital; capitalism; capital enhancement.

Capital enhancement: as preeminent goal, 22; democracy and, 26, 173; education and, 117.

Capital: characteristics of, 159–62;

domination and, 73, 75–76, 119, 209; rights and, 38, 110, 151, 155, 160, 172–73; speech figured as, 157–63, 172–73.

Capitalism, 29–30, 47, 75–77, 105–108, 149, 155, 209; democracy and, 44, 111, 208–209; Foucault on, 58, 60, 75–77, 120, 235 n. 25; *Homo oeconomicus* and, 91; Neoliberalism and, 39, 44, 47, 50, 75, 49, 209, 111, 218–20, 224 n. 6, 232 n. 44; Theology and, 218–20, 278 n. 28; Weber on, 111, 119, 148, 253 n. 76.

Care work, 102–107, 246 n. 71, 246 n. 74. *See also* gender; gender subordination; and *femina domestica*.

Chicago (city), 277 n. 24.

Chicago School, 54, 60, 118, 151; differences from Ordoliberalism, 59–60; historical influences on, 59–60. *See also* ordoliberalism; Friedman, Milton.

Chile, 20, 151. *See also* Allende, Salvadore; Pinochet, Augusto.

China, 25.

Citigroup, 228 n. 27.

Citizens United v. Federal Election Commission, 31, 152–73; civil rights discourse in, 164–67; effects on democracy, 153, 156, 167–68, 171–73; erasing distinctions among individuals, 161, 163, 172; on corporations, 154, 156, 164–66; on corruption, 168–72, 228 n. 27, 258 n. 50. *See also* First Amendment; Kennedy, Anthony; speech.

Citizenship: capacities for, 177, 188; economization of, 39, 109, 151, 173, 179; education and, 177, 180–90, 264 n. 21; governance and, 210–11, 213; neoliberal, 39–40, 109, 177, 179, 211–12, 218, 220; public interest and, 39, 176, 179, 188, 210; sacrifice

and, 109–11, 210–13, 217–20,
277 n. 23.
Civil rights discourse, 164, 167.
Class-action suits, 152–53. *See also*
AT&T Mobility LLC v. Concepcion.
Clinton, Bill, 49.
College de France Lectures (Foucault),
see Birth of Biopolitics (Foucault).
Common good, *see* public good, the.
Competition: as generating economic
growth, 63–64; as installed by
best practices, 138, 140, 148; as
nonnatural, 62–63; as promoting
inequality, 64–65, 72, 143; as
replacing exchange, 64–66, 81;
risk of death and, 64–65, 72, 167;
state's role in facilitation, 60,
62–64, 66, 143, 148–49, 162.
"Conduct of conduct," 21, 48, 117, 148.
Consensus: best practices and, 135–36,
141, 250 n. 43; in Citizens' United,
157, 164; political, 68–69; technology in governance, 35, 127–30, 133,
207, 211.
Cornell University, 267 n. 34.
Crisis, *see* financial crisis.

DEAN, MITCHELL, 115–16.
Dedemocratization, 18, 50, 77, 154, 180.
Democracy: "bare democracy," 202–10;
Citizens United and, 153, 156, 167,
171–73; definition, 19–20, 202–204,
209; economization of, 9, 32,42–45,
110, 173, 207; education and, 175,
177–79, 184–90, 199–200; equality
and, 9, 18–19, 41–42, 44, 64, 87, 94,
172, 177–78, 204–206; erosion of,
17, 42–44, 64, 173, 207–10; governance and, 43, 110, 128–31, 207, 275
n. 16; inequality and, 38, 64, 172,
178–79, 202, 204–205; value of, 11,
44–45, 109, 205–10. *See also* democracy, liberal;democracy, radical.

Democracy, classical republican, 44,
210.
Democracy, liberal: economization of,
9, 32, 42–43, 110, 173, 207; erosion
of, 17, 42–44, 64, 173, 207; governance and, 124, 131; *homo politicus*
in, 35, 95–97, 109; Marx on, 96,
206–207, 244 n. 59; value of, 18,
44–45, 109, 205–208.
Democracy, radical, 9, 18, 44–45, 94,
208–209.
Demos: definition of, 19, 202; economization of, 41, 128, 152–53; erasure
of, 39, 44, 152, 207; *homo politicus*
and, 109; in ancient Greece, 19; sovereignty and, 65, 73, 109, 185, 203,
207; undesirable acts of, 203–205.
Derrida, Jacques, 275 n. 20. *See also*
supplement.
Devolution, 124, 129, 131–34; as a feature of neoliberal governance, 125,
127–28, 131–32; definition, 131–32;
difference from responsibilization,
132, 134; sacrifice and, 134.
Dewey, John, 187, 272 n. 52.
Discourse: definition, 116–17; difference from political rationality,
116–17; emergence of neoliberal
rationality and, 53; irreducibility
of capitalism to, 76; neoliberal
transformation of, 21, 35–36, 47,
52, 71; on civil rights, 164, 167; on
governance, 130, 207; on shared
sacrifice, 213.
Domination: bourgeois freedom and,
76–77, 96; capital and, 73, 75–76,
119, 209; class and, 202, 233 n. 45;
neoliberalism and, 75–77, 119;
Rousseau on, 95.
Donoghue, Frank, 181.
Drutman, Lee, 228 n. 27.
Duménil, Gérard, 30.
Durham University, 270 n. 46.

n. 21. *See also* Citizens United, speech, Kennedy, Anthony.

First National Bank of Boston v. Bellotti, 154, 162–63, 167.

Fitzpatrick, Brian, 152.

Florida State University, Tallahassee, 272 n. 49.

For-profit colleges, 182, 193, 262 n. 9. *See also* proprietary schools.

Foucault, Michel, 53–64, 67–68, 75–77, 81, 85, 111, 121, 235 n. 16, 235 n. 25, 279 n. 43; *History of Seuxality,* 54; *homo politicus* and, 78, 85–86; instrumental rationality and, 119–21; interest and, 56–58, 77–78, 82–87, 111, 235 n. 16, 241 n. 24, 279 n. 43; Marx and, 55, 58, 74, 77, 238 n. 71; Marx and Marxism, 55, 74; "Nietzsche, Genealogy, History," 54; on capitalism, 58, 60, 75–77, 120, 235 n. 25; on governmentality, 55, 59, 73–74, 78, 121; on *homo oeconomicus,* 56–58, 77–78, 82–87, 111, 235 n. 16, 241 n. 24, 279 n. 43; on liberty, 55; on neoliberalism, 47–78 passim; on political rationality, 69, 76, 115–21, 228 n. 29; on popular sovereignty, 52, 55–57, 73–74, 85–86, 117, 126; on social contract, 58, 243 n. 47; rights and, 56–58, 85, 116–17.

Freedom: economization of, 41–42, 108–11, 177–79; education and, 184–85, 190; erasure of, 108–11; Foucault on, 55, 60, 69, 73–74, 76–77, 86, 234 n. 13; liberal democracy and, 18, 44, 181, 205–206; neoliberalism and, 55, 71, 74, 76, 100–102, 108–11, 173; political, 43, 74, 87, 95, 98, 108–11, 173, 185.

Freud, Sigmund, 98.

Friedman, Milton, 49, 57, 100, 122.

GANE, MICHAEL, 223 n. 9.

Gender: discrimination, 153; neoliberalism and, 104–105; of *homo oeconomicus,* 99–107; of *homo politicus,* 99.

Gender subordination: neoliberalism and, 25–26, 44, 105–106, 246 n. 71, 246 n. 72.

George Washington University, 267 n. 34.

Germany, 50. *See also* Merkel, Angela.

Girard, Rene, 217–18, 278 n. 31.

Global South, neoliberal interventions in, 20, 47, 51.

Gomez, Pierre-Yves, 275 n. 16.

Good life, the, 43–44; Arendt on, 43–44, 233 n. 45; Aristotle on, 43–44, 88–91, 189–90, 233 n. 45; difference from mere life, 43–44, 233 n. 45; education and, 189–90; Marx on, 43–44, 233 n. 45; Mill on, 43–44; neoliberal evacuation of, 43–44, 189–90.

Governance: as "soft power," 124–27, 131, 135; as irreducible to neoliberalism, 122; best practices as a mode of, 136, 141; citizenship and, 210–11, 213; consensus and, 126; corroding effects on democracy, 43, 110, 128–31, 207, 275 n. 16; definitions of, 71, 122–25; difference from government, 123–25, 126–28; discourse and, 130, 207; education and, 194, 198, 250 n. 43, 252 n. 49, 254 n. 79; freedom and, 108, 110–11; image of power in, 125–31; legal reasoning and, 152–54; neoliberalism in Euro-Atlantic and, 20–35; responsibilization and, 133; state sovereignty and, 124–25, 177.

Governing rationality, *see* political rationality; normative order of reason.

Governmentality: crisis in liberal, 50,

53, 57–59; definition, 117–18; difference from political rationality, 117–18; Euro-Atlantic neoliberalism and, 47; Foucault's concerns with, 55, 59, 73–74, 78, 121; *homo oeconomicus* and, 111; liberal, 50, 53, 57–59, 86, 118, 279 n.43; neoliberal governance and, 129–30. *See also* "Omnes et singulatim"; political rationality; Foucault, Michel.

Greece, 38–39, 134, 276 n.22. *See also* Southern Europe, crisis in 2012.

Guilford College, 271 n.49.

HABERMAS, JÜRGEN, 68, 92.

Hacker, Jacob, 29.

Halbertal, Moishe, 214–15, 278 n.30.

Hall, Stuart, 48.

Harvey, David, 59, 224 n.6.

Hayek, F.A., 122; Foucault on, 57, 59, 279 n.43; historical influences on, 59, 213.

Hegel, G.W.F., 52, 95–96, 99.

Hirschman, Albert O., 33.

Hobbes, Thomas, 58, 102–103, 245 n.67.

Home ownership, 24–25, 216.

Homo juridicus, 78, 85, 99, 241 n.24. *See also* Foucault, Michel; *Homo politicus*.

Homo legalis, 78, 85, 99. *See also* Foucault, Michel; *Homo politicus*.

Homo oeconomicus: Aristotle on, 43, 87–92; citizenship and, 39; definition of, 79–80, 81–83; economy and, 81–83; family and, 104–105, 246 n.71, 246 n.74; finance capital and, 10, 33–34, 70; Foucault on, 56–58, 77–78, 82–87, 111, 235 n.16, 241 n.24, 279 n.43; gender of, 99–107; historical variability of, 32, 82–83; in contemporary neoliberalism, 10, 31–34, 39, 42–44, 65–66, 70,

78–80, 83–85, 109–11, 177, 244 n.59, 280 n.43; interest and, 32–33, 42, 58–59, 70, 83–85, 91–92, 110, 177, 279 n.43; Marx on, 33, 43, 96; sacrifice and, 213; Smith on, 92–94; vanquishing of *homo politicus*, 35, 41–42, 76, 78, 108–11, 207.

Homo politicus, 85–99, 107–11, 207, 222; definition of, 87; economization of political life and, 109–11; Foucault's neglect of, 78, 85–86; freedom and, 110–11; gender of, 99; in Aristotle, 87–91; in Bentham, 96; in Freud, 98; in Hegel, 95–96; in Locke, 94–95; in Marx, 92, 96, 111; in Mill, 96–97; in Plato, 245 n.61. ; in Rousseau, 95, 98; in Smith, 92–94; sovereignty and, 109–11; vanquishing by *homo oeconomicus*, 35, 41–42, 76, 78, 108–11, 207. *See also* citizenship; *homo oeconomicus*.

Hubert, Henri, 214, 217, 277 n.27, 278 n.31.

Hudson, Michael, 30.

Human capital, 35–41, 109–10, 231 n.36, 247 n.75; citizenship and, 39–41, 71–72, 110, 182; collective life and, 37–41, 71–72, 84, 109–10; education and, 42, 176–77, 181, 184, 187–88, 195–97, 261 n.6; equality and, 38, 42, 191, 247 n.76; finance capital and, 33–36, 65–66, 70; gender and, 100–107; *homo oeconomicus* and, 10, 32–34, 70; invidual sovereignty and, 37, 109–10; labor and, 38, 65; popular sovereignty and, 110; rights and, 38, 100; sacrifice and, 37–38, 71–72, 84, 109–10.

Hume, David, 57.

IMAGINARY, *see* political imaginary.

Immigrants: constructed as dependent, 134; higher education and, 180, 186,

193; liberal personhood and, 206; in 2013 State of the Union, 24–26.

India, 146.

Inequality: democracy and, 38, 64, 172, 178–79, 202, 204–205; economization and, 41–42; effect of neoliberalism, 28–29, 42, 56, 64–65, 143, 219, 226 n. 22, 260 n. 4.

Infrastructure, 42, 105; care work as, 105–106; dismantling through neoliberalism, 104–105, 201, 211. *See also* welfare state; public goods.

Instrumental rationality: difference from political rationality, 118–20; neoliberalism and, 41, 108; Weber on, 111, 118–19, 140; best practices and, 148–50.

Interest: Foucault on, 58–59, 77–78, 83–85, 243 n. 47, 279 n. 43; *homo oeconomicus* and, 32–33, 42, 58–59, 70, 83–85, 91–92, 110, 177, 279 n. 43; sacrifice and, 215–16; Smith on, 32, 84–85, 93, 103, 187; Tocqueville on, 179, 187, 204, 264; transformed in neoliberalism, 33–34, 42, 70–71, 83–85, 168, 177, 241 n. 22.

Iraq, 142–51; agriculture in, 144–46; Bremer Orders and, 142–43; limits to self sovereignty, 142–43, 149–50. *See also* Monsanto; Bremer Order 81.

JACKSON, JACK, 254 n. 2.

Jones, Daniel Steadman, 118.

JPMorgan, 271 n. 49.

Jurisprudence, *see* legal reason, neoliberal.

Justice: as concern of firms, 27; as contributing to economic growth, 26–27, 40, 226 n. 23; citizenship and, 179, 188; economization of, 22, 35, 40–41, 208; erasure

by neoliberalism, 17, 40, 43, 127–28, 131, 208, 254 n. 79.

KANT, IMMANUEL, 99, 113, 140.

Kantian autonomy, 109.

Kantian individual, 37.

Kennedy, Anthony, 154–72, 256 n. 20. *See also* Citizens United.

Keynes, John Maynard, 83. *See also* Keynsianism.

Keynesianism: neoliberalism as a response to, 21, 51, 59–60.

Koch Brothers, 272 n. 49.

Korine, Harry, 275 n. 16.

Krugman, Paul, 29.

Kuhner, Timothy, 155, 256 n. 13.

LAW, NEOLIBERAL: as drafted by corporations, 149, 168, 228 n. 27; as economizing politics, 142–43, 151–56, 162–64, 166–67; characteristics of, 142–43, 148, 151–52, 154–56; dedemocratization and, 151–56; governance and, 66, 71, 129, 140–41; instances of, 142–43; political rationality and, 116, 121.

Lefort, Claude, 32.

Legal reason, neoliberal: as economizing politics, 151–56, 158, 170, 172–73; characteristics of, 151–52, 154–56, 172–73; dedemocratization and, 151–56, 172–73; instances of, 152–53. *See also* law, neoliberal; Citizens United.

Lemke, Thomas, 124. *See also* governance.

Lévy, Dominique, 30.

Liberal arts education: as producing citizens, 177, 183–90; as rivaled by job training, 181–83, 192–94, 261 n. 6; democracy's need for, 175, 177–79, 184–90, 199–200; difficulty in justifying, 177, 180, 182–83, 187–88,

65–66, 70, 78–80, 83–85, 109–11, 177, 244 n. 59, 280 n. 43; individual sovereignty and, 42, 78–79, 109–10; inequality and, 28–29, 42, 56, 64–65, 219, 226 n. 22, 260 n. 4; law and, 142–56, 162–67; legal reason and, 148–56, 172–73; political rationality and, 62, 115–16; popular sovereignty and, 35, 39, 44, 49, 65, 79, 108–10, 161, 172–73, 177, 207; sacrifice and, 109–11, 213–16; the good life and, 43–44, 189–90; the public good and, 39, 43, 108, 127, 159, 168–69, 172; variability of, 47–49.

Newfield, Christopher, 188, 192, 261 n. 6, 264 n. 20.

Nietzsche, Friedrich, 133.

Normative order of reason, 117–18. *See also* political rationality.

OBAMA, BARACK, 49; 2013 State of the Union address, 24–27, 40, 226 n. 13, 226 n. 23; college rating scheme, 178, 225 n. 11; on sacrifice, 276 n. 21. *See also* sacrifice; austerity.

Obamacare, *see* Affordable Care Act.

Occupy Wall Street, 24, 30, 203, 217, 219, 232 n. 40; UC Berkeley and, 250 n. 43.

Offe, Claus, 68.

"Omnes et singulatim," 71, 130. *See also* governmentality; Foucault, Michel.

Ordoliberalism, 49, 59, 60, 64, 66; diferences from Chicago School, 59–60; Hayek and, 59; historical influences on, 59–60, 213. *See also* Chicago School.

PATRIOTISM, 212, 215, 218.

Peck, Jamie, 48.

Pelosi, Nancy, 276 n. 21.

Pierson, Paul, 29, 260 n. 4.

Piketty, Thomas, 29, 226 n. 22.

Pinochet, Augusto, 20, 151. *See also* Chile.

Plato, 19, 21, 89, 91, 254 n. 61. *See also* Socrates; Aristotle.

Polanyi, Karl, 33, 75.

Political imaginary: democratic, 17, 19, 28, 35, 78–79, 152–53, 210; neoliberal, 38, 41, 43, 121, 153, 188; radical democratic, 9, 18, 42, 45, 59, 205–206.

Political rationality: definition, 115–16; difference from discourse, 116–17; difference from governmentality, 117–18; difference from normative form of reason, 118; Foucault on, 69, 76, 115–21, 228 n. 29; governance and, 122–31; law and, 116, 121; neoliberalism and, 62, 115–16; power and, 115–16; subject formation and, 115–16; truth and, 116. *See also* neoliberalism.

Political representation, 87, 179; in Citizens United, 170, 172.

Poulantzas, Nicos, 68.

Professoriate: ability to defend liberal arts, 195–96, 199; adopting neoliberal rationality, 195–96, 268 n. 39, 268 n. 40; negative images of, 181; replaced by adjuncts, 194, 197; undergraduate teaching, 196–97; university governance and, 183, 194–95, 198.

Proprietary colleges, *see* for-profit colleges.

Protests: against austerity, 30, 219; anti-globalization, 30; in Brazil, 220; in Bulgaria, 220; in Southern Europe, 200; in Turkey, 220. *See also* Occupy Wall Street.

Public good, the: citizenship and, 39, 176, 179, 210; education and, 190, 195–96; *homo politicus* and, 39, 87,

Sandel, Michael, 29.
Sarkozy, Nikolas, 49.
Satz, Debra, 29.
Say, Jean-Baptiste, 33.
Schmitt, Carl, 32.
Schneider, Mark, 267 n.32.
Scola, Nancy, 148.
Scott, Joan W., 99, 274 n.14.
Securitization, 72.
Sen, Amartya, 29.
Senior, Nassau, 33.
Shamir, Ronen, 132–33.
Shiffrin, Steven, 257 n.21.
Shinawarta, Thaksin, 35.
Smith, Adam: on family, 242 n.45;
    on *homo oeconomicus*, 32–34,
    92–94, 103, 175; on *homo politicus*,
    92–94; on human nature, 92–93,
    103, 242 n.44, 242 n.45; on
    interest, 32, 84–85, 93, 103, 187,
    264 n.21.
Smith, Jeremy, 144.
Smith, Yves, 30.
Social contract: in Foucault, 58, 243
    n.47; in Locke, 94–95, 243 n.47; in
    neoliberalism, 38, 64, 111, 134, 213;
    in Rousseau, 98.
Social Security, 42, 105, 134, 154.
Social welfare, *see* welfare, social.
Socrates, 189, 218. *See also* Plato.
Soss, Joe, 132.
South Africa, 20.
Southern Europe, 30, 38, 40, 107, 212,
    220. *See also* Greece; financial crisis.
Sovereignty, individual, 86, 109–11;
    Aristotle on, 87–88; devolution and,
    132; economization of, 22, 109–11,
    115, 155, 177, 179; education and,
    185; erasure by neoliberalism, 42,
    78–79, 109–11; Kant on, 109;
    responsibilization and, 133; Rous-
    seau on, 95; secured by political
    sovereignty, 109; Smith on, 92.

Sovereignty, popular: democratic imagi-
    nary and, 44, 79, 153, 206–207;
    demos and, 65, 73, 109, 185, 203,
    207; devolution and, 132; econo-
    mization of, 22, 41–42, 66, 108–10;
    erasure by neoliberalism, 35, 39, 44,
    49, 65, 79, 108–10, 161, 172–73, 177,
    207; Foucault on, 52, 55–57, 73–74,
    85–86, 117, 126; governance and,
    124, 126–27, 177; governmentality
    and, 117; *homo juridicus* and, 85, 241
    n.24; *homo politicus* and, 86–98,
    108–11, 244 n.59.
Speech, 156–72; "political marketplace"
    and, 157, 159, 162–63, 166, 172;
    as capital right, 160, 163, 172–73;
    as form of capital, 157–63, 172–73;
    as needing protections, 158–59; as
    right of corporations, 164–67, 172.
    See also First Amendment; Citizens
    United.
State ex rel. Ozanne v. Fitzgerald, 152–53.
Steuart, James, 33.
Stevens, John, 166–67.
Stigler, George, 49.
Stiglitz, Joseph, 29.
Studley, Jamienne, 225 n.11.
Summers, Lawrence, 106.
Supplement (Derridean), 275 n.20;
    democracy and, 209–10; neoliberal-
    ism and, 210, 215. *See also* sacrifice.
Sustainability: eclipsed by neoliberal-
    ism, 138, 144, 148–49; economic
    growth and, 27, 40; firms' concern
    with, 27; in Iraq, 144–46, 148–49.
    See also environment.
Sweden, 20.

TAIBBI, MATT, 30.
Taxes, 24; in neoliberalism, 28, 49,
    142–43, 212; public higher educa-
    tion and, 197.
Texas A&M University, 254 n.79.

Thailand, 35.

Thatcher, Margaret, 153, 221, 255 n. 9; economic policies, 20, 49; on family as given, 100–101, 103, 107, 245 n. 67.

Tocqueville, Alexis de, 179, 187, 204, 272 n. 52; on self-interest, 264 n. 21.

"Too big to fail," 72, 216, 279 n. 35. *See also* bailouts; financial crisis of 2008–.

Tronto, Joan, 103–104.

Turkey: austerity protests in, 220.

UC BERKELEY, 250 n. 43, 263 n. 18, 250 n. 43, 269 n. 44; corporate sponsorship of research, 271 n. 49; School of Business, 199.

UCLA, 263 n. 18; School of Business, 199.

Unemployment, 63, 72, 131, 191, 218.

Unions, 38, 65, 69, 131, 151–53, 212.

United Kingdom: education and, 23, 134, 196; emergence of neoliberalism in, 48, 100. *See also* Thacher, Margaret.

United Nations, 125.

United States v Automobile Workers, 172.

United States: characteristics of neoliberalism in, 20; education in, 23, 180–200; emergence of neoliberalism in, 48; inequality in, 178, 191; Iraq and, 142–50.

University of California, 262 n. 10, 263 n. 18, 264 n. 19. *See also* UCLA; UC Berkeley.

University of Delaware, 271 n. 49.

University of District of Columbia, 269 n. 41.

University of Kansas, 262 n. 13.

University of Phoenix, 182.

University of Virginia, 267 n. 34.

USAID, 145, 254 n. 79. *See also* Texas A&M University.

WAL-MART, 153, 211. *See also Walmart Stores Inc v Dukes et al.*

Wal-mart Stores, Inc. v Dukes et al, 153.

Wall Street, 30.

Walters, William, 130.

Weber, Max: *homo politicus* and, 99; on market and truth, 67, 75; *Protestant Ethic* and, 67, 75, 148, 253 n. 76; rational action and, 111, 118–20.

Welfare programs, 143, 154, 251 n. 4. *See also* public goods; infrastructure; Social Security.

Welfare state, 28, 125, 130; and neoliberalism, 20, 51, 104, 121, 134, 213; European, 20, 51. *See also* infrastructure; public goods.

Welfare, social, 28, 40, 72, 121, 132, 150, 170, 187, 213.

Wesleyan University, 267 n. 34.

Williams, Raymond, 184.

Wolin, Sheldon S., 29, 92, 204, 274 n. 9, 275 n. 15, 279 n. 42.

ZONE BOOKS *NEAR FUTURES* SERIES
Edited by Wendy Brown and Michel Feher

The turn of the 1980s marked the beginning of a new era in the Euro-Atlantic world: Inspired by the work of neoliberal economists and legal scholars, the "conservative revolutionaries" who came to power during these pivotal years used their offices to undermine the thinking and dismantle the institutional framework upon which welfare capitalism had rested. In their view, the role of the government was not to protect vulnerable segments of the population from the potential violence of market relations but, instead, to shelter the allegedly fragile mechanisms of the market from stifling rules and the disabling influence of so-called "special interests" which ranged from organized labor to protectors of the environment. They also believed that, once markets were properly shielded, their domain could be extended beyond the traditional borders of the private sector.

Eager to blunt the resistance raised by their agenda, neoliberal reformers initiated a series of deregulations, regarding capital flow and asset creation, that were meant to replace social protection and guaranteed employment with abundant and accessible credit—thereby endowing all economic agents with entrepreneurial ambitions and discipline. Yet, under the guise of diffusing the ethos of the self-reliant entrepreneur throughout the entire population, their reforms eventually enabled the speculative logic of financial markets to preside over the allocation of resources on a global scale. Thus, far from restoring thrift and frugality as the virtuous paths to personal independence and lasting profit, the reign of deregulated finance defined success as leverage, understood as the ability to invest with borrowed funds, and compelled the less fortunate to stake their livelihood on perennial indebtedness.

Much more than a mood swing, whereby the advocates of freer markets would temporarily prevail over the harbingers of a more protective State, the policies instigated under Ronald Reagan and Margaret Thatcher, and further refined by their "Third Way" successors, have successively transformed everything from corporate management to statecraft, household economics to personal relations. In the world shaped by these transformations—a world where the securitization of risks and liabilities greatly widens the realm of potentially appreciable assets—even the criteria according to which individuals are incited to evaluate themselves no longer match the civic, business, and family values respectively distinctive of political, economic, and cultural liberalism.

Along the way, the purchase of markets and "market solutions" has expanded to a range of domains hitherto associated with public services or common goods—from education to military intelligence to environmental stewardship. Simultaneously, the number and purview of democratically debatable issues has been drastically reduced by the sway of "good governance" and "best practices"—two notions originating in a corporate culture devoted to the creation of shareholder value but later co-opted by public officials whose main concern is the standing of the national debt in bondholders' eyes.

For a long time, many critics on the left hoped that the changes they were witnessing might be transient. As the unconstrained quest for short-term capital gain would bear its bitter fruits, the thinking went, gaping inequalities and the prospect of an environmental catastrophe would induce elected officials to change course or, if they failed to do so, expose them to a massive popular upheaval. However, neither the steady deterioration of labor conditions nor the increasingly alarming damages caused to the environment has acted as the anticipated wake up call. To the contrary, the aftermath of the Great Recession has demonstrated the remarkable resilience of a mode of government, disseminated across public and private institutions, that gives precedence to the gambles on tomorrow's presumptive profits over the mending of today's social woes and the prevention of after-tomorrow's ecological disaster.

Once filled with the hopes and apprehensions of radical change, the near future has been taken over by speculations on investors' tastes. As such, it mandates the sacrifice of the present and the deferral of any serious grappling with long-term sustainability. Yet, for those who wish to uncover alternative trajectories, the ultimate purpose of exposing the current dominance of speculators and the nefarious effects of their short-termism is not to forego the near future but to find ways of reclaiming it.

Reckoning with the epochal nature of the turn that capitalism has taken in the last three decades, the editors of *Near Futures* seek to assemble a series of books that will illuminate its manifold implications—with regard to the production of value and values, the missions or disorientations of social and political institutions, the yearnings, reasoning, and conduct expected of individuals. However, the purpose of this project is not only to take stock of what neoliberal reforms and the dictates of finance have wrought: insofar as every mode of government generates resistances specific to its premises and practices, *Near Futures* also purports to chart some of the new conflicts and forms of activism elicited by the advent of our brave new world.

Near Futures series design by Julie Fry

Typesetting by Meighan Gale

Printed and bound by Maple Press